MW01049944

Sugar Plum Nut

Yanina Cywinska

AuthorHouse™
1663 Liberty Drive, Suite 200
Bloomington, IN 47403
www.authorhouse.com
Phone: 1-800-839-8640

© 2008 Yanina Cywinska. All rights reserved.

No part of this book may be reproduced, stored in a retrieval system, or transmitted by any means without the written permission of the author.

First published by AuthorHouse 1/7/2008

ISBN: 978-1-4343-4241-6 (sc)
ISBN: 978-1-4343-4242-3 (hc)

Library of Congress Control Number: 2007907600

Printed in the United States of America
Bloomington, Indiana

This book is printed on acid-free paper.

Acknowledgments

To Heidi Smith for her unwavering love and encouragement.

My everlasting thanks to Mercedes Hamlin.

To Paula Telander for being the sunshine in my life.

To Jewish Family Services in Walnut Creek, Kathy Friend and Lisa Bagnatori, for their constant moral support.

I cannot find strong enough words to thank the men of the Nisei 522nd Artillery Battalion who freed me from the Nazi Concentration Camp.

Chapter 1

Yanina Cywinska stepped onto the Golden Gate Bridge and felt the full force of the wind, a wind that began perhaps as a mere breath at some distant point and time, but raged now - a world away - with a hard dulling cold. It clawed at her exposed skin, but she didn't turn her head or push away the light hair that whipped across her face. As she walked to the center of the bridge she felt in her coat pocket for the steak. The butcher had wrapped it twice, once with a sheet of butcher paper and once with the sheet of newspaper announcing her daughter's disappearance. She had bought a small steak for herself at the market, but decided not to go home and eat alone. Now the steak lay warming between the thickness of her coat and the heat of her body. She fingered the loose end of the paper and glanced at the seagulls that appeared from nowhere, floating in an up draft. They bobbed at seeming arm's length just beyond the cars, some with their headlights on and some without, and in each one she knew there was a family, on its way to a home and a warm dinner.

What she noticed most was not the slamming of the wind, but the beauty of the evening. On the horizon the sun was a flaming orange disk, half sunk into the Pacific waters. It was the kind of sunset -- viewed from the Golden Gate Bridge, accompanied by the sound effects of waves crashing rhythmically and the ringing of a lighthouse bell --

that one associates with movies, or the fantasies of young girls. And it filled her with a sense of security and longing.

She stood for a time staring into the sun, San Francisco at her back, and realized that she wanted to escape from that bridge, that cold, and become a part of the beauty and serenity of the sea. As it had many times before in her life, death hovered around her. It made noises not unlike the wind or the flapping of wings, and was almost visible at the corner of her eye. Perhaps there had been no gulls at all.

"I will die here," she said to herself. "I'm tired. I've had enough."

Yanina composed herself for a moment and then, like a prima ballerina, performed a beautifully controlled developpe, gently and gracefully placing her leg on the railing of the bridge. Deep inside she felt as if it were someone else's body, someone she was observing, someone who could not resist the urge to leap into that cold wind in attempted flight. When she looked at the sea below she could imagine herself falling, the air rushing past her ears, the swell of the sea getting nearer and nearer until she could see in the waves the reflection of the sun, the color of the sky, and tiny bubbles of agitation in each ripple.

She still had one foot on the pavement and was clutching the railing with both hands, ready to pitch herself forward when she heard a voice. It was Gerda. Gerda who had died in the camps and spoke to her now from the crack she had opened in death's door. Yanina turned and saw her. She still wore the tattered sack clothing of the camps, the gray hollow eyes and the shaved skull.

"Is this how it ends?" Gerda asked. "The Nazis could not destroy you. They could not crush your body or your spirit, and now you are going to do it yourself?"

"Yes, Gerda," Yanina answered.

"You survived a hell on earth. Death could not touch you. You spat in the faces of the SS butchers, and neither they nor the horrors of their death camps could put out your light. Now you are going to finish the job for them?"

Yanina looked down at the sea and a gust of wind hit her face, blinding her completely. It came with such a force that if someone else had been on that bridge, they too would have been blinded and could not have seen a woman vault over the edge and fall without sound into the waves below.

Yanina was given a new job in the camps -- to get people into the showers, give them towels and soap, and shut the doors. She could not understand why the people were all dead when the doors opened. Death was nothing new. It had been with her for years it seemed, ever since she had first seen the men in black boots the day they came to take her family. It had fallen all around her at the camp in a rain of torture, human sickness and cruelty beyond belief. Already she knew its smell, its taste, and the look of absolute loneliness it brought to the faces of people who know they would soon feel it. But this method was something new.

She was ordered to pile the dead bodies on the trucks parked outside the end of the building. Male prisoners wearing gas masks had separated the tangled mass of flesh, had hosed off the blood and excrement, and had removed the teeth from the dead so the Nazis could get their gold. Halfway through the first day at this new job, the work took on a timelessness. The repetition of handing the prisoners towels and soap; the brief relaxation of their fear as they imagined the comfort of cleanliness; the closing of the doors and the tangle of bodies in one corner of the room when they were opened -- the whole endless ghastly routine made her lose all sense of where she was.

Gerda, a worker, felt sorry for the young Yanina, even amid the horror around them.

"Maybe you should go today and sort out the clothes they leave behind," Gerda said. "Remember, shoes with shoes, purses with purses, underwear with underwear." Then she looked around to see if any of the SS guards were watching. "And talk to no one, child. We are forbidden to talk."

Yanina began the sorting of clothes. So many personal belongings. Pictures of families, jewelry, worthless sentimental trinkets, the odds and ends of a thousand lifetimes. She could not imagine where it all came from.

In time she went back to hauling the bodies. Each day passed the same as the one before, and Gerda would remind her, "Work, girl, and work hard. Unless you want to be considered useless. The Nazis will kill you then."

Yanina piled bodies one on top of the other. Old people, children, wondering who they were, where they lived and what country they came from. Many of them were still alive but she was warned by Gerda not to help them in any way. If she wanted to live, she must do nothing. So Yanina just looked at the faces, and the half-dead looked at her for mercy, for explanation. The guilt of being one that survived ate away at her until one day she felt a desparate cry echo within her empty stomach, "Oh, God, where are you? Where do they get so many people? Why so many children, so many babies? How can you allow this?" But she knew enough not to wait for an answer.

The days piled up like the dead, one after the other, a lifeless parade that blurred her memories, her age. She had become thin as a skeleton and developed sores on her feet and fingers, now three times their normal size it seemed, from cuts and infections. She had only a few teeth left in her mouth and they were cracked and chipped. She became prey to fevers, coughing and chills and any disease that swept the camp. Her clothes were thin and filthy, but they were her clothes, and each day she would secure the tattered rags and straps that were the remants of her brassiere, as privately as the morning would permit.

Yanina lived from moment to moment, never thinking about what lay ahead or what had happened in the past. Like the other women in Auschwitz she was stripped of everything except her soul, and that, the Nazis had seemingly killed. She had no possessions, no friends, no family. Nothing but a fantasy that remained from an earlier time of her childhood: to dance her most loved ballet role -- the Sugar Plum Fairy. This was a fantasy that she had kept hidden during her first year in the camp, something that only surfaced when exhaustion forced her to close her eyes. But as she became deadened from the work and the beatings and the complete unpredictability of the pain, the fantasy gradually became stronger. It took on a life of its own, at times overpowering her and making her dance at its own bidding. The fantasy became real.

She was boasting of her upcoming role in the Nutcracker to the other prisoners when the rumor spread that the whole barracks faced "selection." The directive had come from Nazi Queen Bitch, the brutal matron of the camp, that all of them would be taken to the ovens in the morning.

Yanina knew Queen Bitch only too well, and the thought of her brought her back from the dream. Queen of the whip and the hard pleated skirt. Queen of the granite face that exploded into a twisted terrain of crevices when she screamed, that face of coldest stone surrounded by beautifully soft, absurd blonde curls.

When Queen Bitch showed up at the morning roll call, panic swept the women of the barracks. Their voices rose together in one terrible wail, but before they could even move, Queen Bitch had the Stubendansts join hands in a circle to keep them from running madly out of the barracks. As the guards tightened their circle, the wail grew louder and louder until even Queen Bitch's screaming could not be heard. Yanina found herself pressed between the protruding bones of other prisoners, their gray skin and hairless heads inches from her own, their lifeless eyes and mouths open in pitiful weeping. Then Yanina felt the icy grip of Queen Bitch on her arm.

The Nazi matron pulled her like a rag doll from the crowd, and when she looked up at The Queen, she realized what was to come. That sick mean face, that shadow over the eyes, that stare meant a beating.

"Oh God, if you are there, let me die with the others. Please let it be quick," she thought. Almost before she completed the thought the blows began. The Queen beat her brutally, as she had done countless other times. But for the first time Yanina struck back. Her small fists felt like broken sticks on The Queen's mighty shoulders, and the prisoners' cries turned to cheers. "Bravo, Sugar Plum! Bravo!" she heard them shout.

The cheering only inflamed The Queen's festoring rancor, and that anger became Yanina's hell. As The Queen threw herself upon the tiny prisoner, Yanina fought back, and the two traded blows in a mad fury. Yanina felt like a bag of blood and broken bones and could not resist the urge to fly, to leap from her body and watch the scene unfold like some familiar fairy tale.

In her mind she watched the fighting from afar, and it seemed the two bodies were moving as one, as if they were choreographed, like dancers performing some famous tragic scene, a famed test of wills. The smaller body, Yanina, tried to escape the larger, tried to free herself to breath, to dance alone.

The fantasy took over completely. Yanina knew she had at last been called upon to dance. To her suprise, it was not the role of the Sugar

Plum Fairy, as she hoped it would be, but that of Giselle, one of the great tragic ballets of all time. That's who she saw struggling on the floor -- not herself and the Nazi Bitch, but Giselle and Queen Myrtha, Queen of the Wilis, those ghostly virgins forced to dance even after death.

In the ballet, Giselle was the lone rebel of those dead sisters of grace, the heroine of that tragedy, and the fantasy made Yanina now see herself dancing that role, in swift diagonals across the stage, a blur of human images in white moved by the Queen's overpowering will.

Yanina no longer felt a thing. She only watched. The fantasy had deflected all the pain. Instead she felt the exhilaration of a ballerina on stage. What unfolded before her was the performance of a lifetime -- like Pavlova, like the greatest ballerinas in all of Europe!

Then suddenly it was all over.

As quickly as it began, the performance ended. Queen Myrtha's grip released, her will grew weak, leaving Giselle free to dance her dance, squirming on the floor. The crowds no longer cheered. The audience had already been led like cattle from the theater. Silence took over as the scraping of feet faded away, the silence of an empty house.

Yanina came back to her body, still feeling nothing. At least she had danced her Giselle, she thought, at least the audience had seen. They had cried out for more. "Bravo! Bravo!" they had cried, all of them, all gone now. Yanina hated it when the crowds were gone. Had she danced well or had she failed in her debut? She couldn't know. But they had clapped and cheered at first. She must have performed well. They had cheered, she knew they had.

Suddenly, the beautiful blonde curls were only inches from her face again. A huge face looked down on her.

"I'll be back," she heard The Queen whisper.

Then Yanina closed her eyes and imagined the curtain rising so she could take her final bows.

ᔕ

Lisa thought she was going to collapse. Her muscles were knots and her bones felt like rubber. She had passed last week's audition with flying colors. But now that she had the part and rehearsals had begun, she could barely move. Mrs. Berman was surely watching and Lisa knew only too well that she would never let her rest a moment now that she had been chosen for the lead.

"I don't really want to be Giselle anyway," Lisa thought to herself. "I don't know why she chose me. Caroline was much better in the auditions. Colette, too. My legs are too short and my grand jetes look like the jumps of a high hurdler. I should have stuck to track."

"Lisa Roberts, what is the matter with you?"

It was Mrs. Berman. Now she was in for it.

"Where is your mind, child? Please, let's concentrate. From now until the performance, we must make every moment count. It may seem like a long time until we are on stage, but the months will pass very quickly. Are you with me?"

Lisa looked up from the floor, and with the back of her wrist, carefully wiped a drop of sweat that was rolling down her forehead.

"Yes, I'm with you," she said.

"Alright class," Jeanette Berman turned toward the other dancers, "let's try it again. Now remember, you are the Wilis. You are ghosts. Beautiful girls who have died before their time. You have no substance. You are lighter than air. That's right. Lift, lift. Barely touch the ground. Much better, Lisa."

Lisa hated being singled out in class, being reprimanded in front of everyone. Her cheeks were still on fire from embarrassment. She knew Caroline was looking at her, and probably gloating inside. The whole class was probably gloating.

She tried to imagine herself lighter than air, as the etherial creature Mrs. Berman had described. But when the image of her own body came to mind, it was heavy and dull.

"Lift, lift. That's right. Keep the shoulders down but lift," Mrs. Berman called out. Lisa looked around her and she saw the dancers in the corps complete their graceful leaps. Caroline, who would play Queen Myrtha, was dancing solo off to the side. Around the perimeter of the room she could see the dancers who had other parts in the production. She completed a glisade, then went for the grand jete. It was lifeless, and she came down with a thud, and quickly ran from the dressing room in tears.

Mrs. Berman was quick with her response. "Alright class, that is quite enough for today. Stretch out and then you can go." Without missing a beat she went straight into the dressing room to where Lisa sat, sniffling and sobbing.

"What's this, child? Have you hurt yourself?"

Lisa shook her head "No."

"Then why the tears, eh?"

There was a pause while Lisa found her voice. "I can't do it. I can't. You should have chosen someone else."

"Are you afraid, is that it?"

Lisa shrugged and said, "Yes."

"Use your fear," Mrs. Berman whispered. "Use it. What do you think Giselle is feeling? She is afraid too. Afraid for her Albrecht, afraid for herself, afraid of what Myrtha might do to her. Make your fear her fear. Let all of your feelings become those of Giselle." She sat down and brought her face close to the young dancer's.

"Lisa, you are a beautiful dancer, what are you afraid of? Do not concentrate on what you fear you cannot do, concentrate on what you are doing. Because what you are doing is beautiful. Become Giselle. Know her fears, her emotions. Put your doubts aside and become the poor peasant girl whose heart is broken."

"But what if I can't do it?"

"Child, I chose you for this part because I know you can do it," Mrs. Berman said urgently. "The only thing that can make you fail is fear. So, do not fear. Fear will make you numb, and I want someone who is full of life, so full of life that she is about to burst -- even after she is dead."

Mother

Father

Chapter 2

Warsaw 1929

"Ludwika, wake up. Ludwika please."

He was shaking her by the shoulders, as gently as he could. "Please, Ludwika. We must prepare to go."

"What is it, Vladi?" she asked through the haze of sleep. Even in such a state she had sensed his urgency.

"They are coming. Pilsudski's men. We must prepare to leave. There is a train tonight for Poznan."

Ludwika sat up in bed and rubbed her eyes. "But that doesn't make any sense. What would Pilsudski's men want with us?"

"Don't argue with me woman!" he shouted. "Just prepare youself. I will awaken Tadeusz."

She knew enough not to object. Her husband was a man of few words, but he meant what he said. She could hear him going to wake Tadeusz and from the sound of his hard steps in the hall she knew he was wearing his boots. That meant he was also wearing his military uniform, the uniform he had taken off the day Pilsudski took over the country three years ago, and swore he would never wear again.

Ludwika moved slowly. Getting out of bed was a major effort with the weight of the child holding her down. Vladislav had left a small candle burning on the table, and by its dim light she had to put on her leggings, her shoes, and her most comfortable dress.

Her husband reappeared at the door. "Pick something plain. Look like a peasant. We don't want anyone to know who you are."

Ludwika took hold of his arm as he was turning to leave. "What about the child, Vladi? How will we survive the train?"

He hesitated for a moment. It was a sight she was not used to seeing. His thoughts seemed to sink behind his hard, heavy eyes. "The child, will not come tonight," he said softly. "It must not come tonight."

"You will be there at my side if it does?" she asked.

Vladislav Cywinski looked down at his boots. Then he looked straight into her eyes. "No, Ludwika. You and Tadeusz must go alone. Tonight I am going to see Pilsudski myself. I will not be brought before him in chains."

"Why are they doing this? What do they want with you? You have done nothing to hurt Pilsudski."

Vladislav straightened himself and moved toward the door. "I know that," he said. "But apparently Pilsudski does not." Then he turned and touched her face tenderly. "Quickly now. We must hurry."

Ludwika took down her bag from the mirrored armoir and glanced at herself in the glass. She was huge. The child inside was bursting with life, stretching her body to the limits. It began to kick and poke with its tiny limbs, she could feel it. "There there, my child," she whispered. "My little lullaby. Be calm, be strong. Everything will be fine, my little angel." She rubbed her belly gently and thought of the day when Tadeusz came. That was three years ago when the country was also in a state of upheaval. But at least then she had felt safe. Her family had not been threatened. Vladislav had not joined in the fighting, had not taken either side in the struggle which brought Pilsudski to power. She could not understand why he would want to harm him how. Had they not fought together in the Legions against the Germans? Had he not been loyal to Pilsudski when the European countries gave Poland its independence after the war? Had they not stood side by side in the Battle of Warsaw when the Russians tried to devour the young Polish nation? Perhaps it would be better for Poland to be ruled by someone else, she thought, like before the great war. At least then there was not this constant fighting, this killing.

But she knew she must never admit that thought to her husband. He had fought for years for an independent Poland. He was proud of his noble origins and had learned from his father and grandfather the bitter resentment for the foreigners who divided the country.

He realized his family would probably never regain its noble stature, but he had decided as a young man that armed struggle was the only option to restore the greatness and independence of the nation. Ludwika had fallen for the young soldier before the great war began, and she watched with joy the pride he felt when Poland threw off the shackles of foreign domination after the war ended.

"Mama," a small voice said from behind her. It was Tadeusz "Where are we going?" Ludwika bent down as best she could and held his little face in her hands. "We must go on a train. You like trains don't you?"

Downstairs she could hear voices. Vladislav's was getting loud in an argument with someone whose voice she did not recognize.

"Come, Tadeusz. We must hurry."

She stuffed her bag with a woolen shawl, a change of clothes, and brought some extra things for her boy as well. She also took the small quilt he had used as an infant in case the new baby arrived before she could return home. It was the arrival of the child that she feared most. This baby's birth had been so well planned for. Doctor Ratkowski had been calling on her regularly this past week and had assured her he would be there for the labor and delivery.

When she came to the top of the stairs with Tadeusz, Vladislav and another man were arguing at the dining room table. "But, Kromer, he knows I am not in league with the Nationalists," her husband shouted.

"Does he?" Kromer asked. "You name was on the list the Nationalists had prepared of persons who would support an overthrow of the Sanacja Regime."

"That is impossible," Vladislav objected. "The Nationalists have approached me many times, and I have always turned them away. I am no friend of Dmowski and his people."

"Yet you have not in three years offered anything but protests to the way Pilsudski is running the country."

"Josef knows very well why I have not supported him. I contacted him personally after the May Coup to protest his disrupting of the principles on which this nation was born. But I have done nothing to oppose him. I have retired from the military and have been living here quietly with my family. Besides, I am not the only one of his friends who have objected to his methods. Sikorski and Wasilewski have been more vocal than I."

Kromer lit a cigarette on the lamp that burned on the table. "This is true, Cywinski. But neither of their names turned up on a list of Nationalist supporters."

Vladislav Cywinski stood up abruptly and began pacing back and forth in the dimly lit room.

"Don't take it so personally, Cywinski," Kromer said. "He is not directing the purge against you alone. All of the Nationalists will be hit."

Vladislav turned and slammed his fist on the table. "I am no Nationalist!"

Kromer took him by the sleeve and his voice softened. "I know this, Vladislav. Why do you think I am here? I don't want to see you killed, but Pilsudski has no choice. The Nationalists and their Camp of Great Poland have been getting stronger and stronger. Pilsudski knows he must put an end to them before it is too late. The survival of Poland is at stake. You know we could not survive a civil war. In order to avoid that, he must crush the Nationalists, and he must do it tonight."

Vladislav relaxed a bit and sat down at the table. He took one of Kromer's cigarettes and lit it, sending spirals of smoke through the light. "Kromer, I must see Pilsudski myself. I must explain to him that this list is a big mistake. He knows I would never take up arms against him."

"Take your family and leave Poland, Cywinski," Kromer said. "Perhaps in a year or two this will all blow over."

Vladislav reached across the table and grabbed Kromer by his coat, pulling his face close to his own. "I am going with you tonight, do you understand me? I am going to personally explain to Pilsudski that he is mistaken."

Kromer pulled away from his grasp and dusted his lapels. "Have it your way then. But what about your family?"

"There is a train for Poznan in less than an hour. When does the attack begin?"

Kromer took a watch from his pocket. "It is very late. Pilsudski's men are already on their way. You'd better get your wife and child down to the station right now. But tell them to stay low. It is likely word has spread among the Nationalists that a purge is coming. They may also be heading for the trains. Believe me, when the fighting starts, it will be an ugly scene."

Kromer stood up and buttoned his coat.

"Get your family to the train, Cywinski. Then meet me at the Cathedral. If you are not there in one hour, I am leaving without you. Then you will be on your own."

Ludwika stood at the top of the stairs and watched as Kromer left the house. Vladislav turned and looked up at her. She could see the hardness in his eyes. It was the look she had seen many times before, when he had left her to fight battles in defense of Poland. She had hoped she would never see that look again.

"Come," he said gently. "There is little time."

Vladislav loaded her small bag on the duroshka and helped her into the seat. A cold wind had come up and was whirling snow through the air. The covering of snow on the ground made it appear lighter than it should have been, he thought. He turned to Tadeusz and pulled up his collar and tucked his hair beneath his cap. "Be a brave soldier, my little son," he said. "You must take care of your mother." Then he hoisted the boy into the duroshka.

Ludwika felt a pain in her heart. Driving away from their home she wondered if they would ever return. They had worked so hard for the things they had. It was a nice home, located on the outskirts of Warsaw. They had some wealth, what little they had been able to keep from Vladi's father. Things had been peaceful these past three years. She had born Tadeusz, she was ready to bear a second child. At last they would have complete family. Now this. Would there never be peace in Poland?

Vladislav had the horses running at full speed. The rumble of their hooves and heavy breath were the only sounds on the empty streets he had chosen to take. To him it seemed the whole duroshka was traveling in a cloud. Perhaps it was just wishful thinking. But the whirling snow and steam puffing from the horses breaths and backs seemed to blur all the buildings and the streets in front and behind them. He realized then that his eyes were tearing from the cold. He looked at his wife and her eyes seemed to be full of tears as well. She looked so frightened there with Tadeusz huddled against her huge belly. He knew he had no choice but to supply the strength for all three of them. He only hoped Ludwika could manage the trip to Poznan without him.

They were less than a mile from the station when the shooting began. The first crack of a rifle sent a bullet of fear that seemed to go through each of them. Tadeusz began crying and clung even tighter to his mother. Vladislav slapped the horses with the reins for more speed. The first gunfire, though unmistakable, was quite distant. The second was much closer.

"We haven't much further to go," Vladislav said to Ludwika as strongly as he could. But she didn't need to look up at him to sense the fear in his voice. New gunfire was accompanied by a scream of horror, and from a side street, Ludwika could see the yellow flicker of flames from the windows of someone's home.

She thought again of her own home, of all of her clothing, her safety and security going up in flames. She knew she mustn't show her fear to Tadeusz, or even to Vladi, but it was all she could do to keep from screaming at the top of her lungs. The duroshka jolted her as they took a corner and she felt a deep pain in her abdomen.

"Vladi, the child!" she cried.

"The child mustn't come," he shouted. "Not tonight!"

Each burst of gunfire startled the horses and Vladislav struggled to keep them in line. Ludwika held Tadeusz, sobbing now against her chest, and gently stroked her stomach. Your father is right child, she thought, touching her belly. You must not come tonight. Dear God, please not tonight.

When they arrived at the station, there was already a mass of people crowded around the train. They gathered in small groups and spoke with their eyes -- ashen looks of fear and silence. The number of people there told Vladislav that word had already spread among the Nationalists that the purge was coming. He jumped out of the duroshka and came around the other side to help his wife and child. He noticed his hands were trembling as he lifted them down to the ground.

Ludwika took hold of her bag, then turned and looked at her husband. They held that glance for the longest moment. She spoke first. "Will you be able to convince him? When will you come to Poznan?"

"Pilsudski will believe me," he said. Then he reached out and touched her belly. "You will be alright?"

Ludwika took his hand away and brought it up to her lips. "Yes, we will be fine," she said, kissing it. "Now hurry.

Kromer will not wait one extra minute."

Vladi kissed her quickly, knelt and hugged Tadeusz. Then he turned and disappeared among the crowd.

The station was electric. The train had been there for some time and people began beating on the doors of the train to get in. When they were finally opened, it was mayhem. Ludwika had to pry with her elbow to wedge a place for her and Tadeusz in the rush to the train. The strain made her break out in a sweat, despite the icy winds. When she finally fought her way into the train she had to hurry through three cars to find a seat for the two of them.

The shooting was more frequent and sounded nearer by the moment. She could see on the faces of the men and women aboard that train that they were frightened. But no one wanted to look at anyone else. Some feared they would be mistaken for Nationalists. Others, themselves of Nationalist sympathies, feared their fellow frightened passengers would blame them for the attack.

Ludwika was grabbed by another deep pain that seemed to blot out all sensations. It lasted only a moment and was gone. Gunfire rang out through the Warsaw night and the passengers reappeared around her, cringing at the sounds of battle. "When is this train ever going to move?" she asked herself out loud.

"They are getting nearer," a woman behind her answered. It was Nadia Vychek, from the bakery. Her husband, the baker, was there with her. Ludwika turned and offered a weak smile, relieved to see someone she knew.

The pain hit again, and this time it made her double up in her seat. She knew in her heart that the contractions of birth had begun, but she did not want to admit it with her head. "Not yet, child," she whispered. "Please, not yet."

Gunfire was closing in on the station. The shooting was continuous now, and Ludwika figured that the Nationalists must be fighting back. She stroked Tadeusz' head and told him not to worry, twisting a small lock of his hair between her fingers. People on the train were near panic and Nadia's husband stuck his head out of the window and began shouting at the engineer. The crowd echoed his calls and in an instant it seemed the whole train was crying out for even the slightest inch of movement. A bullet ripped through the window across from Ludwika sending glass careening off the seats, the ceiling and her shoulder. She reacted with great agility and brought Tadeusz to the floor beneath her.

Tadeusz was bleating like a lamb, and there was a great rush of feet as passengers tried to find some way off the train. "Don't cry, darling," Ludwika consoled him. "We must be brave, like your father said." The gut wrenching pain struck again, pulling her away from her thoughts and the chaos of the train around her. The contraction ended and another quickly began. From the distance of her pain she noticed more gunfire and shattering of glass. She heard more passengers in panic and even thought she saw the heavy soled boots of a soldier running down the aisle. She tried to comfort Tadeusz, whose mouth was wide open in fright. Then suddenly he was gone! Someone had taken him. "No!" she cried. "My baby! No!" Then, just as suddenly, she found herself being dragged up off the floor, and pulled down the aisle. Most of the seats were empty now, but doubled up in pain she could not see who had hold of her arm. Ludwika recovered her balance enough to look down as she prepared to jump from the train, and below her she saw Nadia Vychek holding Tadeusz, and recognized the baker reaching out to help her to the ground.

"Quickly," he commanded. "Get under the train. You must hurry."

The pain came again, but this time Ludwika was on her back. Nadia had laid her coat on the ground for her and had given her a belt to bite so that she wouldn't scream.

Ludwika Cywinska didn't know how long she lay beneath that train. She was only aware of the pain, and the taste of leather in her mouth. She knew that there was fighting, that people were dying very near to her, but the presence of Nadia made her feel safe. She could barely make out her face through the blackness under that train, the lunging of her belly, and the tears in her eyes, but it was an image of some saintly aid, she was certain. The baker held her shoulders throughout the delivery while Tadeusz huddled behind one of the black train wheels.

Ludwika had nearly bitten through the heavy belt by the time the baby came. Through the delirium of her relief she saw Nadia holding up the tiny child, wrapped in her own shawl. "It's a girl, Ludwika! A beautiful baby girl," she said.

Ludwika reached out with all her strength, and when she felt that tiny body that Nadia handed her, she sank back to the ground in exhaustion. "Oh my little child," she whispered. "My little Yanina. My sweet little Yanina," she cried, pressing the child against her neck.

My Parents' House

Chapter 3

Harold Berman opened his eyes. The dim light through the curtains told him it was morning, early morning. Certainly too early to be getting up. Although he had his back to her, he knew his wife was awake too. He could feel her trembling. The bed reverberated with her movements, and he figured she was sitting up, holding her head in her hands. He could hear her quick, hard breathing.

Jeanette brought her knees up so she could rest her head against them. Harold heard her taking deep breaths, trying to calm herself. He heard her feet dragging through the sheets. All of her movements, he felt, were tense and rapid. He had not yet turned to look at her.

"Harold? Are you awake?" she asked. Her voice was weak and quivering. "Harold, please. Please wake up."

He didn't stir.

"Harold, I've had another dream," Jeanette said. "I'm frightened."

"What do you want me to do about it?" he snapped at her over his shoulder. He put his head back on the pillow again, but knew it was no use. Then he tossed off the cover, got out of bed and walked into the bathroom without even looking at her.

Jeanette was still staring at him as he left the room. She wanted to scream, "Help me, please help me!" She just needed someone to tell her what was going on inside, someone to listen at least. But she knew now it wouldn't be Harold. Not today. Not any day, for that matter.

Jeanette put her head back into her hands and sank down on the pillow. But she didn't dare close her eyes. The demons of her dreams were still whispering in that internal darkness. If she closed her eyes, they might rise out of the fetid swamp of her subconscious again.

In the dream she was running. The train was leaving and she had to catch it because her parents were on it. She did not want to be left behind. She ran as fast as she could and got closer. She reached the door and grabbed the bar on the side to lift herself onto the step. But when she put her foot there, it slipped right off. And when she looked down she saw the step was covered with blood and glistening human entrails. The train was moving so fast now and she had to get on, but every time she put her foot onto the step she slipped on the blood and fell off again. The train was getting away from her, taking her parents with it, and the terror was too much to bear.

Harold turned on the shower, then stopped. He wrapped the towel around his waist and slowly stepped back to the edge of the bedroom door. He could see Jeanette clutching her pillow, rolled up in the bed as tight as a fist. The blankets were stretched across the diagonal of the mattress and he sensed the whole bed was shaking, ever so slightly. He didn't make a move, just stared. Perhaps she had fallen back into sleep. Maybe she would wake up and forget the whole thing. Her back was to him. He couldn't know that her eyes were wide open, carefully studying the small flower patterns on the wall.

At the school it was completely different. For Jeanette ballet was life in all of its beauty: the essential movements of the body, the strength of muscles and motion, the leaping music, the irresistable flight of the soul. The moment she stepped into her school she felt released, however briefly, from her anxieties and doubts. In truth, she internalized them, turning them into the energy of dance, the understanding of character.

It was something she always tried to impart to her students, that turning of their own emotions into the emotions of dance. That's why she needed experienced dancers for her production of Giselle. Not just experienced in dance, but experienced in life. No one could really dance Giselle, she believed, unless she had had her heart broken. In Leningrad, they had said no one could dance Giselle unless she had lost her virginity. There was that much need for maturity and understanding in order for the dancer to touch, as Giselle, the depths of love and sorrow.

That's why the decision to chose Lisa for the role had been so difficult. Jeanette was just not sure about her. The girl could dance, there was no question about it. Her discipline and technique were marvelous. But did she have the real depth of emotion to become Giselle? Jeanette had decided to take the chance.

Lisa was an experienced dancer. She had studied at several schools, including San Francisco ballet, and had performed in several productions. But never in a lead role. Consquently, Lisa had doubts about herself. The doubts must be eliminated. Doubts and fears served no purpose but to destroy. It was Jeanette's job to get rid of those fears, to release Lisa's soul so that she could allow it to control her finely trained body.

Jeanette felt sure the production would be an excellent one. Her two finest dancers, Lisa and Caroline, would play Giselle and Myrtha, Queen of the Wilis. She had hired Christopher and Robert as the male leads. They were true professionals and their expertise would elevate the entire production. Her students would be able to fill in the other roles, as peasants and Wilis.

Students always amazed her. Their attention and earnest desire made teaching a wonder of large and small satisfactions. Some students -- she could see from the first day she met them -- were living in a world of fantasy. They had neither the physical capabilities nor the true desire to become dancers. Earnestness was not enough. Others had the talent but needed rigorous training to bring their bodies to their potential. Then there were those with the gift. But too often they needed to be guided through their own self doubts and moodiness. It had been quite different in Russia. Only in America do the children have the wealth and freedom to indulge in such emotional garbage, Jeanette often told the class.

Then there was Francheska, her own daughter. It was so hard for Jeanette to be objective about Francheska. She knew her daughter was talented -- she had worked with her for years. She had even arranged for Francheska's audition with the San Francisco Ballet, and there was a good chance she would win a scholarship. But Jeanette had no way of knowing what Francheska would do. She had become so rebellious and unpredictable. Jeanette had such a difficult time influencing her, that she felt like she had lost her daughter completely. Everyone reassured her that the breakdown in their relationship was just the result of adolescence, but she knew better. She knew the real reason behind her daughter's unruliness and strange behavior.

Francheska had been the love of her life. In fact, she still was. But it was a one way street these days, and the way was blocked with frustrations and fights.

In school, Francheska at least had enough pride to maintain good work habits. The pressure of competition with her fellow dancers kept her in shape. Jeanette was especially pleased with the way she danced the Wili scenes. All of the girls were doing well, but Francheska's dancing the role of a dead virgin, the seductress of the living, was especially evocative. She only hoped that it wasn't her motherly bias twisting her judgement.

Jeanette always arrived at the school two hours before her dancers came. It gave her time to go over the progress of the production with Kirsten, her assistant, and also time to warm up for class. So far they had raised about half of the money needed to perform Giselle. Where she would get the rest, at this point, she didn't know. She and Kirsten had written letters to a number of the companies in San Francisco. They had contacted the doctors, professional people, and wealthy patrons on their "possible donor" list, and many had responded. But expenses were getting higher every year. Renting the stage, paying high wages for stage hands, hiring scenery painters and costume makers — it all added up to a tremendous sum of money.

Jeanette wasn't even sure anymore what had prompted her to organize a performance of Giselle. The idea had seemingly welled up out of her soul. She found herself obsessed with the image of the dead young heroine, so fragile, so ethereal, hovering over the place that marked her own grave, her one true love downstage, with the threatening power of the Wili Queen right before her. It was an image from her memory somewhere.

She recalled the excitement of her students when she told them she had decided on performing Giselle. Some of them didn't even know the total story. They knew it was a classic ballet, and their enthusiasm to be a part of it was limitless, but she did have to recount the story of Giselle to all of them, just to be sure.

It is the tale of a peasant girl, who has fallen hopelessly in love with a young peasant boy, she told them. Only the boy, Albrecht, in reality is a duke betrothed to a young noblewoman. He too, is in love, and has donned the peasant disguise so that Giselle will love him in return. But a jealous hunter, Hilarion, also loves Giselle, and is bent on revealing the duke's deception in order to win her.

When the truth is shown, Giselle is heartbroken.

Inconsolable, she goes completely mad, grabs the duke's sword and tries to pierce her own heart with it. She finally dies of a broken heart.

It is after death that Giselle becomes a Wili, one of the dead virgins who haunt the forest glades, doomed to dance eternally. Giselle rises from her grave at the command of Myrtha, Queen of the Wilis, whose will is the driving force that makes all the Wilis dance. First Hilarion comes to visit Giselle's grave. The Wilis capture him, seduce him into dancing with them, and then make him dance until he dies. When the young duke, Albrecht, comes later than night, the Queen and her Wilis command Giselle to make him perform his fatal dance. But the love between Giselle and the duke is strong, even in death, and she protects him. Again and again the Wilis try to kill him with dance, but Giselle is able to keep him on his feet. Through the entire night she protects him until at dawn, when the Wilis and their Queen are forced to flee, he is finally saved. And as the sun breaks, Giselle returns at last to the earth, leaving the duke weeping on his knees beside her grave.

When the auditions began, Jeanette spent days studying the dancers' movements. As they danced to her commands she formulated the choreography. At first, it was inside her head -- the steps, the leaps, the movements of the peasants as they harvest grapes, the haunting grace of the Wilis, winged creatures of the dark. She had memorized the classic choreography from her studies in Russia and Europe. This she adapted to the abilities of her dancers, the way they moved, their training, their ability to act.

Her students were good. Many had studied elsewhere and had joined Jeanette's school to learn Russian classicism. Most were good enough to get a part in the production, be it Wili or peasant. Jeanette had had to cast the parts of Bertha, Giselle's mother, and Bethilda, the duke's betrothed.

She was happy she had hired Christopher and Robert to dance the male leads. Christopher would be the handsome Albrecht, Duke of Selisia, and Robert would be Hilarion, the jealous hunter.

Once the students had all arrived, stretched and warmed up their muscles, Jeanette went to the record player and gently placed the needle on the recording of the ballet's score.

"Alright," she shouted, her voice rising above the din of the dancers' conversations. "Today we will start with the Wilis. Let's go. Dona, Amy, let's stop the talking. We must work. You, too, Francheska.

"Now remember, you are young virgins who have had life taken away from you before you really had the chance to live. You have all the youth and beauty of young girls, but you are dead. You are spirits. Ghosts. You hover in the air above the ground and seduce the living with your pure beauty. Remember, your feet float above the ground."

Caroline, Queen of the Wilis, took her part to the left as the Wilis lined up diagonally across the floor. Jeanette put the needle down and the dancing began. But it was only a few bars before Caroline faltered and the dancers had to take it from the beginning. Caroline faltered again and Jeanette stepped onto the center of the floor to show her the exact opening steps.

"Pas de bouree across the stage as if your are a floating torso," she said.

It was when she had the entire group's attention that Jeanette began to tremble. At times she could not believe that anyone would follow her movements, that anyone would really want to be like her. In her class she felt admired and respected. The students were so attentive to her every move that if she inadvertently scratched her nose at the end of a dance sequence, they would do the same. She had total control. Here in the school, at least.

It made her realize how safe and powerful she felt within the world of ballet and how helpless she felt outside of it. The events in her life had never given her much reason to feel confident. Only ballet could do that. It was only the total immersion into the characters, the steps, the sweat and the music of ballet that freed her.

Jeanette glanced around in astonishment. All faces were on her. She began to feel the fear but fought her own inner impulse to question: "What are you doing here? What right do you have to lead these young people?" For an instant she felt as if she were on an icy lake, instead of a dance floor, the thin frozen skin that held her feet about to give way and send her plunging to the bottom. Then in the next instant her body was moving.

She was dancing and the doubts were gone.

"Now you try it, Caroline," she said softly.

Me at 8

Me at 16
Liberation Day

Chapter 4

Ivan snapped the reins and the duroshka brought them within sight of the house. Yanina noticed how beautiful the front of her home appeared -- the doors so tall and delicately sculpted with large brass knobs that reflected the mid-afternoon sun. From the moment she had received word in Leningrad, she had been afraid. To be brought home before her this year's studies at ballet school were completed meant something serious had happened.

The crack of Ivan's whip, the clatter of hooves and the sudden wind that whipped her hair across her face combined to magnify her apprehension.

"Why am I being brought home in the middle of my studies?" Yanina asked Ivan. "Is someone ill?"

"Oh, no, no, Yanina," Ivan laughed. He was a large man with a thick beard that rested on his chest. "Everyone is in excellent health. Please, do not worry."

As the duroshka came to a halt, Yanina saw her mother fling open the doors and come running out of the house to greet her. She was followed by Yanina's brother, Tadeusz.

"I am so relieved you arrived safely, Yanina," her mother said. "There was no problem with the trains?"

"No, Mama. Everything is fine," Yanina said. But inside she did not believe it was true.

Yanina had heard about the problems in Poland while she was studying, but it did not seem to concern her. The Kirov Ballet in Leningrad was the safest place in the world, she was certain. It was a place where she could work alongside the greatest dancers in the world, and if she practiced hard enough, could someday maybe join their ranks. It was a place where she slept and ate and studied, and when she performed well, the teachers praised her, even though she was not yet eleven years old.

Yanina had been in and out of the Kirov once before. Her mother had enrolled her there when Yanina was only six, using her influence and connections in the world of theater to get her daughter into the school. But after a few months, the school directors decided Yanina was just too young.

She was enrolled again at eight, again through her mother's influence, and again younger than any other student at the school. This time she stayed, spending much of the next two years living away from her home in Warsaw. She was fluent in Russian now and had not been back to Warsaw in almost six months.

Since war had broken out in Europe, there was an air of great tension at the school. A number of the students had left for their homes immediately. But many more had stayed, concentrating more heavily on their dancing.

To Yanina, still one of the youngest students in the Kirov, the stories of soldiers and war seemed just another problem for the adults -- one that she hoped would quickly go away. It didn't. And now she was being brought home in the middle of the school year. She was happy to see her family, but what she really wanted was to be back at school.

The whole situation began to make Yanina afraid. She had tried to ignore the soldiers who guarded the train stations -- the Russian soldiers in Leningrad, and the black booted ones who greeted the train in Warsaw. Soldiers were nothing new to her, but the ones in Warsaw were different. They were Germans, and she had never seen German soldiers before. At her home, everyone around her seemed nervous and upset, and that made her even more confused.

Finally her mother cut through the tension with a warm hug. "Come, my darling," she said. "We are so happy to have you home."

Yanina relaxed a bit. Her mother had always been able to make her feel good. Still, the sensation that something extraordinary was happening continued to cast a weird light on the way Yanina saw her family, the horses, her home. And as she walked upstairs to her room, she could not get over how beautifully the stairs curved, how red and vivid the Kashan carpet looked. When she reached the top of the staircase she looked down again at the front doors. She saw them for the first time as the most splendid of doors -- hand carved and richly detailed in white and gold. Their strange beauty, intensified by the sunlight pouring in through the still opened entrance, made her feel more fearful and odd.

Soon it was dinner time and, as always, no discordant conversation was allowed. It was a rule of the house, Vladislav Cywinski had always required his family to enjoy lengthy dinners, elegant affairs that featured all of the family silver, crystal, china, linen and baskets of fresh flowers. Everyone was dressed in his or her finest clothes. Yanina's father demanded they all sit proud and straight, but no one sat prouder than he with the aura of complete command that had always been his trademark.

No matter how many tragedies befell the world around him, Yanina's father kept them locked outside his door when his family dined. Even if he, himself, suffered financially, or was threatened by the political climate, he more urgently sought out the pomp and elegance to remind him that nothing lasts forever. His wealth and social position could easily be stripped away, as it had been many times during his life.

His family had been nobility, but the privileges that had come with it were taken away when he was a child. Those were the years when Poland broke down the traditions of the privileged classes in an effort to establish social equality. As a young man, Cywinski had fought for the formation of an independent Poland and had fallen in and out of favor with the various ruling regimes on several occasions -- sometimes viewed as a staunch ally, sometimes as a dire threat. Through the decades of social upheaval in Poland he had always survived, rebuilt his home, and reestablished his family's security. He had been forced to do so just ten years earlier, when he personally convinced Pilsudski, the country's president, of his loyalties to the country. He had nearly lost his family and his life that night and never forgot that although he had become again a man of influence in Poland, his position could never be guaranteed for long.

That's why his extravagant meals were so important to him, and why they were to be conducted as a time of warmth and joy. Yanina had learned at an early age that personal problems were not to be discussed at dinner. She had also learned not to take the problems of the family beyond the front door. "If you want people to like you, you have to be likable," her father told her. "You must be lively and interesting. People don't want to hear about your troubles."

The dinner ritual ended as always. Each member of the family took up an instrument -- Ludwika, her violin, Vladislav, the piano, Tadeusz sat on the right with his flute, and Yanina on the left with her harp. That night the family played Chopin. A trained musician, Vladislav had taught them all how to play. He had carefully instructed them how to release the most emotion from their instruments to match the thoughts and feelings of the composer. He told them stories of each piece and each man who wrote it.

He was an accomplished pianist and knew personally some of the greatest composers of Europe. As he spoke of Chopin that night, Yanina sat in awe of his strength and power. He seemed the most important man in the world, a man who surely knew the answers to the most difficult questions. Sitting at her father's side that day, her fears finally left her.

The sitting room filled with the melodies of Chopin's melancholy music. Each member of the Cywinski family was deep in concentration when the booming at the front door brought the music to a sudden stop. For an instant there was complete silence, just the echoing of that great sound inside their chests. Then the thunder came again and the front doors flew open with a third great boom.

Frozen in her seat, Yanina saw a dozen men dressed in uniforms and a dozen gun barrels pointed at them. The men shouted in German, and as they stomped into the room Yanina heard the clicking of their guns as they were cocked -- a sound that seemed louder even than the booming at the door. Fear made her numb. She was unable to respond to their demands. She looked at her father and he too seemed unable to move. Finally Cywinski stood up and the soldiers pushed him toward the door with their rifles. One soldier grabbed Yanina by the shoulder and ordered her to stand in the corner. She felt then that it was only a matter of seconds before they would all be shot. "What are you waiting for?" she cried out. "Why don't you kill us all now?"

"Shut up, you swine. Shooting is too good for you Jew lovers."

Yanina pulled away from the soldier and spat at him. "Go away!" she shouted. "Why have you come to our home? Why have so many of you come her with your guns? We have no weapons, we are not guilty of anything."

Her father stepped closer to silence her, but to Yanina it still seemed so odd. With her father at her side, she felt it was all so silly, like a childish argument at school that could be settled with shouting. "Go away from my house."

One of the German soldiers answered her protests with his gun barrel. The blow hit Yanina square in the forehead. Blinded with pain, she felt a cool liquid running down her face. Her father held her in his arms and trembled. When she touched her face she saw there was blood everywhere, dripping down her dress and onto the carpet. Yanina looked at her father and saw his face was white with fear. He had a look of total helplessness.

Yanina felt as if the floor had disappeared. She was floating in the colorless dread of complete abandonment. The sight of her family stricken in fear was too much to understand. Especially her father, her strength, who had been there her entire life to protect her and guide her.

Yanina felt her will crumble and she shrank into a subservient child. She followed her family, passing the beautiful staircase with its red carpet. She stood for an instant in the doorway of her home, so grand, so opulent, so beautiful, she thought. And she felt the deep terror that this was the last time she would ever pass through those doors. She ran her fingertips over them, as if to help her remember them forever.

Outside the roses were bursting, and their aroma was more intense than she had ever noticed. Birds whistled and chatted as if the world were beautiful and completely unchanged.

The family was pushed into a large gray truck and all the light was shut out as the Nazi soldiers closed and locked the doors. Vladislav wrapped his arms around Yanina while his wife tried to comfort Tadeusz.

"Papa, can I get my ballet slippers tomorrow?" she asked. But Vladislav Cywinski had no words to say.

The family was taken to a building that Yanina had never seen. They were let out of the truck and through a door that led down a narrow hallway with iron doors on each side. They were all still too numb to speak. Then the soldiers forced them into a small room. Before closing the door, one of them grabbed Vladislav by the shoulder. "You. Come with me."

Vladislav turned to his wife and children. They clutched at his coat and tried to kiss him. Yanina hung onto his leg until the soldier kicked her away. The door was slammed and bolted and her father was gone.

In the cold and dark of that room, lit only by a tiny window at the top of the wall, sleep came to the family more as an escape than from fatigue. Yanina woke hours later to the sound of her mother crying. She was holding in her hands the unfinished Easter dress she had managed to grab before they left the house.

"Come, Yanina," she said through her tears. "Try on the dress. We must have it finished by Easter."

Before Yanina could act, the doors flew open and two soldiers entered. It was morning and Yanina thought for an instant that they must be bringing food. But instead, the soldiers told Ludwika Cywinska that they were taking her children.

"No, no!" she screamed. "Don't take them away. They are so young. I have to take care of them, please, please!"

Yanina and Tadeusz were quickly pulled away from their mother, despite their crying and kicking. Again they were loaded into a truck, this time with dozens of strangers, Poles who were just as confused and frightened as they. Later, they were taken to another building they had never seen. It was an enormous place with many large rooms and bunk beds, and many many people who had been arrested.

Once again the two children found themselves being forced into a cold, dark room, not knowing where they were or why their lives had changed. No one had fed them all day, and to the sounds of people fighting over scraps of food, they fell asleep with nothing in their stomachs but fear.

In sleep, Yanina's life was beautiful. She was still at ballet school, preparing herself for auditions for the school's year end production.

She was treated tenderly but still made to understand that the rigorous training of ballet would lead to a life of discipline, of transforming her body into a thing of perfect human expression and beauty. It was what she wanted more than anything in the world.

A horrible ringing awoke her and over the loudspeaker she heard the soldiers ordering everyone to line up. Many people had satchels and small bags of their belongings, and these they would be able to keep, they were told.

In a large hall they were lined up and finally given some bread and water. Rather than rejoicing, the people ate in slience, in small bites and sips, like animals fearful of an attack. Then the large doors to the outside world were opened. When Yanina saw them she thought of the doors to her home, their white and gold splendor. These doors were even larger and they were made of iron.

Outside the building the prisoners were lined up with eight people to each line. Soon there were rows and rows of people, and guarding each ten rows was a Nazi soldier in an impeccable uniform of gray and black, machine gun pointed and ready. The prisoners were mostly children and old people. They were ordered to march, and to march quickly. Yanina, in the early stages of puberty, had a more womanly form than other children her age, and as they marched, she became more and more afraid. During the lining up she had become separated from Tadeusz. Now he was nowhere to be seen, no matter how much she strained. She also heard rumors from some of the other captives that the girls and women might be attacked. As she marched she began hiding behind people, hiding her body from the soldiers' views by staying in the center of the pack.

Just after the march began a man fainted near Yanina and was dragged to the fields and shot. The echo of the machine gun made her scream for her mother. She cried and pleaded for God to bring back her parents. She knew if they would return, everything would be alright. Suddenly she felt someone's hand over her mouth.

"Shut your mouth or they will kill you," a voice urged. "Don't you know they are killing everyone who becomes a problem?"

"I want my mama," Yanina wimpered. "Please. I want my mama. Where is she? Why has everything changed?"

Yanina turned to see who was behind her. It was a woman about her mother's age, with black hair and deep sad eyes. "I don't know, child," the woman said. "But I do know this -- if you don't stop your crying, you will be killed."

Yanina turned her face to the ground and marched. The prisoners were far from the city and for an instant, Yanina thought she recognized the village they were passing. From behind her Yanina heard one of the prisoners cry out for water. He cried out desperately with all of his strength. Yanina heard the soldiers shout to each other and suddenly the march came to a halt.

All of the prisoners turned to look as one of the Nazis took the haggard man out of line. "You want water, Jew, is that it? Sure, you scum, we'll give you water," the soldier shouted.

The soldier motioned to the water truck and it pulled up close to the line of prisoners. A Nazi on the back of the truck handed the hose to the other guard.

"Come here, Jew. I'll show you how we give the Jews water!"

The Nazi pushed the old man to the ground and forced the hose into his mouth while another soldier held him down. He held it there as the water flowed from the truck and the old man fought and tried to free himself. Finally, he went limp. His body twitched and jerked as water came out of his nose and his stomach exploded within him.

"Anyone else want water?' the soldier called out. "We'll give it to you gladly' he said, laughing.

Yanina could not understand. Everything had been turned around. Suddenly everyone was cruel instead of nice. Suddenly the world was filled with hatred instead of love. What had happened?

The Nazis ordered the prisoners to march again. They marched all day and into the dusk. Yanina had given up thinking. She felt only the pain of her tired body and the thirst, the endless thirst. She saw only the shining black boots of the soldiers. No matter how dirty the roads were, no matter how long they marched through fields and ditches, the shining black boots shone -- reflecting the sun, and as night fell, the moon.

The march continued all through the night. More prisoners collapsed and were shot. Children cried and many were picked up and carried by the stronger adults. When morning came, Yanina found herself on the outside of the line, marching in step with a young Nazi soldier, just a few feet away. Looking at his face, Yanina wondered how he could do what he did. How could he be a party to such cruelty. Their eyes met and held for a long moment. Yanina thought he wanted to say something to her, like:. "Isn't it a lovely day?" It just seemed so natural a question to ask, two people walking side by side on that bright morning. But he didn't ask, and a distant spray of gunfire brought Yanina back to the reality in which she now lived.

The sound of the machine guns was frequent and got louder as they marched. The prisoners entered deep woods and the guards watched more closely so no one would try to escape. When the guns sounded, Yanina counted to herself until it began again. There was an eerie regularity to the shooting. After it stopped, Yanina would count to fifty, and then it would begin again. The pattern continued the whole time they were in the woods. When they came out of the trees into a wide field, Yanina heard trucks, many, many trucks, starting and stopping their engines and she wondered why they had been forced to walk so far when there were so many trucks.

"Halt!" shouted one of the soldiers. The command was followed by more shouts of "Halt!" down the line as everyone was brought to a stop. The soldiers divided the prisoners into large groups and then they ordered one of the groups to follow them. Again came the shooting, only louder this time. Yanina counted to fifty and like clockwork, it began again. Still she reasoned the gunfire could not mean anything bad because no one screamed or cried for help. There was just silence, and then the machine guns' quick thunder.

Finally Yanina's group was separated from the rest and ordered out into an open field. The Nazis carried their guns and whips and when anyone fell or even slowed, they felt the bite of that whip. The shining boots were right next to Yanina as they distributed shovels to the prisoners. "Dig!" they ordered. "Dig, dig, faster, faster!" as the whip would crack over their heads.

"I hope they know they must feed us to get work out of us," the man next to Yanina said. The thought of food lightened her heart and she felt a surge of hope. Her body grew stronger and the ditch deeper and deeper. After what seemed like many hours, the ditch was complete and the prisoners made steps out of the dirt so they could climb out.

Yanina looked down and it seemed like the ditch never ended. It was so long and deep and seemed to pass out of sight. As she climbed out of the hole, the Black Boots ordered the people to undress and neatly pile their clothes in categories -- shoes with shoes, pants with pants, underwear with underwear -- and then Yanina noticed heaps and heaps of clothes piled neatly everywhere in that field. The piles of clothes made her realize others had come before her. What had happened to them?" she thought. Why must we be naked in front of each other?

A family began to gather together near her and Yanina watched them hug and kiss each other. She looked again for Tadeusz, but was afraid to call out his name. Her crying alarmed the family and they took her hand and told her that her brother would return soon with her mama and papa. The kind words reassured her and she watched the family more closely. The mother held her boy, maybe eight years old, who was trying to control his tears. She pointed to the sky and stroked his head, speaking softly to him the whole time.

Yanina noticed the white-haired grandmother too. She was holding a little baby, and her white hair hung down her back. Yanina was fascinated by the sight. For years her own grandmother had refused to let Yanina touch her white hair, bound neatly in a bun, and the curiosity was often more than the little girl could bear. Now, here in front of her, was a woman who could easily be her grandmother, and her beautiful silky hair flowed like water down her back. Yanina moved closer to the woman. She stood directly behind her, trying to find the courage to reach out and run her hands through all that hair.

Then the shooting began. The old woman was suddenly falling onto Yanina and the two of them tumbled into the huge ditch. Bodies, more bodies fell on top of them until all of the sunlight was blocked out. Yanina realized she was alive and was going to be buried under all of the falling people. She fought her way up, pushing aside the bodies, blood smeared all over her. Many of the people were still alive and their eyes stared in pain and disbelief. She could see those eyes were searching for help, but there was nothing she could do. Some of the people moved their heads and hands in desperation. From above, the Black Boots, pistols in their hands, peered into the pit and began to shoot anyone that showed signs of life.

Yanina froze. She lay that way for the rest of the day and into the night, not knowing whether she was asleep or awake. She didn't move or make a sound. The only thing she could hear were the occasional moans from the ditch of bodies, and distant machine gun fire in the night. When it was completely dark she dared to move. She began to crawl and climb over the dead to find the steps they had dug into the side of the ditch. She could not find them. When she tried to climb up the side, she slipped in the bloody bodies and loose dirt. Everything around her was wet and slippery with blood and the torn pieces of human beings. She knew she had to get out of that hole, but every time she stepped on a body to try to reach the top, she slipped back into the hole again. In a state of near panic, she piled bodies -- one, two, three, four...all the way to ten -- in one corner of the ditch to climb on. When she finally made the human steps high enough, she climbed out of the hole and could see in the distance groups of Black Boots gathered around a huge bonfire, playing their harmonicas.

Yanina crawled away from the ditch on her belly. There were no trees or hills to hide behind, so she crawled on her belly for what seemed like miles. Finally she began to run on all fours, still terrified by the faint sound of the Nazis, getting farther and farther away. As she crawled, she felt a huge pile of cow manure, the first soft feeling against her nearly raw hands. A few feet ahead she could see a great mound of hay. She crawled up to it, then she covered herself with hay and fell asleep.

Yanina in the Fountain of Bakhchisarai

Yanina in Swan Lake

Chapter 5

"All right, class. Let's all come to the center of the stage," Jeanette said. "Peasants, take your places. We'll start with the mad scene."

She called them by their stage names. "Okay, Wilfred get behind Albrecht. Hilarion, over there by the cottage."

Then she went to the record player and lowered the needle. The music crashed ominous chords and the dancers began. She was very excited by their progress. The ballet was coming together nicely and the characters on stage began to come to life:

In the ballet, Giselle and Albrecht gazed intently at one another, each holding the other closely in an embrace of love. Hilarion the hunter ran out to the lovers and jealously forced them apart, telling Giselle that Albrecht is in truth the Duke of Silesia. He showed her Albrecht's sword as proof. Robert, as Albrecht, mimed his character's horror. He knew the truth had been revealed and that Giselle would never believe that he really loved her.

Wilfred, Albrecht's attendant, entered and moved to protect his master as Hilarion continued his insistent revelation to Giselle. She, of course, could not believe what he was saying and danced over to her Albrecht so he could tell her it is not true. Albrecht could only bow his head sadly.

Then Albrecht, enraged, grabed the sword and attacked Hilarion, but Wilfred prevented him from commiting the killing.

The sword fell to the ground.

Hilarion was overjoyed that he had revealed his rival's deception. Christopher played it beautifully, literally jumping for joy. He danced about the stage and blew his hunting horn to summon the prince, not even noticing that his revelation has broken Giselle's heart. She was weeping in her mother's arms when the prince and his daughter, Bathilde, arrived.

They were surprised to see Albrecht in peasant clothing, and when he knelt to kiss Bathilde's hand, Giselle broke free from her mother's embrace and confronted the noblewoman. Albrecht tried to intervene, but before he could, Bathilde displayed the ring on her finger. She and Albrecht have been engaged.

The Mad Scene began. Lisa, as Giselle, was heartbroken. She was so devastated, in fact, that her reason began to crumble. The dance required a great deal of mime and Lisa performed it well. She threw herself at her mother's feet, as Jeanette had shown her. Bertha tried to comfort her, loosening her hair, and Albrecht came over to swear his love was true. But Giselle was inconsolable. Her grief was so great that it drew the pity of all of the characters on the stage.

Giselle's face has gone blank, her eyes dead. Lisa concentrated hard. As Giselle she staggered helplessly across the stage, bringing her pathetic and expressionless face close to the peasants and the courtiers alike. Her movements broke into a grim parody of the happy dances she had shared with Albrecht. She bent down to pick an imaginary flower and crouching near the ground played by herself another game of he-loves-me-he-loves-me-not.

Jeanette could see that Lisa's movements were greatly improved. She was beginning to touch the "unhealed wounds" within herself and transfer them into the utter grief of Giselle, just as Jeanette had hoped she would. There was still a bit of hesitancy, but the emotion was there.

It made Jeanette think of her own emotions just prior to class. Before the students arrived, she had gone over in her head Giselle's great mad scene. But all the thoughts about suffering had opened up her own wounds. In a moment, she felt the chaos of emotion sweep through her in an uncontrollable wave. Giselle's madness became her own. Faces of her past welled within her. Horrible faces of death and suffering. Human screams filled her ears and the sadness of an entire continent raged inside.

She stood with her head against the dressing room wall, hoping for the wave to pass. It was not something she wanted to face again. The emotions were too great. They had to be brought under control. She banged her head against the wall three times, as if to shake away the fear and unbearable madness. She had worked so hard for so many years to put this past out of her mind, out of her system. She knew she had to balance her emotions with the power of her intellect.

But the feelings were running in all directions and their force made her stop still. She held her face in her hands and stood rigid against the wall. More than anything she feared that it would all be too much. The madness of her past made her want to stand that way forever. Ever still. Immobile. To just be free from it all, that is what she wanted.

But she knew she could not give in. She fought the fear, the desperation. If she gave into them she would never be able to survive. She would never be able to work. Her whole body was trembling and sweat dripped down her temple in a tiny river. She continued to fight to get her past under control. She knew that if she remained immobile, she was already destroyed.

While she struggled in her office for her sanity, Jeanette could hear the students arriving for class. The battle had lasted only fifteen minutes, but to her, it seemed like a lifetime. She learned to control that life, to put it into an order, to build from it a structure that could stand -- she only guessed how long -- despite the horrible truth that its foundation was unbearably decayed. In those fifteen minutes she built that life once more. Then she collected herself, wiped her face with a towel and got ready for class.

"What's this I see?" She shouted at the dancers. "There should be no one standing around leaning on the bar. How much time do you think we have? Does any one of you believe we have time to waste?"

Now the class was nearly finished. Her students showed that they were learning quickly and learning well. Once again, dance had given her strength and satisfaction -- a world so beautiful that it gave her the power to keep reaching outside of herself.

Chapter 6

Yanina awoke with the smell of dung in her head. But it was a pain in her leg that brought her back from sleep. Something was poking into her leg. Someone was sticking her in the leg with a pitchfork, she realized. She jumped up out of the hay, and like a shot was running across the field. The man quickly caught up with her, and grabbed her around the middle, pinning her arms to quiet her. She fought more from the shame of her nakedness than from the fear of dying. When she was finally subdued, he held her, and wrapped his coat around her.

"Please. I want to help you," he said. His words were comforting and reassuring, and she was so tired. Yanina let him lead her across the field to the road where his buggy was waiting.

"Is she a Jew?" the woman in the buggy questioned. "I don't want a Jew in my house."

"Please, Mariola," the man said sharply.

"But she is blonde and blue-eyed, she can't be a Jew," the woman said.

"Are you a Jew?" the man turned to Yanina.

"What is a Jew?" she asked. "Is that something bad?"

"What are you?" the man questioned more urgently.

"I am Polish," she said.

"No, I mean the religion. What religion are you?"

"I am a Roman Catholic from Warsaw."

"That is good," said the wife. "Come here and let me care for your wounds,"

The peasants took her to their home. For the first time in days, Yanina felt the warmth and comfort of a home; the rich smells of food seemed to come from all corners of the house. When the peasant woman served her that first meal, Yanina grabbed everything in sight, pushing the food into her mouth as fast as possible, clutching the next bite in her hand.

In the time she spent with the peasant couple Yanina found herself in a world that was totally new. She was still too frightened to consider what had happened to her since her return from ballet school, too confused. None of it had made any sense -- so she blotted everything out. She would have to begin all over again. It was as if she were a baby now, reborn, having to learn all over the meaning of objects, their names, their value. Places, too, were all strange. She recognized no towns, no names of streets, no houses or school buildings. She knew nothing of the people with whom she spoke, not the peasant couple or the other villagers she would see on occasion from their door. People were certainly the strangest phenomenon of all. Who were they? Why did they do the things they did? Everything she had learned before seemed to count for nothing.

Food became her most important possession. It was warm and comforting and gave off vapors that filled her head and heart. She found herself stroking it, loving it, keeping it in her mouth longer and longer.

Words also had to be relearned. They carried great weight, old words, words she had never heard before, which seemed to count for everything. Jew. Someone feared and punished, she learned, someone undesireable. Nazis, too. Germans, the Black Boots who had come to change the world. She overheard the conversations of the peasant couple, she heard the fear in their voices, their late night whispers and secret prayers. She also learned that they were looking for her family. The search had been going on for weeks when Roman finally came to her with good news.

"We have found your Aunt Stasia, your father's sister," he said. "She told us to bring you back to Warsaw."

Yanina was heartened by the news. Yes, she remembered her Aunt Stasia. She had seemed a nice person. Yanina and Tadeusz had visited her often when they were very young and had always given them gifts to make them happy. Perhaps the rest of her family was there in Warsaw too.

"When are we leaving?" she asked Roman.

"In the morning," he said. "You need sleep. It will be a long drive."

The morning came, and from her sleep, Yanina allowed herself to retrieve her past. She began to look forward to being in her home again, to seeing her father and mother and brother. She was certain they would allow her to return to ballet school in Russia where she could continue her studies.

On the journey to Warsaw she began to feel that maybe all the troubles were over. The war was over, the cruel Germans had disappeared, and life was as it used to be. She could not wait to see her room, her dolls and friends. As they traveled through the night, she could hear trucks going in a seeming endless parade, and the thought of the trucks and the machine gun fire from just a few weeks ago made her shudder. She hoped somehow that it was all past.

A few kilometers outside Warsaw, they were stopped by the Black Boots.

"Are there any Jews here?" they shouted.

"No," said the man. "Not any at all."

A Nazi soldier came closer and looked into his face. "Okay, move on. Move! Get out of the way."

When they got into Warsaw they found Aunt Stasia's flat. She took Yanina from the peasant couple. She thanked them for their help and sent them off. Then she showed Yanina the attic flat where she and her husband lived.

Yanina's hopes of a return to the life she had known quickly came to an end. It was as if she were on some kind of spiral, as if the world or she -- there was no telling any more -- were spinning out of control.

Aunt Stasia was a mad woman. She had lost most of her family, she lived in constant fear. Yanina, and the possibility of feeling something for her, was a burden Aunt Stasia was unable to accept. The flat was dark and dismal and pervaded by a strange silence. Aunt Stasia's husband never spoke to her, and she never spoke to him. He only drank. He sat by the window as Poland quickly fell under the Black Boot of Germany, watching it all fall helplessly, and drank.

Warsaw was gripped in the chaos of war: Germans everywhere, Jews being hauled off to the ghetto, anyone who resisted quickly eliminated. Aunt Stasia saw only her lost brother, Vladislav, when she looked at Yanina. She saw her life of resentment at his successes and power, and her lack of either. She saw her own pain and frustration and turned all of her rancor on Yanina.

She put the young girl to work immediately, she spat at her and threatened her with beatings.

To Yanina it was all so unbelievable. She began to feel as if she were in a cruel fairy tale. All the stories from her childhood were coming true. Here she was, helplessly taken away from her family, at the mercy of a evil and insane aunt in an underworld of fear and danger.

"You are a spoiled brat!" Aunt Stasia screamed. "You and your father and your family so high and mighty. Your father such an important man, a political man, a military man. What did he ever do for anyone but himself? Where is he now that the Germans are destroying our country?"

Yanina did not understand. She knew only that the fairytale she had entered was as terrible as anything she could have imagined. Aunt Stasia was more evil than any stepmother and there was no one to turn to for comfort.

Each morning the wicked aunt pulled her out of bed by her hair, and she sent her off to work in the nearby village. Each night, it seemed, she beat her with a wet rope and sent her out in the pitch dark to buy bootleg liquor for her husband.

Perhaps I have done something very, very bad, Yanina thought to herself. There is no one here who loves me. I must be very ugly. I must be very bad.

The beatings continued, but with more intesity. Aunt Stasia took all of her pain out on Yanina, who would run from corner to corner of the rooms trying to get away. Aunt Stasia's eyes looked puffy and black as coal, lips thin, her brows as thick as a man's.

One day Aunt Stasia's husband pulled Yanina aside to warn her. Aunt Stasia was out of the flat, and he took the opportunity to pull

Yanina close to him and breathe his heavy alcoholic breath into her face. He was very drunk and was shaking, his voice near tears. "You must leave here," he said. "She beat you again, didn't she. Run away, Yanina. Get away from her, she is a witch! She is insane!"

He paced back to his window and took another drink. "I am leaving soon to fight the Nazis underground. I hate to leave you alone with her. You must run away. She is mad. She will kill you," he said.

But Yanina did not leave. There was nowhere to go. She took a job that Aunt Stasia had found for her at a paper factory in Warsaw. "It is right downtown and you will be helping the owner of the factory," Aunt Stasia had said. "The pay will be good. But you must get up at four in the morning to get your chores done here first."

Aunt Stasia's insanity grew more intense, and so did the beatings. Yanina's fear of her became larger and larger. Her only escape was when she was in her bed at night and her mind would fly to the ballet school in Leningrad, where she had been cared for and she knew what to expect. Best of all she could dance. Some day she would be a prima ballerina.

But then the morning would come, the dream would end, and she was forced back into the nightmare of real life.

In the factory, the work was not difficult, and at least there, Aunt Stasia could not beat her. Her boss was a woman. She liked Yanina very much and kept a close eye on her. The woman entrusted Yanina with special jobs, and even asked her to help clean her flat above the factory.

Yanina thought the woman was very beautiful, like a princess. She had wonderful clothes, scarves, and jewelry that Yanina would inspect whenever she had the chance. She spoke softly and was kind, and her kindness made Yanina wonder why her aunt was so mean.

Yanina decided to try to win her Aunt Stasia's love by bringing her gifts. At first it was small things -- napoleons, chocolates and silk scarves. But Yanina had to steal money from her boss to get them. In time the gifts became larger, and the thefts did too. The gifts began to work. Aunt Stasia at least stopped beating. But to Yanina, it still seemed there was no way to please her. It was such a confusion to the young girl. When she thought of her family and how they seemed to adore her, how she could do no wrong, she could not understand how she had changed so much. Why had she become so ugly, so terrible that her aunt hated her? She became obsessed with trying to make Aunt Stasia happy.

One day she stole a beautiful blue satin slip and silk stockings from her boss. She took them in the morning and kept them tucked inside her shirt while she worked. At the end of the day her boss called her into her office and told Yanina that she knew she had been stealing, and worse, that she had told her Aunt Stasia about it.

On the way home Yanina was terrified. When she got up to the door of the flat, Aunt Stasia flung it open and stared at her. "How could you do this to me!" she screamed. "Now she will fire you and we will have nothing to live on. We will starve!"

"But I wanted to make you love me, Aunt Stasia. It was for you, so you would like me and love me," Yanina answered.

Aunt Stasia took Yanina by the collar and dragged her up the the flat. "You are a thief!" she shouted. "You are no good, rotton, no good to anyone."

"No, no, I am good. My father told me I was very good. My family likes me very much. Why don't you like me? I do everything you want me to do. Please like me," Yanina pleaded. Then she threw her arms around Aunt Stasia's legs and begged. "Please love me, please Aunt Stasia."

As she hugged her aunt and pleaded for acceptance, Yanina felt a blow on her head that sent her reeling. Aunt Stasia grabbed her by the throat and began to choke her. Yanina struggled to free herself from her aunt's grip. Then she cried, "Stop it. You are going to kill me. My father will be very angry if you kill me!"

"You little brat! I'll show you what it means to be angry!" She grabbed Yanina by the shirt and banged her against the wall. Yanina recovered from the blow and ran for the stairs. She stumbled half way down them and slammed against the door, knocking it open. She ran into the street and could hear her aunt calling, "Come back you brat, come back!"

The words rang in her ears and she remembered her uncle saying, "Run away, get away from her. She will kill you."

Yanina escaped into the streets of Warsaw. Free from her brutal aunt, she walked. She walked day and night. She wandered around the city, hungry most of the time, except when she could steal food from a garbage can, or beg for something to eat from a shopkeeper that still managed to run his business. She slept in doorways, in corridors, covering herself with newspaper to keep warm. Even the cold and hunger were better than the beatings.

Then the explosions came. Yanina awoke on a stairway one morning to the deafening blasts of German bombs. She found herself high on the stairs and there were no walls anymore, just a crumpled mass of bricks and wood. She heard screaming, moaning. The stairway hung suspended in the air and bombs kept falling. Everywhere she turned her eyes she saw them. She could not move. She sat there watching the airplanes and the bombs falling. People running, fire in every building. Warsaw was collapsing into rubble and still the bombs kept falling. Then a siren cut through the chaos and the attack was over.

When the silence and dust settled after the bombing, Yanina found herself more hungry than afraid. She got down to the street and began looking for a market or a restaurant. But there was nothing left. Just rubble. As she wandered through the destroyed buildings she heard a child crying, buried somewhere, and crying. She listened for the sound and started to dig with her hands and push the dirt with her feet. Sweat ran all over her and dust stuck to her wet forehead and neck. The cry was muffled but distinct and she was sure she was digging in the right place. Yanina looked for help but all she saw was people running and crying out in desperation. No one even stopped to help her dig. Finally she discovered a cellar door beneath the crumbled building. She had to move more rocks and more broken boards before she could get it open. Inside she found a little boy with only a few scrapes and bruises. Behind him she could see his family crushed in the collapsed building. He was frightened, but seemingly unharmed.

Yanina took him in her arms and caressed him. She yelled for help but no one seemed to notice. She scrounged through the rubble for food, but there was none to be found. Suddenly a woman ran up to her and took the child from her arms. She was hysterical and wept tears of thanks for saving her son. She explained how she had left the boy with her parents while she went to work.

"God will be good to you all of your life for digging my child out, for saving him," she cried. "You didn't let him suffocate like my parents did. Oh thank you. God will bless you and keep you safe."

Then she and the child were gone.

Yanina walked until she found a street untouched by the destruction. It seemed not all of the city was being bombed, just certain areas. She jumped on a trolley and rode it from one end to the other several times, hoping she would not run into Aunt Stasia. She decided she would rather starve than go back to her. The trolley stopped suddenly because there was a huge building on fire and the street was blocked. Yanina asked a woman next to her why no one called the firefighters. The woman told her that it was a hospital for the insane and the Nazis were burning it down. Yanina looked at the barred windows and she could see fingers and hands trying to pry the bars open. The people inside were screaming, helplessly screaming, and Yanina could only sit, feeling so alone, wondering what was happening.

Finally the trolley moved again and when it came to the end of the line, all of the remaining passengers were told to get off. Yanina walked down a street that looked so peaceful and friendly, untouched by bombs or fire. The street was cobblestone and the houses had lights on. It was near nightfall and Yanina looked through the windows of the homes watching the people eat their dinners. The sight of them hurt so badly. Yanina could not understand why these families were able to stay together while she had lost her parents and brother. She stood and cried by the side of one house until she heard someone at the garbage can. Then her hunger told her what do to.

She waited until the man had gone back inside the house then she searched through the garbage. There she found bread with butter smeared on it, a chicken leg and almost a whole pear. It was so good to eat again, it felt so comforting and tasted delicious.

As she sat on the grass beside the house a small cat came out of the bushes. Yanina reached out and the cat rubbed its back against her fingers. Yanina picked it up and put it in her lap. The cat was the first companion she had had since she was separated from her family, and she named it Murca.

"Now, Murca," she whispered, picking up the cat and stroking its back, "I don't know what is going on, but I know that someday I will find my parents and my brother and my house. And I will go back to ballet school. I am going to bring you home with me so you can be happy there like I was, and you will have plenty of food. I will take care of you, okay?"

The cat purred as Yanina scratched its chin and neck.

"Tomorrow you can go with me to find my house. It is someplace outside the city and it is very beautiful. Everyone will be waiting for me and they will be mad at me for being gone so long and for being so dirty," she whispered. "Now it is time to go to sleep, Murca."

During the night it rained and Yanina held on to the wet cat. By morning they were both completely drenched and shivering. Yanina walked through the streets in the morning and Murca followed her. When the cat would begin to wander, she would pick it up and hold it to her chest. The rain continued and Yanina searched for a familiar street that might lead her to her father's house. Late in the day she recognized a candy shop where her father had taken her many times.

"Murca, we are very close to my house. Stay close to me, I don't want to lose a friend."

On the porch of one of the houses on the street Yanina noticed a line of clothes. "Look, Murca, dry clothes. Let's grab some."

She took as many as she could and dried her hair and the cat's hair. She took a sheet from the line and tore it into strips which she wrapped around her feet for shoes. From the towels she fashioned a coat. Yanina felt warm again and Murca was purring loudly as they ran away from the porch. Then she saw the iron gates surrounding her house.

Yanina felt a surge of hope. She was home. Everything would be okay. At the sound of the dogs, Murca jumped out of Yanina 's hands and ran off into the night. Yanina just stared and then she ran back through the gates toward Warsaw.

The next morning Yanina was on the trolley again. No one saw her get on or asked her for money. People around her looked frightened and unfriendly. When the trolley made its next stop, Nazi soldiers boarded with their black boots and machine guns. They grabbed several men and forced them off of the trolley.

"Please, leave me alone. Please, I have done nothing!" one of the men cried.

Yanina climbed up on the seat to look out of the window. The Black Boots dragged the men when they resisted, while their wives and children cried out from the trolley.

"Josef! Josef! Papa! Papa!"

But the Nazis tied the men's hands behind them and stood them against the wall of a building, facing the trolley full of people screaming hysterically and praying. Yanina was struck by how clear everything looked. The wall of the building was full of sun and so very white, and the men stacked up against it stood out like figures on a stage, their horrible faces contorted in fear or begging for mercy. Then the Nazis stepped back and fired. The thunder of the guns was deafening, but only lasted a brief moment. It was followed by the most unbelievable silence, as clear and complete as the sun on the wall, now spattered with red blood in complicated designs, as if it were graffiti.

The trolley emptied. Only the sound of shoes on the grit of the street interrupted the silence. The Nazis were already gone. Then the women bent to gather the brains of their dead husbands, picking them up and wrapping them in their kerchiefs.

Even the children remained silent. No tears, no crying -- just the shock and terrible realization of total helplessness.

Chapter 7

Yanina walked. She walked until she had huge calouses on her feet and her skin on her shins was split from the dirt. She hadn't bathed since she left Aunt Stasia's and her hair in long blonde braids was matted together with filth. No one noticed her because everyone in Warsaw was stuggling for their own survival.

The killings knotted Yanina's stomach, but as the days passed she got used to it. Each time the Polish people fought back and killed the invaders, the Nazis retaliated by killing ten Poles for every German. Death was so commonplace that she became totally numb to it, as did most of the people in Warsaw, thinking only of survival, of where to hide safely and what to eat.

Yanina grew weak from the hardship and lack of food. Her sight was blurred with dust and dirt and she began to wish that a bomb would fall on her. She found a bombed-out church and decided that she could walk no more. She didn't know how long she lay there, drifting in and out of consciousness, drifting in and out of sleep. Above her she heard a woman's voice:

"Yanina? Yanina, it's you! My God, I don't believe it, it's you! I thought they killed you with the rest of the children. Someone help me take her home. Quickly, she is dying. Help me."

Yanina felt herself carried in strong arms. She had no will of her own, no strength. Her body was weak and smelly and aching. In those arms she felt so far away, so tiny like a little bird she remembered holding when she was younger, protecting it from danger. She felt that at last someone had come to protect her.

"Mama, Mama, why did you leave me?" she cried. "Why didn't you come and get me, Mama? You did not like me, is that why you didn't come? Don't you love me anymore?" Yanina went on in her delirium until she fell into a long sleep.

It was two days before she awoke, and when she did, she screamed, "I heard guns! I heard bombs! I saw fires!"

The woman who looked down on her was blond and very beautiful. Her eyes were deep blue and filled with compassion. She was Yanina's aunt by marriage. She cuddled Yanina and told her she had had nightmares from the fever.

"Where are we?" Yanina asked.

"We are in hell, my little girl," she said sadly. "But you are safe for now. You must rest."

"But what is happening?" Yanina asked.

"The Germans are destroying us. They are killing everyone. Especially the Jews, who are now walled up in their ghetto, starving, dying."

Yanina flinched when she heard that word Jew again. It is surely bad to be a Jew, she thought. But she remembered that her father had helped a Jew. That's what the Black Boots had said.

"You must stay here by yourself tonight," Aunt Maria said. "We are going to the ghetto with medicine and food. We will return in the morning."

Yanina nodded and lay back down to rest. But once they had gone, she got dressed and took some money from their room. Then she went outside to find the trolley.

As she rode the trolley she noticed it for the first time -- that terribly long high wall, that seemed to extend for miles. On top of the wall were wires and many broken bottles. The buildings that she could see behind the wall had broken windows and looked burned out from fires and bombs. She saw one building that was still burning, the red blaze lighting up its windows. As the trolley slowly made its way through the city traffic, she sat against the window, with her head hanging out in fascination. She heard screams and cries for help. The building was burning at the bottom, and on the upper floors she could see the desperate people clinging to the balconies and windows screaming in vain for help. Yanina thought they were calling directly to the people on the trolley with her -- the Polish passengers, the Nazis. But no one noticed. No one even gasped or looked shocked.

It was beyond her understanding -- all the people with a see-nothing, hear-nothing, say-nothing reaction. In fact, no reaction at all. Just silence and indifference. Yanina looked up at the building, looked at the people on the trolley, and looked up at the building again wondering if the people saw anything or heard anything. They were all so blank. As she looked at the building again, a woman with two children in her arms jumped out of a window and from somewhere the Nazis sprayed them with machine gun, splattering pieces of their bodies in every direction.

Yanina knew there were Jews in that building, and Jews behind that wall. And she knew there was no place of safety for them. Either die by fire or by shooting. She was confused that everyone around accepted the suffering of others so quickly, and so silently. But she soon found out that not everyone ignored the Jews' cries for help.

The next morning at her new family's home, she was told that even she would be needed to help in providing aid to the Jews in the ghetto.

Her new family worked with the underground of Poles who did the best they could to supply the basic necessities for survival to the Jews in the Warsaw ghetto. The work was dangerous and required strict secrecy, and had it not been for the state of desperation of the people behind those walls, Yanina, a girl of 11 years, would never have been allowed to participate.

Aunt Maria explained to Yanina the danger of trying to help the Jews. It meant death if the Nazis found out. But the family's involvement was such that either Yanina must help or go back to her Aunt Stasia.

"I will do whatever you ask," Yanina said. "Please don't send me back to Aunt Stasia."

So the work began. Yanina learned that there were secret ways in and out of the ghetto and that the underground was trying to prepare the Jews for an armed uprising against the Nazis.

Yanina was proud to be part of such a courageous undertaking. She was needed and she liked it. Her first job was to deliver medicine and bundles of flat dry bread to the Jews and to bring back furs, jewelry, gold teeth, silks and anything of value to secure weapons and more medicine.

Yanina followed her aunt and another man from the underground through the dark of the night. There were no lights in the city and to Yanina it seemed there were bombs going off everywhere.

"Quickly, get inside this hole," said one of the man, pulling up an iron plate that revealed a small hole in the ground.

Suddenly, Yanina was terror stricken. "I can't," she stammered. "I won't fit and it's too dark."

"Get in or get out of the way!" the man shouted. "You could bring attention to us. The Nazis will kill us all if they find out."

Then the man knelt down so he was face to face with her. "You must understand there are spies everywhere. They will turn us in for a loaf of bread. Make up your mind when you get in that hole that it is dangerous, and that you may never come out."

Yanina looked at him, eye to eye, trying to control her fear.

"The ground may collapse and you could be burried alive," the man continued. "Or if the Nazis locate the hole they will let loose a gas that would kill everyone. Or you could climb out of the hole and they could already be waiting to shoot you as soon as they see you.

"Do you understand?"

Yanina nodded her head, picked up her knapsack and pushed her body through the narrow tunnel. She was still terrified but forced herself to go on. There was no way back, only forward. Yanina felt squeezed by the walls of the tunnel and wondered how her fat aunt had made it through. Finally, after timeless crawling, she came to the end and pushed on a wooden board above her head.

She lifted the square board and could see she was in a bombed building in the ghetto. There was a man waiting with a Star of David on his jacket.

"Bless you, my child," he said softly. "Bless you for caring about us. Quickly, come in. Doctor Varner is waiting for medicine."

When Yanina came all the way out of the hole another man protested. "You are only a child. Why do they send you?"

"Oh I wont't tell anyone, I'm smart," Yanina said. "They can torture me to death and I will not tell."

"You don't have the strength. You could tell out of fear and ruin everything!"

"No, I am strong. I am very strong," Yanina said.

The man stormed off and left Yanina standing there. When she looked around the room she saw people lying on the floor amidst the rubble. Some were burned, some shot, some dying from disease.

The ghetto was a slaughterhouse. The sick had little help; the old, little strength; the young were scared. Everywhere there was death. People were starving and dying from lack of water. The smell of corpses was everywhere -- the smell of death, the sound of fear, everyone alive wondering why they were chosen for destruction.

Finally the rabbi came up to her and told her she could not return, and that if she did, he would have her killed.

Yanina was totally confused. At first, the sight of these suffering people made her feel powerless and guilty. But at least she was helping them a little. Now, their own rabbi was telling her never to come back again.

"You are too young and too small. You are only a child and a girl at that," he said. He was a tall man with a great beard of black and white. "We are preparing for a fight with the Nazis and may all be killed. But we don't want them to find out before we even get the chance to try to die with honor."

Yanina did not know what to do. She stood silently as the rabbi covered a table in the room with a huge white cloth. The his wife placed on the table beautiful silver, gold jewelry and diamonds. People came into the room one by one and placed their valuable possesions on the table for Yanina to take back in exchange for medicine and food.

Even at her young age, Yanina felt the anger and the guilt. She could not understand why these people were being slaughtered. And though she was risking her own life to bring them meager supplies, she realized it would never be enough, no matter how many trips she made. The Nazi cruelty and the constant killing were overwhelming, and she felt totally powerless to do anything about it.

She became angry, especially with God. Where are you now? she wondered. Why don't you stop all of this? I have been good and believed in you, why won't you help us stop the killing?

The prayer of the young girl was interrupted by the sound of footsteps just outside the building. Suddenly the sound of Nazis was everywhere.

"Geh links, nach rechts," one of them shouted. "Go to the left, go to the right. Get them, kill them all!"

The Jews acted fast. Somehow the wall by the fireplace revolved and they fled through the opening. The rabbi grabbed Yanina and pulled her through just before the wall was pushed back into place. Yanina found herself in a small room with no doors or windows. There were fourteen of them in the room --some children and an eight month old baby.

The rabbi spoke quickly. "I tell you people, if you have to sneeze or cough, don't do it. You will give us all away and we will be killed. Silence! Hold your breath."

There was no room to sit, so they all leaned against each other waiting, and waiting. They stood silently, afraid to shuffle their own feet. On the other side of the wall they could hear the Nazis searching the room. Some of them looked up the chimney and fired their guns to kill anyone who might be hiding up the shaft.

The gunfire startled the little baby and it let out a cry.

"Was ist das?" one of the Nazis shouted. From the other side of the thin wall Yanina could sense them listening. Inside the room the mother had put her hands over the infant's mouth to silence him. She stood in the far corner and pressed her entire body around the child. Yanina could see the infant's arms and legs moving to free himself, but the more he struggled the more the young mother pressed his mouth.

The Nazis were looking everywhere, shouting loudly now and the people inside the tiny room trembled at their every move. Then suddenly they could hear the Nazis' boots going down the stairs and out of the building.

For the first time, it seemed, everyone breathed again, waiting a few moments to make sure the soldiers had gone. Before they even left the room, the mother began to speak.

"Wake up, Joseph. Wake up." She was shaking his little body. "It is all over. We are free, they did not find us. Why don't you wake up? Joseph, wake up."

Then she turned to the rabbi. "I can't wake him up, Rabbi. He is so lifeless. I can't wake him up."

No one in the room spoke. They all realized that she had smothered the child to keep him from wimpering, to silence him so they would not be discovered. The mother was the last one to understand what she had done. She looked at her little boy and began singing him a soft lullaby in Hebrew. She caressed his body, stroked his hair and spoke his name.

"Joseph. He is so tiny. I was so tense with fear. I pressed too hard and too long. I have killed my own child."

As they re-entered the large room, the young mother sang her lullaby again. The rabbi stood by her, but the others moved away to allow her time for grief.

Without warning, the young woman began screaming and ran out of the room, down the stairs toward the Nazis. "I have killed my son because of you. I have killed him, you pigs, you murderers!"

They could hear her on the street now screaming and running. Then came the sound of machine gun fire.

The rabbi took out his prayer book and prayed for God to forgive the young mother and give her a resting place with her child.

As the group stood silently and prayed with him, Yanina felt the frustration and helplessness again. She could do nothing, and it was killing her inside.

Soon after, Yanina's aunt and the man from the underground arrived with food, medicine and supplies. They spoke with the rabbi telling him that they were returning to the city that night and would be back in one week with arms and ammunition. As her aunt spoke the rabbi gathered the jewelry and gold and packed it into Yanina's bag. Some of the people had even pulled out their gold teeth and donated them so that the underground could afford the weapons necessary to fight back against the Nazis.

"Help us," the rabbi said. "Don't forsake us. We are going to fight. And when we die we will take many of the Nazis with us."

Yanina returned to the city that night with her aunt and their companion. Warsaw was still chaos but it was better than the world inside the ghetto. They arrived at their home. Yanina ate a good meal and slept in a warm bed.

Over the next few days she stayed huddled in her room as the underground members met to discuss their plans. She heard them talk about the special German unit called the Einsatzgruppen who were shooting so many of the Jews. The shootings were having a bad effect on the minds of these soldiers, so the German command had devised other ways to kill the Jews. They were gassing them in vans and there were even rumors that the work camps were being transformed into death camps, she heard them say.

She also heard them say that they would not allow her to go to the ghetto again, that she was too young and it was too risky. But then she did go again, several times. The need was great and she was small and agile.

Different people met her each time she brought the food and supplies. She learned that the people she had met the first time had all been found and killed.

One night she returned from the ghetto but there was no one to meet her. She waited for hours outside the wall, but no one came. She sat by the hole and then went to the church where they sometimes met, but there was no one there either. The complete loneliness frightened her so she found her way back to her aunt's house, looking for her new found family. She banged on the door, but there was no answer.

Then suddenly a Nazi grabbed her by the shoulder. "Come with me," he ordered.

"Why?" she said. "I have done nothing."

"You know these people that live here? What are their names?" he asked.

"I don't know them," Yanina said.

"Come with me," the Nazi said pulling her along with him. Another of the soldiers protested that she was only a child.

"She is no child," he snapped back. "How old are you?"

"I don't remember," Yanina said.

The soldier slapped her across the face.

"You're lying!"

Yanina held her hands to her head. "I don't remember. I really don't remember."

"Are you with these people?" the soldier questioned.

"No," she said again. "I was hungry and lost. I was just looking for someone to help me."

The Nazis took her to their headquarters and searched her. When they emptied her pockets they found one of the gold teeth.

"You are an underground worker like the others, yes!" the officer shouted. "Only Jews pull out their gold teeth to pay for help. Tell us about your friends in the underground."

Yanina stood looking at the soldier's desk. Then she looked up at him. "I don't know anyone," she said.

Then she felt the butt of a rifle against her mouth. The blow knocked her to the floor and split her flesh open, breaking her teeth. She didn't know where she was. All she knew was the pain.

The Nazis kept her there for days. Yanina was in and out of consciousness, not knowing how long she would have to endure their torture, their beatings. Sometimes they tied her to chairs and pulled her body apart. Sometimes they beat her with a whip.

"Are you a Jew from the ghetto?" someone demanded.

Through her swollen lips she managed to answer, "I am a Catholic. Leave me alone."

One day the beatings stopped and the Nazis decided that she was not Jewish, that she was a blond haired, blue eyed Pole so they set her free. But it was really no freedom. Her body was pained and bruised and the cuts in her flesh were already infected. She went to where her aunt's house was, but the building was flattened. The whole block had disappeared. Everywhere there was shooting and explosions.

Yanina was lost and frightened and starving. She could find no one she knew, so she just walked through the streets. She felt chilled and lay down in a garbage heap beside a building, covering herself with newspapers. She developed a high fever and became delirious, crying out for her mother. She never came after me, Yanina thought, because I always made her angry. My brother did not like me either. They don't want me back. They could come and get me, but they don't want me, she thought.

Yanina felt for sure she was going to die. But she did not die. Her wounds began to heal. She began walking through the streets again, weak and tired, but strong enough to run and hide every time she saw one of the Black Boots. She ate out of garbage cans or stole from other people on the street.

Inside she still felt the guilt. Her thoughts were always on the Jews in the ghetto or wondering why her parents would not come to get her. Her father had always taught her to be helpful and she had tried to help the Jews in the ghetto. Why didn't he come back for her?

One day Yanina noticed a crowd of people looking up at a tall building with bars on the windows. They were shouting things to the people in the building, and the people were shouting back.

A young girl from one of the windows yelled, "Mama, get me out of here. Please get me out!"

Yanina saw the mother in the crowd calling back to the girl. The mother was crying, and Yanina thought that the girl must be very important because someone cared about her. Someone cried for her.

She went and stood by the weeping woman. Her husband returned and explained something to her about the Nazis. Yanina asked the woman for some food. The man and woman looked at Yanina, who was about the same age as their daughter, and asked if she had someone in that building.

"No," Yanina answered. "I'm just lost. I don't know where my family is. The house is burnt down, the Nazis took everything. I'm hungry and weak."

The man and his wife stared at the young blonde girl for awhile without saying anything. Then they whispered to each other. The woman pulled a biscuit from her pocket and gave it to her. While Yanina ate the man and woman spoke quietly. Then they told her that they had decided to take her home with them.

Their home outside of the city reminded Yanina of her father. They rode out of Warsaw in a duroshka, and the sound of the horses and the bell made Yanina think of how she used to wait every day for her father to come home. There was a huge rock on the bend in the road and she sat on it, waiting for the family carriage to bring her father home.

He would have the carriage stopped, lift her off of the rock and onto his lap, then gently pull on her long, blond braids.

"I love your braids, my little duck," he said. "Don't you ever cut your hair. Never."

As she rode she thought about how he used to make her sing songs for him and he would give her money for candy as a reward.

"You will be a beautiful opera singer some day," he said. "But first you will go to finishing school and ballet school to learn to be a great lady, so you will marry well and make your husband proud."

The stopping of the carriage brought Yanina back to her senses. The family's house was warm, and the colors and rugs suggested it was the home of a wealthy peasant or a merchant.

She was given a bath, a wonderful soothing bath that she hoped would never end. Afterwards, by the fireplace, there was a table set and she ate meats and cakes with the man and woman. The atmosphere was calm and kind, as if nothing was going on outside the peaceful little village. Yanina could hardly believe such places still existed.

After dinner they showed Yanina to her bedroom. The bed was of the softest feathers, and the pillow too, and the covers smelled of fresh air. Yanina's body felt so clean and cared for and the man and woman kissed her good night when they left the room. Yanina was asleep almost instantly.

It was a rooster that woke her in the morning with the sounds of birds chattering and cows lowing -- like some kind of symphony, she thought. The sun shone through the window and Yanina studied the patterns it made on the feather covers. She stayed in bed all morning drifting in and out of sleep.

It was nearly noon when she got up and went into the parlor where the woman was ironing an outfit for her of thick white linen and embroidery the color of a spring garden. The blue of iris, the yellow of daffodils, the green of the leaves -- the simple beauty of it all was a sharp contrast to the cruelty and ugliness Yanina had witnessed for so long.

The woman asked Yanina who she was and she told her about how her parents had disappeared. Yanina said she didn't understand what had happened to them, but that they probably didn't want her back because they didn't like her. She told the woman that once she stole a beautiful lily from the church and her father was very angry with her. He made her take it back, go to confession and then kneel down with her arms in the air for a whole hour. After that he told her that she was bad and that he was ashamed of her.

"Now he won't come and bring me back home," Yanina said.

The woman answered that these were sad times and that it was impossible for a girl her age to really understand what was happening.

The next morning they told her they all had to go back to Warsaw to pick up their daughter. They packed bread and dried meats for her to eat, along with money and extra clothes. For most of the ride there was silence among the three people and an air of sadness. Then the woman began apologizing. "We're so sorry," she said, "so sorry it has to be this way."

"You are going to give me a home and food to eat aren't you," Yanina asked. But the woman became silent again.

As they approached the city, they could see the fires and smoke of Warsaw under siege. Yanina was terrified again at the sight. They rode up to the prison and entered through a huge gate with guards everywhere. The man showed some papers to the commander and they were escorted to a large office with bars on the windows. Yanina was too afraid to speak. She looked up at the woman for comfort, but she would not return the glance.

There was a long discussion between the man and the commander of the prison, and an exchange of money and papers. Then the man told Yanina she had to come with him. She didn't understand why and didn't ask. As she got out of the durashka, she looked at the woman, but the woman still averted her eyes. The man walked her gently over to a woman guard, and gave Yanina a small bag. The guard walked her inside through the door of the building. Then Yanina saw another guard bring out the man's daughter. They hugged and kissed and cried and embraced each other, and walked quickly over to the girl's mother. Then the doors closed and Yanina was inside the prison.

She was too numb to speak.

"Come this way," a woman guard said and took Yanina to a large room filled with bunk beds and women. She was told to take a shower with a group of women and they were all de-liced with a white smelly powder.

When night came, Yanina sat on a bed she had been assigned and dug into her sack full of food that the man and woman had given her. It was so good. There was bread and ham and even a knife to slice it. She had apples and raisins and buttermilk. It was a feast. The prison supplied them with no food so she was thankful that the people had given her so much to eat.

In the morning all of the prisoners lined up in a corridor and then went to the windows, grabbing at the iron bars, calling to their loved ones, asking to be taken out of there, asking for more food, praying and crying. Yanina stood against the wall and watched it all. The loneliness swept over her, more painful than the blows of the Nazis. Yanina began to cry out for her mother. She went to the bars and tried to rip them out, crying, "Mama, where are you? Please come and get me. I promise I will be a good girl."

Her chin barely cleared the bottom of the window and as she looked out she saw a huge crowd below, waving and throwing messages tied to rocks. In that crowd Yanina recognized a small dark figure. It was her Aunt Stacia. Immediately, she jumped away from the window. Then she peeked out again and stared at her with disbelief. She was a tiny figure in a huge crowd. She looked like a child, lost and limp, her tiny head crowned with black. Piercing black eyes searched every window. What could she be looking for, Yanina thought.

Aunt Stacia stood there, never budging from her spot, never moving. Finally, Yanina climbed up onto the window sill to let Aunt Stacia see her. She felt proud and defiant because Aunt Stacia could not reach her, could not even touch her. Their eyes met. Yanina could feel her aunt's stare go right through her as if to ask Why? Why are you here? You are not a Jew! They will kill you! She stared with tears in her eyes as if she knew Yanina's destiny, as if she knew that her brother's family would never forgive her for what she had done to his child.

That night Yanina could barely sleep. She had nightmares about her Aunt Stacia buying her out of prison or finding someone to exchange for her.

In the morning there was a roll call. All of the prisoners were counted and told to get dressed, put their scarves over their heads. The huge gates of the prison were open when they went outside and all of the women were lined up, five to a row. At every tenth row there was a Nazi, on the right and on the left, with black boots shining, a machine gun and a whip.

As the group marched slowly out of the prison yard the people outside rushed toward them, grabbing their relatives, kissing them good-bye and crying. The Nazis pushed them away and warned them they would be shot if it happened again.

Yanina felt a surge of relief that even then Aunt Stacia could not touch her. But she was there, walking beside the group, right near Yanina, who kept her eyes to the ground so she would not have to look at her evil aunt. Then Yanina said out loud, as if speaking to the ground and to her aunt at the same time, "I must be a very bad person. You beat me so much. I must have been bad. My father and my mother must think I am bad because they never came to get me. And now the Nazis think I am bad too."

Yanina looked at her aunt and she saw a tiny person running to keep up with her. Aunt Stacia was crying. Her face was all wet with tears. She reached Yanina and handed her a small envelope. In it were pictures of her father, her mother and her house, wrapped in waterproof paper so they would keep. As she handed it to her, Aunt Stacia squeezed Yanina's hand, and at that moment, that one moment, Yanina's fear left her. She wanted to run and help her aunt. For that brief moment she felt that maybe Aunt Stacia did care, maybe she did love her. It was as if the sun was suddenly shining on her, warming her despite the cold outside. Maybe everything will be alright, Yanina felt. Maybe my life will be alright.

Chapter 8

The train station was filled with cattle cars, cars of thick wood and barred windows. The Jews were hearded onto the platform. Already there were hundreds of other people there, families and children, frightened and lonely and insane people. The entire station was encircled by hundreds of German soldiers, machine guns pointed and black boots shining. On the track a train waited, stretching out of sight. The Nazis aimed their guns at their prisoners and slowly closed the circle, forcing them into the cattle cars. Those that moved too slowly felt the butt of a gun, and anyone who actively resisted was shot.

It had taken over an hour to march in a long line from the prison to the train. Yanina was exhausted and felt her brief moments of hope vaporize as she took in the desparate scene that appeared before her. She was forced into a car with a hundred other people. The fear was so thick that the crowd seemed about to explode. People could barely hold in their fears, just as the car could hold no more people. And when the explosion finally came, it sent bodies running in a stream of panic and screaming. The Nazis turned violent and shot those within easy range. Then to demonstrate their control, they took five young Jews from the crowd, three small children and a couple of teenagers. The crowd settled down, listening to the five young victims crying out for their parents to save them.

There were two iron poles about ten feet apart at the station, and on top, an iron bar connecting them. The Nazis lined up barrels below the bar and had the five children climb on top of them. Then they tied their hands behind them, tied their feet together and looped a rope around each of their necks. The children continued to scream and beg for mercy, some praying, the oldest yelling and spitting at the soldiers. Then the Black Boots kicked away the barrels and hung them before everyone's eyes.

The crowd fell completely silent. Yanina, who had been standing near the doorway of her car was pushed to the back as more people were forced inside. Then the single door was shut behind them and in a few minutes the train began to move. The slow heavy train wheels rolled and the brakes screamed with an intense rage that struck all the prisoners deaf and dumb.

Yanina stood rigid against the back of the car. The smell of the engine smoke reached her nose and her mind flew back to the time her family spent so many hours on the trains to Vienna, where Yanina learned to drink coffee. It was the city where she wore her jeweled gown and danced waltzes with her brother and father at the Imperial Ball at the Hapsburg Palace. The marble grand staircase was lined with members of the Imperial Guard in colorful uniforms of red and gold and their drawn sabers reflected the fabulous huge crystal chandeliers. The ballroom was enormous, lavishly decorated with the riches of past royalty. Yanina and her family danced to the playing of the Vienna Philharmonic Orchestra, performing the works of the king of waltzes -- Johann Strauss. Yanina's gown would float and spread in all directions at each turn as her father whispered, "You are my princess, my daughter." And Yanina would respond, "You are my prince, Father," She looked at him with his uniform and chest filled with bright medals. He too had a saber that reflected the elegance of those days.

The train hit higher speads now and Yanina came out of her reverie. She looked around her and counted one hundred and ten people in the car -- women, children, men of all ages with their belongings and suitcases. The cars were made to hold eight horses, but the Nazis had managed to crowd one hundred and ten people inside.

During the first few hours no one spoke. The prisoners were polite and tried to make way for each other. In a short time, however, the difficulties of basic human living thrust themselves upon the crowd. There were no facilities for urinating or defecating, and no way to dispose of the human excrement. Some mothers had cooking pots among their belongings which they let people use, holding up a blanket as a curtain. One man used his pocket knife to cut a hole in the floor of the car, so they could empty the waste, but there was no water to rinse the pots or paper to use for wiping. Some of the prisoners banged the walls and yelled for help, afraid of the inevitable health problems, but there was no answer.

Despite the mounting terror, the Jews tried as best they could to be courteous and helpful. But as time passed the social manners cracked. Soon there were serious fights, the children cried, the sick moaned and called out, the older people lamented. The stench was unbearable.

Those still in good health began to notice their own discomforts and fought to protect themselves. Men, women and children struggled hysterically for every square inch of space. As night fell, with fights breaking out one after the other, Yanina began to feel as if she were being smothered to death. She too began to fight and scratch those around her for her own precious space.

By the end of the first day several people died -- a man who had been arrested and taken from his hospital bed, a child was trampled to death, a woman had a heart attack, one of the others was smothered. Out of desparation for some kind of order, the prisoners managed to designate a few of the stronger among themselves to take charge. There was a doctor on board and he chose captains; two women were chosen to help with weaker people.

"We must survive this," shouted one of the captains. "We must start a heavy program of hygiene and discipline. We have a few decaying bodies among us, we are without medicine and we have some very sick people here."

The food began to run out. The guards had given the prisoners nothing, and the little bits of food that some of the Jews had managed to bring with them were nearly depleted.

Then one day the head SS guard appeared at the small barred window at the front of the car. "We want gold and diamonds and watches. All of your fountain pens and your leather briefcases. When all of these have been collected, you will be issued some water."

The Jews looked at each other and their lips were parched. Everyone gathered the goods for the Nazis. "We need two buckets of water," said one of the captains. "We have one hundred people here." But the two buckets were not enough. Everyone was allowed only a drop.

Thirst became one of the lesser threats. Illness was spreading: dysentery, children with scarlet fever. One man suffered a heart attack and his son had no pills to save him. He held his father in his arms and watched him die. Suddenly, the train stopped, the door opened and a Nazi soldier entered. The son charged him screaming, "My father is dead! We have many dead on this car."

"Keep your dead," said the Nazi. "You will have many more soon."

Even after all their tribulations, the prisoners were shocked by the indifference. More died, and the survivors became completely numb. No one discussed the seriousness of their plight out of fear of starting panic. The train stopped again. Hopes rose among the prisoners that they would at last be able to get out of the cattle car and breathe fresh air. But these hopes were soon dashed when one of the Nazis told them they would spend yet another night in the car. The living huddled into one corner as best they could to avoid the decaying bodies.

In the morning the doors were opened. "There will be no discussions, no talk," one of the Black Boots ordered. The prisoners were ordered to align in straight columns. Everywhere Yanina looked there were prisoners. Thousands of them, and the columns stretched for hundreds of yards. The Nazis began to choose among them, sending some to the right, some to the left. Children and the older people were sent to the left, and at the moment of parting came the horrible shrieks of despair, terrifying cries that rang out through the Polish countryside. Those that resisted were beaten brutally. Yanina's turn came and she was pushed to the left. Then an officer, a tall blonde Nazi, looked closely at her as he passed. "You are no child," he said. "Look at those breasts. You are strong enough to work." Yanina stepped to the right, and it was a step into the living. The others were considered useless to the Germans -- old people and children too young to work. They were soon killed.

The camp to which the survivors were taken was six by nine miles in area. It was surrounded by cement posts, fourteen feet high and sixteen inches thick. The posts were placed four yards apart and strung with row after row of barbed wire. On each post was an electric lamp that shone into the camp. As long as those lights were on, the fence was charged with electricity. A tall gate stood at the entrance to the camp above which were the words: "Arbeit macht frei." -- "Work will make you free." The camp was called Auschwitz.

Yanina entered the camp and actually felt a brief moment of hope. Work after all was not frightening. At least you must be alive to work. The rumors that had spread among the prisoners were of death and torture. Work was not a threat.

Outside the camp was a town called Birkenau. There was smoke in a constant line to the sky billowing from the chimneys in the town. The smell was unbelievable, the sky always black.

Even in the camp the prisoners were allowed to carry a few personal items. Yanina clutched the photos of her father, mother and home that she had received from Aunt Stacia. Others hung onto photos too, bits of memories, a kerchief from a lost wife, a child's wooden toy. Inside the camp there were row after row of low slung barracks buildings -- lagers. The buildings seemed to stretch as far as the prisoners could see.

Yanina and the others felt death all around them. It left an odor, a stillness that was sensed by the body rather than the mind. The Star of David was everywhere, on thousands of people. Everyone was given a number, tatooed upon their wrists, and these numbers replaced their names. "I am not a Jew," Yanina told a Nazi officer in the processing office. "I am Catholic. Please let me out of here. There has been a mistake!"

"Shut up, you scum, and get moving," he replied.

"But there has been a mistake. I should not be here," she cried.

"You won't be here for long. When you get too worn out to work, it's off to Birkenau," he smirked, and his fellow officers laughed too.

After being numbered, the prisoners were ushered into another room where they were ordered to undress. "Up against the walls," the Nazis ordered. Then the guards struck their naked bodies with truncheons. The Jews tried to hide their most precious belongings in their fists, and some put diamonds in their mouths. Prayer books, pictures, papers were protruding from their white knuckles. Yanina was pulled by her hair into a small room where there were two men with huge scissors.

When she saw them she clutched her hair. "You can't cut my braids," she pleaded. "My father loves my braids. He'll kill you if you cut them!"

The Nazis came at her with the scissors. Yanina ran around the room as they chased her and pulled at her hair. "No, no, you can't! My father told me not to ever cut my hair! Leave me alone!" she cried.

She was hysterical, screaming her hate at them, resisting with what youthful strength was left in her body. She still believed her father was coming, and when he saw what they were doing, he would be furious. He would kill them all. The Nazis subdued her and held her tight against a chair as the scissors crunched in her ear. Yanina's mouth found one of the soldier's arms and locked into the firm muscle with its teeth. A blow to the head and a rag stuffed into her mouth ended the struggle.

With her head held down she could see her hair falling on her lap, and with each piece that fell, she shook and fought with all her strength. She was clipped and cut and as the hair fell, parts of her being began to go too. She felt it slip, the pain, the rage and frustration. The total helplessness began to give way to feeling. She felt herself being bathed in shower of tears, and the hurt began to wash away with each moment.

Finally she was led into a corner of the room and she heard the Nazi officer order one of the guards to teach her discipline. Yanina lived through the beating, the lashes of the Nazi whip, as a spectator, far across the room, as if it were a downstage aside, while she at centerstage prepared for a performance. She imagined her legs lifting into the air in a high alaseconde as the orchestra played and the audience applauded and applauded. As the beating ended, she felt as is she were still observing, watching them lead a young girl into a long low building. Inside there were endless, poorly made, wooden bunks, stretched before her, filled with skeletonlike bodies. She thought perhaps these were the Wilis from Giselle, the other beautiful young girls who were taken from life, but their costumes were too grotesque. Where were the delicate chiffon gowns that were made to stream through the air as they danced? Where were their leaps of fantastic seductive beauty? These faces were not those of highly skilled dancers, and it was not the rhythms and melodies of the orchestra that brought her dancing across this stage. Rather it was their desparate chanting, their screaming: "Twelve thousand bodies a day are being burned! We are next! We are useless! We are starved and thirsty and have no strength. They will get rid of us now. We can no longer work. We have nothing to eat! You will be next. You will be worked to death, starved to death and killed finally in those ovens of gas. Twelve thousand a day! See all those clothes? They brought them back for you. See all those clothes? Those mountains and mountains of clothes?"

These are clothes of the dead before us. Look there out the window see the park and the trees on that big hill -- Oh you mean next to the Bierstube, yes next to the restaurant for the officers they also picnic on that hill with their families and drink beer and dance polkas how nice said Yanina innocently -- The woman shifted, so you know what is underneath that hill? Do you see the smoke from the chimney? Do you see the iron gates below? Yes yes I see all that -- well that is the gas chamber and the ovens -- first they push in twohundred people like sardines in a can then they gas them then they burn them to ashes then they use the ashes for the plants above and they can eat dance and picnic after they murder people.

Chapter 9

By the time Jeanette had changed her clothes there was nobody left at the school. She hated this time of day -- after everyone had gone, when there was no sound but the wind against the windows and her own shoes squeaking on the floor. The emptiness of the school loomed so large and the wooden dance floor just cried out to be trampled by dancers' feet.

Jeanette spun into a pirouette, then brought it out into an arabesque. She walked across the floor and peeked into the locker room. Yes, everyone was gone. Then she turned and leaned against the door jam. Why was it always so painful when her classes were over? Why did the nagging ache of not knowing her own past keep coming? Where was her family? Who was her family?

She slid down into a squat, still leaning against the wall. She had heard stories about her family, about their position and place in Europe before the war. But it never meant anything because she could not remember any of it herself. She could not remember a face, could not remember a name or relationship. She couldn't even remember her real name, even though that, too, had been told to her on a few occasions. It just never seemed real. All she knew was that at one time her family really loved her. Then they stopped. They abandoned her. She never knew what she had done to make them stop.

Of course the memories of the war were with her always. They were a collage of images, of unspeakable tortures and traumas, of soldiers shouting and shooting and people crippled by sadness. Those memories left her fighting another war each day -- a war for her own sanity.

Outwardly, she could keep her life in order. It was her mind, her intellect, that got her out of the house and to the ballet school where she could lose herself in the attempt to create something beautiful. It was that intellect that forced her to link into the mechanization of every day life -- the founding of the school, the paying of the rent, the hiring of Kirsten, her assistant, the negotiations with costume makers and scenery painters for her productions, the fund-raising, the petitioning of patrons and businesses, the lunches with the high society of San Francisco.

It was that impulse, that will, that had driven her life for years. It had given her the strength to survive the chaos after the war ended, when it seemed that only luck had kept her alive. A young woman, stripped of her childhood, she had put an advertisement in a Nuremberg newspaper for dancers and had formed a ballet company that went on to tour the small towns and military camps of post-war Germany and France. It enabled her to focus on tasks immediately before her with a power and determination that consumed her and those around her.

For it was only the total immersion into activity that kept back the swamp of her emotions. It was as if the life she had constructed was built without foundation. As much as she fought to manage the details of her life, she fought even harder to keep them from being swallowed by her fear, her anger, her guilt, her disgust. These were the swirling fetid emotions that she tried each day to seal off by doing, by action.

All of this activity took place outside her home. Inside, the emotions overflowed uncontrollably. What made it most difficult was that she had no support from either her husband or her daughter.

Harold Berman could not understand her at all. Her first husband had been insane, and now she was married to a man who was emotionally impotent. Years earlier, before they were married, he swore his love to her. But soon after their new life together, he became cold and distant. He was a man of few words who did not want to admit he was Jewish and was troubled by his relationship with his family. Jeanette envied him his family -- his seemingly loving mother and father, his aunts and uncles, his two sisters. But Harold wanted to put as much distance between his family and himself as he could.

Jeanette had tried to become the perfect wife, the perfect mother. Francheska was nearly nine years old when she married Harold and Jeanette's goal was to make everyone around her happy. She wanted to join a church for the family, but Harold did not want any part of religion, especially not his own faith. She tried to get him to adopt Francheska, but he responded with silence and indifference. She found herself angry and frustrated at his complete inability to act, his refusal to participate emotionally in their relationship.

"If you love me as you said when we were married, why aren't you affectionate with me or Francheska?" Jeanette asked him.

In a rare moment of honesty, he replied, "I don't know how to show affection. My family never showed it to me, so don't expect me to show it to you."

He was silent always. Jeanette wanted to grow, to be a part of the community, to build roots and live near his family, but one by one her desires were squelched. She began teaching ballet in their home and Francheska decided she wanted to become a ballerina. Jeanette plunged into ballet to replace the fulfillment that was missing at home. She opened a studio and it grew rapidly. She was proud of her accomplishments, proud of her school, but Harold became more distant and silent.

The more she tried to get him to respond, the more he would punish her by withholding his words and emotions. Her anger turned into guilt. She could not make him happy so there must be something wrong with her. By nature, she was warm and affectionate, but he made her feel ashamed of her warmth, ashamed of her affections.

The lack of communication led to a confusion of emotions. She could not understand why she was being rejected.

Nightmares began. In her dream she would see a young blond girl watching a man and a woman, stretching their arms out of an enormous pile of ashes, crying out for help. The girl could do nothing to help them. Jeanette would wake up screaming and feel guilty all day. She wished for her husband's arms around her.

She wished he would talk to her, soothe her, comfort her. But he withheld affections and remained silent, magnifying her guilt. She needed him so much, needed someone to help her understand the pain that was pouring out of her, but his rejection made her feel worthless.

None of her friends ever realized what was going on. She had been taught as a child not to discuss family problems with anyone. The conflicts of the home were to be left in the home. Her life became two worlds: the outside world of action, dance, involvement with other people, and the inside world of frustration and pain.

Jeanette entertained her husband's friends and no one suspected the war that was going on inside her. Strangers and friends were good to her. They made her feel good about herself. So why was it so hard with her own husband?

The nighmares increased, dominated by bad sweet smells. In her dream she would be standing as if in quicksand, but the earth that sucked her down was made of human suet, melting, and she was slowly, helplessly sinking into the human fat, melting with the sweet color that steamed and bubbled around her.

She would wake up screaming for help and Harold would just sit there astonished, looking at her as if she were crazy. She desperately wanted him to say, "It's going to be okay, you're safe here with me." But nothing.

Jeanette's guilt turned to depression.

One day it all became too much. She began to hit him, throw things at him. He just took it, casually shielding his face with his arm. She hoped he might hit her back. At least physical punishment was something she understood. It was something she had experienced throughout the war and after the war. But he did nothing.

At one point he told her that it was fear of losing her that made him act the way he did. "You don't love me," he said meekly. "Someone will come along and you will love him and I will lose you."

"But I would never leave you," she said. "I want to stay married to you."

Jeanette began to hope that she might be getting through to him when one day he said, "Give me a chance to love. I know nothing of love, not with my past. Please teach me. Give me reason to stay. Let me be close to you."

Jeanette told him she loved him. She told him she needed him and wanted him to be proud of all the things she had done. But as she expressed her needs, he began to withdraw. The next day it was as if he had never spoken those words.

She found she could not build a family with him. She could not share his family and was jealous that he even had a family. He was immobile and she felt the burden of being the boss, the decision maker, the disciplinarian.

She was constantly depressed within her own home. It was as if she were alone, fighting her own image in the mirror. After the battles, exhaustion would follow and she would give up completely.

Outside the home she managed to keep her life moving forward. She could cope with anything: the rigors of hours of dance class, the emotional problems of her students, the pressures of putting on productions. Inside she was completely exhausted, but outside she put up the front of being happy and no one suspected a thing. It was funny how so little had changed in those years, Jeanette thought to herself. She was still strong and vibrant at her ballet school, but as soon as classes were over, depression began to set in. She knew that by the time she got home she would be a wreck.

The conflicts with Francheska made it that much harder to bear. She and Francheska had been so close at one time. Even when Jeanette was struggling with Harold to get his emotional support, at least Francheska had been at her side, loving her.

She thought her mother was the most beautiful woman in the world. She wanted to be just like her and quickly developed into a promising dancer, even at a young age.

Francheska had been one of the only reasons Jeanette had been able to go on with her life. Their love and affection for each other filled some of the gap that was missing from her marriage. But now that had all changed.

It had been Harold's doing. His single act of cruelty had ruined everything. In retrospect, Jeanette guessed he must have been jealous of the love she and Francheska shared. What other reason could there be for doing what he did?

Whatever the reason, she had lost Francheska completely. From the day of Harold's act, the closeness between then was gone. Francheska became defiant. She fought her mother at every turn, rejected her, gave her the silent treatment and sided with her father.

Ballet was all she had left. The chance to get away from her home and involve herself with trying to create something beautiful was all that sustained her. Francheska still studied with her and showed the ability to become a true professional, but the bond that had once existed between mother and daughter seemed cut beyond repair.

Chapter 10

The barrack was a vast building of rough boards carelessly built. It was known as the lager, and resembled a stable for farm animals. The lager was divided into two parts and in between was a huge brick stove nearly as tall as Yanina. On either side of the lager were three tiers of bunks, like wooden cages, measuring twelve by six feet -- the hole. Twenty women or more were huddled together in them, lying on just wood with one filthy blanket to each cage, wet with the stench of urine. The filth in the lager was unbelievable. And the women were grotesque shadows of human beings -- shaven heads peeking out from behind the boards, wild bulging eyes and voices mumbling or screaming the sadness of the insane.

Each lager had a Kapo, a prisoner like the others who had been given the power to keep them all in order. Yanina quickly learned that the Kapo was one to be feared.

Each dawn brought roll call. The prisoners stood straight and stiff for so long, Yanina felt she would collapse. After roll call they were given breakfast. It consisted of luke warm water that was slightly colored. Nothing more. The Nazis called it coffee.

After breakfast, the prisoners were divided into groups and given job assignments. Yanina's job was to clean the yards outside of the lager and it was there that she met Natasha.

Natasha and she had been classmates at school in Warsaw. Like Yanina, she was Catholic and the two of them quickly made arrangements to share the same hole.

It was so good to see somebody from home, Yanina thought, a place she had nearly forgotten even existed. Over the past countless months of surviving the destruction of Warsaw, it seemed her memories of home were in truth a fantasy from her early childhood. But seeing Natasha renewed Yanina's hope and kept her memories alive.

Natasha was taller and bigger than Yanina, and she felt that Natasha was protecting her as much as she could, especially from one insane Polish woman who had been a doctor.

The woman began following Yanina every day, wherever she went. She would reach for Yanina's crotch or her breasts and several times tried to pull her into her hole where she slept. Yanina was totally frightened by her. The doctor would stare at her from accross the room with a weak half smile that made Yanina's insides crawl. Several times Natasha pushed the woman away from Yanina, and one time even hit her to try to drive her off.

One day the woman came up behind Yanina and began to kiss her on the neck and shoulders. Yanina pushed her with all of her strength and knocked her to the floor. The mad doctor became enraged and flung herself at Yanina, grabbing hold of her throat. Yanina struggled but the woman squeezed harder. Yanina couldn't understand why everyone just stood by instead of helping her. They even seemed to be laughing at the two people wrestling in the dirt. Finally, it was Natasha who came to Yanina's rescue, pulling the woman away and threatening her so she would stop her attack.

At lunch, the prisoners were given soup. The soup was made of water and more water and the flavor was unbearable. It was hot, though, and the prisoners sipped it. To hold the soup, many of the women used the same tin cans that they used for peeing into at night. The soup was always a surprise, for there was always something new in it: tufts of hair, pieces of metal, rags, keys, and quite often, dead mice. Natasha and Yanina shared one of their two tin pots for the night, and used the other for eating soup.

In the afternoon, Yanina was given the job of making leather briefcases and lampshades. The work was hard and the Nazi supervisor was a woman with a face of stone. She was a large woman and her plump body stood in sharp contrast to the prisoners, most of whom looked like skeletons. No one was allowed to talk, but Yanina momentarily forgot the command and asked another prisoner for some thread. Then she felt the whip across the back of her neck. Its tip wrapped around her face and cut a long slice above her eyebrow. Yanina instinctively grabbed her face to protect herself and didn't see the boot coming toward her ribs. The kick knocked her down and when she looked up she saw the checkered skirt and the shiny black boot of the Nazi woman.

"Silence!" she screamed.

The day passed from moment to moment and Yanina concentrated on her work. When evening came, it was time for dinner, which consisted of seven ounces of black bread made of flour and sawdust. That was to be Yanina's menu for years. When she ate, she realized why nobody lasted more than a few months. Their bodies became useless for work, their minds unable to function.

That night the Kapo went into a rage, screaming at everyone in the lager.

"You think they will let you live, you're crazy. We will all be killed like my parents -- gassed or burned to death. I have been here awhile. I have seen it," she jeered at them, pacing wildly.

"The people that were put to the left in the railroad station have all been killed -- liquidated, burned the same day you arrived here. Come to the door. I will show you. Look. We call it a bakery so no one panics and causes chaos. See, first they burn children under twelve, then older people, then useless starved people. All of those that were put on the left side of the station were sent diretly to the crematorium."

The prisoners had roll call twice daily and they were often inspected by camp officials -- people whose names Yanina learned quickly and never forgot. There was Doctor Klein, and the SS woman, Irma Griese. They assisted with roll call and chose people for the crematorium. Yanina looked in awe at Irma Griese, who was so beautiful, she thought. Doctor Mengele was strange, however. His eyes were wild and made Yanina extremely uneasy. He never spoke a word, just pointed while whistling under his breath. He pointed once more to the right and to the left and Yanina stood there waiting her turn, hoping she would not be chosen to go left.

After roll call, the prisoners were allowed to go to the toilet or to wash. The toilets were concrete with a single hole in the middle. They were cleaned by the intellectual prisoners -- the professors, the doctors, an added humiliation as a gift from the Nazis. Yanina never got near the bath. The water was on only two hours each day and the line was so long and she was so small that she never tried to fight her way to the front.

There were 30,000 women in the camp and the more the Nazis killed, the more they brought in. The toilets became kind of a club house for the women, a place where they were able to talk freely, get things on the black market from prisoners who had gained privileges and had access to goodies. Bread was the most common currency for buying black market goods, such as cigarettes.

Because of Yanina's age and size she rarely got to the toilets. She was constantly dirty and lice ridden. All the prisoners were covered with lice. Their pastime on weekends was to pull lice off their bodies and clothes and put them on the table and kill them with a rock. The women would award prizes to the one who killed the most lice.

The lager had many informers. For a bit of bread a woman would tell on anybody that broke the rules. Yanina learned early to keep quiet and keep to herself. Natasha and Yanina would warn each other if they saw the Kapo coming. The Kapos got their privileges by working with the Nazis. They were dangerous and feared by all of the other women.

But most of all, the prisoners feared the uncrowned queen of the camp. The Queen Bee. The Queen Bitch. She was cruel and without mercy and reigned as the supreme mistress of thousands of prisoners.

In the daytime, Yanina moved from job to job. Sometimes she made lampshades, sometimes briefcases, sometimes it was garbage collecting. Her most frequent assignment was gathering corpses. The work consisted of gathering dead bodies and putting them on a wheelbarrow, then wheeling them to the trucks where they would be thrown on top of other bodies and taken to the creamatorium for burning. So many of the prisoners were dying of disease, starvation, suicide. Sometimes they were only half dead, foaming at the mouth and moaning as Yanina loaded them onto the trucks.

The Queen Bee entered the lager one day and pulled Yanina outside for no reason at all. She began beating her with her fists and her whip. The beatings continued until Yanina fainted. Then the Queen would have her helpers pour water over Yanina so the beatings could start again.

Later, when Yanina came to on the hard wooden floor of the lager, she turned to Natasha. "Why me? Why did she pick me?" she asked her friend.

"They want us all to give up," Natasha said. "They want to break us like dogs. I don't think we'll ever get out of here."

From her delirium, Yanina blurted out, "I will. I will dance the Sugar Plum Fairy someday. You will see, Natasha. I will do it."

As the days became more unbearable, Yanina's fantasy got stronger. She really believed she would dance the Sugar Plum Fairy. It was the one role she wanted to dance more than any other. One she had never danced at school in Leningrad but had always longed to perform -- the beautiful fairy of Tchaikovsky's Nutcracker. She would dance it in the lager at night, imagining herself on stage. At first the other prisoners hooted at her and told her go back to her hole, but gradually she began to amuse them all. She became known throughout the camp as the Sugar Plum Nut.

Gradually, the insanity that went on in Auschwitz and Birkenau disappeared for Yanina. She concerned herself only with the task at hand -- eating bread when bread was given, hauling corpses when the dead piled up, escaping beatings, and imagining she was a ballerina. The passage of time and the magnitude of the Nazis' brutality were too much for the young girl to understand.

One day the Nazi guards came to Yanina's lager and all of the women were forced to walk in front of the guards naked. As the women ran, the soldiers grabbed their breasts and pulled them or pinched them. They reached for their crotches and grabbed their buttocks. Yanina felt the greatest shame. Then the guards chose some of the women to take with them.

Yanina learned the women were taken to the pleasure camps. They were small cages with bars, small cells with cots where the Nazis would rape the women and young girls. Sometimes they would beat them with leather, hang them by one leg, torture them, cut their breasts into four pieces with knives.

Many of the women died from the rape, nearly all from the torture. Yanina was chosen as one of the prisoners who had to haul off the bodies of those who had died. The women still imprisoned in the cages looked like wild animals to her. Some were pregnant and the rumors told that if the child was a boy it would be taken away to be raised as Hitler's child. If it was a girl, it was killed or used for experiments.

Sometimes the Nazis brought in husbands to watch their wives being raped and tortured. The husbands would just go insane from helplessness. One day one of the Jewish women held her husband up with words of love, telling him to close his eyes and not watch.

"It will all be over soon," she said. "We must survive this. Please don't let these swine destroy you. They are sick people."

Finally the Nazi, angered by her words, took out his bayonet and cut her throat, then continued his sex act on her. When he was finished he called for Yanina to take the body away and hurry if she wanted to live.

That day Yanina could take no more. When she was through with her work she ran back to the lager, screaming for Natasha. She was hysterical with fear and sadness. She tried to describe to Natasha what was going on in the pleasure camps but all she could do was scream out her disgust. She didn't notice that the Queen Bee was standing right behind her.

"I have been waiting for you," the Nazi Queen said. "I have a special treat for you today."

Yanina shuddered. Then she was forced outside of the lager and pushed ahead by the Queen who cracked her whip just over her head. She took her to the outskirts of the camp to a place where the Nazis had built a hole in the ground the height and width of a normal human body. It was made of concrete and there were spikes sticking out from all four the sides and from the bottom. The Queen told Yanina to get in, and then she slamed the iron grating top and locked it with a lock.

For days Yanina stood in that hole, no place to move, no food, no water. Sometimes it rained outside, sometimes there was sun, but Yanina just grew weaker, slowly collapsing. But each time her body lowered a spike would jab into her so sharply that she would stand erect again from the shock. Several days seemed to pass and she grew too weak to stand so she just hung by her arms from the iron top. When they came to get her finally, the Nazis had to drag her back to the lager and throw her in.

Natasha came over to her and gave her water and offered food for Yanina to eat.

"If you don't eat, if you stay weak like this, they will take you to the gas chamber. They will kill you, so hurry, eat."

But Yanina could not.

At the next morning's roll call, all of the prisoners held Yanina up and Natasha pushed her to the inside of the group so she would not be noticed in such a weakened state. The Nazi guard was pointing to the right, to the left, and as he passed by Yanina and Natasha he paused and then pointed to the woman next to Yanina. To the left, his finger decided.

Once more, Yanina had been spared. For what? she thought. One more day to live, but for what?

Yanina gradually regained enough of her strength to keep from being chosen for the ovens. Her ballerina fantasies took over more and more of her life. She spent all of her free time dancing in the lager, dancing the Sugar Plum Fairy and telling the other women that she was a famous ballerina and that her father and mother were just on the other side of the wall. They love me very very much and I am a prima ballerina, she said. Sugar Plum Nut, the prisoners continued to call her. The faces changed daily in the lager. Old faces disappeared and new ones came in to replace them, but they all called her Sugar Plum Nut.

When she wasn't dancing, Yanina spend the rest of her time, it seemed, fighting off the advances of the mad doctor. Her hatred for the insane woman intensified, but she still did not understand the woman's sexual motives.

One day, after work, she returned to the lager and before her hung the mad doctor, strung from the ceiling with a cord. Her head was twisted, her tongue hung out and her feet dangled in the air. One of the other prisoners told Yanina that she had hung herself and was dead.

For Yanina, weak from starvation, the surge of hope was shocking. She felt such joy and strength in her body because she was finally free of the doctor woman and that strange embarrassing fear that she had lived with for so long. Yanina was so happy that she danced right there while the woman was hanging. Hope was renewed. Another day I will survive because I am free of her, she thought.

As she danced and twirled, chaos broke out around her. The other prisoners in the lager had taken down the body and surrounded it. Then women came in from another lager and fighting broke out. Yanina was still too little to see above the heads. As soon as the body had hit the floor the woman had lunged for it. Yanina tried to put her head between the crowd's feet, but still could not find out what was happening. Then she saw the women go wild, tearing the doctor's body apart, fighting over her. Yanina was shocked. She thought she was the only person who hated the doctor.

"Hey, don't you want a piece?" one of the human skeletons near her shouted.

"Piece of what?" Yanina asked.

"A piece of meat. Aren't you hungry? There is no food left in the camp, haven't you heard? You better grab what you can!"

The women were tearing the human body apart and eating it. As the woman handed Yanina a piece, she pulled back with an absurd comment.

"No, my mother only serves beef," she said.

Finally the Black Boots arrived.

"You filthy pigs! You dirty Jews! You cannibals! Out with you, you swine! Out! Get ouside, you animals!" they shouted.

The name calling struck Yanina as odd, coming from the Black Boots whose intentional cruelty far surpassed the desperation of these women. As a punishment, the whole lager was denied food and water for three days. They were forced to stand day and night in a roll call position. Many of the women died from starvation, pneumonia and weakness. But soon the lager filled up again. More prisoners arrived daily and the Nazis needed all available space. The trains kept coming.

Chapter 11

Even amidst the unimagineable horrors of Auschwitz there can come a moment of human tenderness, a moment that comes like a sudden wind clearing the rancid air, a brief glimpse of the reality that must surely lie outside the terrors of that war, in some peaceful human place, because it had existed before the war began. That moment came for Yanina in her third year in the camps.

She had been assigned to work in the infirmary. Rumors in the camp said that if you worked in the hospital, things got better, you got better meals. The SS officers came to find infirmary workers and Yanina had a new job. The chance to escape the daily killing and the beatings of the Queen opened a crack of hope in Yanina's defenses. She began to dream of returning to ballet school where life was so beautiful, so full of fun and laughter.

Lager 15 was the new workplace. The Nazis had recently completed the building of a new infirmary and in no time it was filled to capacity with more than six hundred sick and dying. But the sick didn't seem to get any better. Patients would disappear. Screaming of the most hideous nature could be heard from behind closed doors. The new workers learned quickly that the infirmary was not built to save lives, but to experiment. The experiments were most gruesome. Twins were very popular with the German doctors. Children would have their eyes removed and put into another's body, to learn if they could see. People were tested to find out how much stress a human body could take and survive, to see how the mind would bear pressure and unbearable noises.

The test of human resistance to pressure was unbearable to watch. If the bends didn't kill them, the victims would slowly recover in a state of physical and mental confusion and then the doctors would finish them off.

*

Yanina was assigned to help clean up after the experiments, performed by a group of SS doctors from Dachau. She had to clear the bodies killed in low pressure experiments, and bring them into another room where the doctors would cut off part of the skull.

It meant setting up the head on a small metal platform and holding it while the doctor cut out the top part of the skull.

Yanina had seen the infirmary as an opportunity to return to the world of the living, to recover a sense of her own humanity, and help the dying get well, but the facility turned out to be another tool for murder, only more complex. Debility, disease and despair surrounded her once again. In a desparate moment, she made the mistake of approaching Doctor Klein, asking for medicine to help the poor souls around her.

"Don't you know it is forbidden for you to approach me?" he suddenly said. "Sergeant, come here!"

Doctor Klein called a young German officer and ordered him to carry out the appropriate punishment. As the young blonde officer approached her, Yanina looked at his face and for the first time since the Nazis had entered her life, she saw a human being behind the uniform. The soldier looked back with such compassion and sadness that Yanina felt he must be a friend. She felt that she and the officer exchanged many words in that brief moment, though nothing was spoken. As he escorted her, she could feel the difference in his movements. He did not push her, but led her out of the room with regard to her body, with patience and even warmth. Yanina looked again at his eyes, and she could see in them feeling, real human feeling. The officer realized it, and turned away.

The soldier's face was thin and sharply chiseled, and Yanina, who lived in a state of adolescent fantasy, began to feel it was the handsomest face she had ever seen. A surge of warmth and passion took over her body, a feeling she had never before experienced. The further they walked, the gentler he became. His body was close to hers, his grip tightened on her hand. Yanina's heart which had for so long held her raw emotions in check, burst with a love and warmth and hope that this young man had come to save her and together they would leave that horrible place.

As they walked, he said gently, "I was assigned to punish you. That means I have to beat you with this whip."

"I don't care," Yanina heard herself saying. "You can do anything you want to me."

He looked at her sharply, and then glanced away. "I am a Nazi SS man, don't you fear me?"

"I feel safe with you," Yanina whispered, averting her eyes.

They were behind the building now, and out of sight of the other soldiers. The young soldier stopped suddenly. He seemed to shake as he put his hands on Yanina's shoulders and made her face him. Then he took her in his arms and held her. He kissed her first on the forehead, then on one cheek, then on the other.

"Look at you," he whispered. "You are so wasted. You are a skeleton. There is nothing to you but bones. I am afraid to squeeze you, afraid I will break you." The soldier sobbed and Yanina could see tears ready to pour out of his eyes. "Why are we punishing you people so much? Why is this going on? You poor little girl."

As he felt the condition of her body, he cried desperately. The guilt was too much for the young man to bear.

"I can't beat you. I can't. I will break you to pieces." Then he took Yanina in his arms and kissed her. As he did, Yanina felt a passion and throbbing in her heart that was beyond her understanding.

"I am sorry for all this," he said

"Don't be," she said softly.

"Have they raped you? Have the SS used you sexually?"

"Thank God they spared you." The young guard was trembling, but not nearly so much as Yanina, who felt herself drowning in a sea of passion that left her weak and soft.

Suddenly he pushed her away. "My God! What am I doing? The punishment is death if any of us mingle with a Jew."

"I am not a Jew," Yanina said urgently.

"But you have a number on your arm. Who are you if you are not a Jew?"

Yanina looked down at her feet. She thought of them laced tightly in her toe shoes, she thought of her once strong body and the elegance of dance. "I don't know who I am," she whispered. "But I do know this: I am a ballerina, a prima ballerina, and I must dance again soon. I must."

The young SS guard looked around the yard to see if anyone was watching them. "It doesn't matter who you are. I must beat you or the Nazis will arrest my mother and bring her into this camp. She would never survive here."

The young guard turned to Yanina desperately. "Please, I am going to beat you. Scream loud and remember that I don't want to do this. Pretend hard, yell as the whip hits your skin."

Yanina screamed. She screamed with all her might as he beat her. And when he was done, she looked into his face and saw it was wet with tears, his eyes begging forgiveness. Then he ran. He ran without looking back, as Yanina lay there reliving every moment of the totally new feeling inside, deep within her heart, which he had left behind.

The pain of the infirmary became for a time more easy to bear for Yanina, if only because she would see her young soldier often. He would stand and stare at her. Their eyes would meet and hold, revealing a storm of emotions that was nearly too much for them to understand: fear, guilt, love, tenderness, compassion. Then the reality of the slaughterhouse would break them apart. But even after he was gone, Yanina felt something she had thought was completely lost -- hope.

Late one afternoon Yanina walked toward the fence where she saw a small kitten meowing and playing. She sat there for a long time thinking. The kitten was on the free side of the fence. Yanina wanted to stroke her, but was afraid she would come too close to the electrified fence. "I wish you could talk, kitten. Then you could go to the village and tell the people they are killing us here. Go tell someone to save us."

The cat ran off, chasing after a moth, and Yanina wished she was that cat or that moth. As she sat there daydreaming, she felt a strong hand grab her shoulder. She turned and there he was, standing over her, the handsomest soldier she had ever seen. She stared at him and he stared back. Yanina felt that wave of helplessness come over her again. She wanted him to lift her up and carry her away. The soldier took her hand and in it he put a large chocolate. Then he walked away. Yanina ate the chocolate and the taste was beyond anything she had imaginied. It was as sweet and rich as the desserts she had eaten in Vienna, as satisfying as the most luscious Swiss creations.

When she was finished she sat still by the fence until she heard the trucks coming to take the infirmary workers back to their lagers.

One morning at the infirmary the young SS guard gave out the assignments to the workers. Then he turned to Yanina. "You, come with me," he shouted, his voice loud and cruel, pushing her with his gun barrel. He took her into a private room and closed the door. Then his touch became tender. He pulled medicine from his pocket and treated her wounds. His eyes were wild with terror.

"I want to save you," he whispered. "I must save you." Yanina could not see the true desperation of his spirit. She saw only that he was being kind, that he acted as if he loved her.

"The Nazis will kill you. Take me back, this is useless," she protested weakly.

"I am useless now anyway," he said. "These hands have killed. I have become a part of this brutality. My soul is dead. You can not believe what it is like inside of me," he said weeping. "My hands are forced to pull the trigger during the day and hold a pencil to study mathematics at night. It is too much to take."

The young guard wept bitterly even as he tried to keep silent, holding his face in his hands. "It will live with me forever, and if I survive, holding a pencil will bring memories of today. Black ink, murders and love -- love for a person I cannot save." Yanina tried to comfort him. It was a terrible irony that she should be consoling an SS guard, but Yanina was not feeling that way. She was stripped down to her barest emotions for the first time in months. But she still had a limited sense of reality. The young soldier's compassion had swept her into irresistable flight, a fantasy of hope.

"I am only twenty and this is for my education, to work in a camp, to kill innocent people, to beat you. It is an education that will never leave me. I want to die with you," he wept.

"I am not going to die," Yanina protested. "I have made up my mind. I will live to be one hundred. I will dance ballet on the greatest stages in all of Europe."

The soldier grabbed her by the sholders. "You poor little thing. You have no chance here. Neither of us do." He let go of her and walked to the other side of the room.

"What is your name?" Yanina asked.

The young soldier hesitated. Then he said, "It is Hans. And you. What is your name?"

Yanina didn't answer.

"What is your name?" he asked again.

This time it was Yanina who hesitated. She looked at her feet, then at Hans. "I don't know," she said finally. "I know only that I am a ballerina, a prima ballerina, and someday I will dance the Sugar Plum Fairy. It will be the greatest performance of all time. Greater than Markova. Greater than Karsavina."

Hans came across the room and took her arm, looking at her with great pity. "Of course you will. I know you will," he said softly. "Sugar Plum it is then. That is what I will call you. I am going to take you away from this infirmary work, Sugar Plum. It is too much for you."

Then he took hold of her and came close to her ear. "But remember, don't believe me when I am mean to you. I must do it. I must convince the SS I have the proper cruelty, so they will trust me."

Within days Yanina was taken away from the infirmary. She was assigned odd jobs around the camp, cleaning yards, cleaning the lagers. She missed Hans. She longed to see him again, and when she realized he was nowhere to be seen, that he was back at the infirmary and she would not be going back there again, she began to see him in her dreams. She imagined him congratulating her after performances, greeting her back stage as she toured the great cities of the world.

One day Yanina found herself working at the gas chambers. The new prisoners were brought into Auschwitz every day, they gave up their clothes, accepted towels and soap, and in a few moments,Yanina and the other workers loaded their lifeless bodies onto the trucks headed for the crematoriums.

Yanina was in and out of her dreams when an SS officer saw her working at a slow pace. He grabbed her by the collar and shouted at her. "You want to know what your future is? Is that it? Come, I want you to see for yourself!"

He took her by the shirt and dragged her into the building, pushing her up the stairs. Yanina tried to resist but it was no use. "Look here," he shouted as he pushed her head into a small window criss-crossed with wires. "Look."

Yanina kept resisting and he kept pushing her face into the window. He held it there as he proceeded with his job, which was to release a bag, wait and then open a small set of doors. As he held her there, she moaned with disbelief. All the time she wondered what was happening in the showers. It was all before her eyes now. Hundreds of people -- children, men, women, old people, couples, totally naked, holding towels and soap. Their faces were relaxed as the doors behind them were shut. They stood there, packed like cattle, looking at each other, wondering how they were going to take showers with no room.

The SS officer said to Yanina, "I am waiting for the heat to rise, the heat from their bodies. It helps the gas kill faster."

Yanina could not believe her ears and tried to pull away as he banged her face back into the tiny window. The expressions on all the faces below changed to disbelief, then to horror, then to panic. It became a room of mouths gasping for breath, bodies grabbing each other's throats, scratching at each other's faces, putting out eyes with panic and disbelief. All of them were moving forward to the little window, reaching, gasping, as if to get a chance to open the window and be saved. Women, men, children were choking to death. As the cloud spread all over the room, the bodies fell, piling up in the corner near the window. The room suddenly seemed so empty, except for that one corner. Yanina screamed and screamed with horror. The SS man dragged her by both arms as she screamed and choked and grabbed her throat, experiencing the same symptoms as the hundreds who had just died before her eyes. The SS man threw her outside into the dirt, laughing hysterically.

As she lay there choking, several Black Boots joined the SS man, exchanged greetings and began to discuss a concert and the dinner they had attended the night before. They spoke of their children's new school clothes, and their wives and how much they enjoyed the ball following the Chopin concert. They appeared to each other so civilized, so normal, so educated, as if all of this around them had never happened. Yanina finally caught her breath and crawled to her lager.

But from that moment, she lost her speech completely. For months she did not say a word. She was assigned a new job, this time in Birkenau, full time, gathering the corpses, piling them on top of the trucks, some still breathing, still reaching with stretched fingers for help, for mercy. There was none anywhere. When she could no longer bear it and tried to revive a child that showed signs of life, an SS guard pointed his pistol over her shoulder and blew off the child's head while she was still holding it. In an unbelieveable instant she was left with a tiny headless body in her hands, blood splattered all over her. That was the extent of the mercy.

"Never do that again," The guard shouted at Yanina, his pistol pointed in her face. "Or next time it will be you that is thrown onto the truck."

New prisoners arrived on the trains each days. There was much talk of Europe. Some of the news was comforting, news of it all ending soon, of Americans and Russians surrounding the camp, trying to free everyone. Sometimes they heard bombs. A French Jew who had recently arrived told the other prisoners to hold on, that they would all be free again soon. Notes and letters circulated throughout the camp. There was a new buzz among the prisoners, a slight energy of hope.

The Nazis became meaner. Killings and exterminations increased by the thousands. The death trains arrived day and night and the prisoners were ordered to increase the speed of their cremations. The prisoners guessed that the SS were killing everyone as fast as they could, so there would be no witnesses to their atrocities. Yanina hoped she would not get ill, that she would remain strong enough to be needed. The Nazis were selecting huge groups of people at random, sending them to the chambers and to the crematoriums.

Yanina had to work the ovens now. She became one of the Sonderkommando, the most disgusting job of all. It meant 12 hour days at the ovens, piling bodies for cremation as fast as possible, some still barely breathing. Yanina would stroke their hands as if to comfort them. The guilt was unbearable, the helplessness, the pain. Still she did not speak.

The Sonderkommando were forbidden to have contact with other prisoners or to even talk to each other. Many went insane. Often a husband was forced to burn a wife; a wife, her husband; a mother, her child; sons and daughters, their parents. The killing went on by shooting, hanging, gassing and injections. The crematoriums were huge, working day and night, consuming unbelieveable amounts of bodies.

Each unit had two ovens, a huge hole and a gas chamber. All had very tall chimneys, sending black rancid smoke billowing into the sky. The Sonderkommando burned 380 bodies each half hour, and the secret shop talk was "How many did you burn today?" When they totaled their work, it came to more than 18,000 a day. Two shifts working, 9,000 a shift. The trains arrived three times daily, thirty to fifty cars long, stuffed with Jews, political prisoners, Russion POWs, Greek Jews. Jews of all nationalities, it did not matter anymore who you were.

It was madness. Chaos. The SS were insane and wanted to get rid of everyone. The special reclamation service functioned without stop. Dentists pulled gold and silver teeth, bridges, crowns, and plates with no injections to deaden the pain. Others gathered rings and valuables that had been overlooked.

Yanina had new work again, more disgusting than the last. Huge casks were used to gather the human grease which melted down at the ovens' high temperature. The grease was used to make soap. The ashes were given to farmers in the surrounding areas, or were dumped into the rivers. Yanina was emaciated. Most of the Sonderkommandos lasted only three weeks and then were gassed. New workers came to replace them. Yanina's prison garb was changed so often, no one knew who she was. Perhaps she survived so long because she was blonde and blue-eyed -- the looks of a perfect Aryan, not a Jew. For a time she wore a Star of David, then an 'R' for Russian, then a 'P' for Polish. The colors of the insiginia varied with each prisoner's category. There were colors for prostitutes, for saboteurs. A black triangle was for work escapees, the green for common criminals, and the rose for homosexuals. Many of the prisoners who survived in Auschwitz were gentiles. The Jews, immediately on arrival, were exterminated. Many non-Jews were killed daily too. Toward the end there was no checking process for who was who. If you were herded into a truck or train, you were exterminated.

Yanina heard that the year was 1944, and could tell from the weather that it was nearly summer. The five creatoriums, the mysterious white building, the death pits were used to full capacity. There were mountains of luggage at the train station for weeks, and not enough workers to clear it out. A large transport of Greeks were assigned for extra shifts, at least four hundred of them. They came from Corfu and Athens and refused to work. With dignity and decorum they refused to be part of the killing. They preferred to die first. They did. The Nazi soldiers opened fire on them, and this act of courage, this demonstration of character, seriously disturbed the German soldiers. They shot and shot their machine guns until there was nothing left but human hamburger.

The madness increased. Fear of the end of their power drove the SS crazier than before. They were loosing control, becoming careless and disorganized. One day during the chaos Hans appeared before Yanina. They were near the infirmary. He took her aside and explained that the nurses took the insane prisoners to another clinic for experimentation, and then return in the evening. "I will get you a German nurse's uniform and you will go with them," he said. "Don't panic. The nurses told me that the insane are very difficult, that they attack and spit and urinate at you."

Hans looked deeply into her eyes. "Do you understand what I am saying to you?"

"Yes," she answered. It was the first word she had spoken in months.

"Good. Your job will be to pin the insane down and keep them under control. Don't come back. Escape during the experimentation. The nurses tell me, they go for beer across the street, while waiting. Go with them -- but disappear. Don't go in. They will get wise to you because you look too tattered and thin."

"My Sugar Plum," he shook his head about to weep. "You must get away from here."

In addition to the uniform, Hans gave her a diamond ring, a broach, and earings to look more prosperous. He put makeup on her to make her appear more healthy, and told her to sit erect.

The trucks were being loaded with the insane. "We will meet again my little one. Take care of yourself. Remember, I live in Heidelberg. When this is all over, we will meet there."

The truck began to move, there were soldiers everywhere. "Hans," Yanina called. "What is your last name?" But he did not answer. He was moving away from the truck for his own safety, looking so mean and cruel, so much like the other soldiers.

The truck arrived in a small village and Yanina jumped out of the back, shouting, "Raus, Raus (get out, get out)." When the prisoners were taken inside, the nurses decided to go for their beer. Yanina was already outside, hiding on the side of the building. When the nurses left, she ran. She hid from people, who seemed to regard her with great suspicion. She had some money that Hans had given her and she spent many days eating small bits of food and staying inside the room of a small inn she had found.

It was too much to believe. She was free! Free because of her love. She stared at her ring, shining so bright. Perhaps she should go now to Heidelberg and wait for Hans, she thought. But she did not go. The good food, the comfort, the escape from the horror of the camps began to add up. Yanina felt secure and relaxed her caution. She began to stroll the streets and shop for clothes, and even eat outside in the cafes. No one would miss her in camp, there was too much confusion. In the village, so long as she kept covered and wore her hat, no one would notice her. She could put on weight, get healthy again, be free. The people in the village were busy with their own lives, she thought. They will never notice a young German nurse as being unusual.

Yanina indulged in her new freedom, and became more careless. Her German was good. She could converse with the villagers, the restaurant people, the children. No one would doubt she was a German, she thought. The rich foods, and overeating caught up with her. She had severe stomach pains and stayed in her room for several days. When she started feeling better, she decided it was time to get rid of the uniform and buy some civilian clothes. Passing a dress shop Yanina liked the dress in the window and went in, the store owner showed Yanina some new clothes. She pointed to the dressing room and gave her three dresses to try on. Yanina asked not to be disturbed. The excitement of new clothes went to her head, and when the dress she had with her turned out to be too large, she called out to the shopkeeper to bring a smaller one. The woman walked in on her in the dressing room and froze for an instant, staring at Yanina's frail figure, her short hair, and the blue number on her forearm.

"I hope this will fit better," she said haltingly. "You are so thin, perhaps I can find something even smaller for you. If not, I will call my seamstress and she will make something fit," the woman said.

Yanina tried on the new dress and heard the woman phoning someone from her little office. The new dress fit much better. It was still a bit large, but would do quite nicely, Yanina thought to herself. When she came out of the dressing room, she was smiling ear to ear.

"I am so sorry," the woman said trembling.

"But it doesn't fit too badly, does it?" Yanina answered.

"I am sorry, so very sorry," the woman said again. She kept staring and shaking, apologizing again and again. "I am sorry. I will be killed. My family would be killed if I did not report you. Please forgive me, we are too old to go to the camps. This is wartime."

Yanina stood with her mouth open, realizing what the woman was saying. Then the SS men came and took Yanina away.

"God forgive me," the women wept as they left the shop.

YANINA
CYWINSKA:
COMMITTED
TO
EXCELLENCE

Me Teaching Ballet Class

Chapter 12

For Jeanette Berman, the toughest part about putting on a ballet was getting the money to finance it. The most satisfying part was that it consumed her time and attention, and kept her from sinking back into the abyss.

Giselle had its problems. Besides the funding, which Jeanette hadn't solved yet, there was Lisa. She still struggled with her confidence, especially in the mad scene. Jeanette had worked with her for months on the scene. She had coached her through the steps, and blocked the scene so that Lisa knew where each step began and ended. It wasn't so much the difficulty of the steps that confused Lisa as it was her acting.

One day Jeanette brought in a mime teacher to help the dancers with their movements, their drama. The teacher began simply, asking each dancer to come up before the group and mime the act of eating an apple. He did it for them first, carefully picking up the apple from the imaginary table, grasping it gently and firmly in his fingers and delicately pressing his lips and teeth into the flesh of the fruit. He even wiped away the single line of juice that ran down his chin with a straight and deliberate backhand.

Lisa was chosen to go first, and the request terrified her. Jeanette noticed her tentative steps as she moved to the front of the class. She was red with embarrassment and even made a couple of false starts toward the imaginary apple on the imaginary table before her body went limp and she ran from the class in tears.

Jeanette caught up to her in the dressing room.

"I didn't know you were going to make me act alone," Lisa whimpered.

"It looked to me like you could handle it better than anyone else," Jeanette said.

"I'm sorry I failed you, Jeanette. You have so much confidence in me." Lisa leaned her head against the wall, and continued crying.

Jeanette came closer and touched her on the shoulder. "Breaking into tears is the best thing that could ever happen to a dancer," she said softly. "It allows you to release your fears, your anxiety. Now you are free to act your part, to go into it fully without emotional interruptions. Are you up to it?"

The words gave Lisa a little strength, but she couldn't answer because she was sobbing. Finally she shrugged her shoulders.

"Are you up to it?" Jeanette asked again.

"Yes, I'm up to it," Lisa said meekly.

Then she looked up at her teacher. "How do you get the confidence? How do you get the strength? I've tried not to be afraid, but it's so hard."

Jeanette made Lisa sit down on the bench, and then she sat down next to her.

"You give yourself permission to like yourself and to love yourself," she said. "You accept who you are. You look into the mirror and say, 'This is it. I'm going to like it.' Only if you do that can you go forward in life without turning to your parents, your friends or men to prop you up. Your progress is fueled by magnificent failure.

"Your strength has to come from within. Lisa. You have to decide you are going to live your life to the fullest and hope when the end comes, you will be remembered for doing your best."

The other dancers had seen it before. In fact, it had happened to just about everyone of them at one time or another. That was one of the risks of ballet: challenging yourself, daring yourself to succeed and daring yourself to fail. When the failures came, the pain was unbearable. They all knew that's what had driven Lisa into the dressing room. They also knew that no one could give you the strength to rebound like Jeanette.

That was her specialty -- the pep talk that really touched the heart, that really made you believe in yourself.

When Jeanette and Lisa came out of the dressing room, they were hugging, as if they were sisters -- two survivors of the emotional wars of ballet. The other dancers broke into applause, and Lisa, smiling broadly, readied herself for the mime lesson.

Acting was especially important in Giselle because the part required two distinct portrayals of the character. In the first act she is the young innocent peasant girl, so full of life that she cannot contain it. She is fragile of heart but her spirit and love for Albrecht are so great that she bursts into dance to express it. The second act is Giselle the shadow, Giselle the ghost. Though her body has died, her fleeting spirit returns to the stage, still passionate enough to save Albrecht from the punishment of Myrtha, Queen of the Wilis.

The mad scene is the focal point of Giselle's transition from innocent flesh to irresistable spirit. The mime that Lisa learned would help her to physically articulate Giselle's desparation, her mad attempt to hold onto Albrecht's love. In the scene she pulls at her hair, loose now around her shoulders. She stumbles in a trance from Albrecht to her mother to the other peasants, limp from her loss, her eyes hollow as if she were already dead.

Mime training would give Lisa power and expression in her hands, her arms, her face. Jeanette knew she had the talent to pull it off. She just needed to keep the girl's confidence peaked so she wouldn't slide into the well of doubt that could ruin her performance, and the ballet. Jeanette needed a young body with an adult mind to really perform Giselle.

Preparing the dancers was only half the battle of putting on the ballet. Jeanette had already spent months interviewing the artists who bid on creating the scenery. She reviewed countless portfolios of costume designers looking at their past work and their sketches and ideas for Giselle. It was not only the design of the costumes that mattered, but the material they would be made of as well. How would the material feel on the dancer's skin? How would it move and flow? How would it look under the stage lights during performance? All of these questions had to be answered before the designer could be chosen. Then came the task of keeping the designer on schedule, the measurements, the fittings, making sure half the costumes were complete two months before the production went to stage.

Jeanette had already signed a contract for use of the facilities at a local junior college. With the use of the stage, the school provided a stage manager and lighting people. Like everything else in the production, renting the college facilities cost money, and the money situation was still not solved.

After class, Jeanette had fund raising appointments. Francheska met her at the school and the two of them planned to make the first call. Jeanette already had commitments from several local corporations in San Francisco she had contacted. They had agreed to sponsor the production and had given money to the non-profit ballet company she formed. But she needed more.

That's why she had arranged to meet with Mr. Pearson. He was a wealthy patron of the arts. When she called and explained her reasons for wanting to see him, Pearson said, "Yes, I've heard of you. I may be able to help."

He had suggested they meet at Tadich Grill in San Francisco. When Jeanette and Francheska arrived, Mr. Pearson introduced himself. They took a seat in a booth along the wall.

"So this is your lovely daughter," he commented.

"Yes," Jeanette said. "Francheska, this is Mr. Pearson."

He was a tall man with an insipid smile. Jeanette tried to ignore his smile and avoided his eyes as she asked him for a donation for the production of Giselle. It was not that she was embarrassed to ask, it was just that his smile would not go away. And the look on his face was so patronizing, as if he were amused that she had interests all her own and was passionate about them.

Jeanette made her pitch, explaining that the name of his company would appear prominently on the program. It would be good advertising and would be tax deductable as well. She didn't tell him how much she needed his donation, that she had run out of sources and feared the ballet might have to be cancelled if he didn't contribute.

Lunch arrived and Jeanette ate quietly. Pearson took over the conversation, talking about himself, his business, his list of daily expenses, all the while flashing smiles at Jeanette and Francheska.

Jeanette was impassive, but Francheska met the smiles head on, looking him right in the eyes and smiling back defiantly.

"You and your daughter are so beautiful," he said to Jeanette. "If your ballet is as lovely as you two, I am sure it will be a tremendous success."

After they had eaten, Francheska excused herself to make a telephone call. It was then that Pearson reached across the table and took Jeanette by the hand. She pulled it away immediately, but he was undaunted and the insipid expression on his face turned a bit more lascivious.

"I think we should spend some time together," he said slowly. "I would like to get to know you better. Can you have dinner with me tomorrow night?"

Jeanette was shocked, but held her emotions in check. "Are you married, Mr. Pearson?" she asked.

"As a matter of fact, I am," he said.

"Well, so am I. And I want you to know that seeing you again is entirely out of the question. It's not proper and it's not right."

"Come now, Jeanette," he said, "we are both adults. You know as well as I that marriage is a convenience of social law. People like us sometimes have to go above that law."

Jeanette was adamant. "I view that law as something greater. The answer is No!"

Pearson paused to sip his coffee. When he set the cup down he was wearing that insipid smile again.

"I would think that someone in need of financial support for the things she so loves would be more generous with her time," he said. "You really could use some improvement in your fund raising abilities, but don't worry, I am a patient man."

Francheska had just returned when Jeanette stood up. "Thank you very much for lunch, Mr. Pearson," she said curtly. Then she took Francheska by the arm and stormed out of the restaurant.

"Mother, what is the problem?" Francheska asked once they had gotten out to the street. "I leave you alone for two minutes and you go and offend the man. How will you ever get enough money to stage Giselle?"

Jeanette was fuming. All of the outrage she had held inside in the restaurant was pouring out of her.

"The man had the gall to ask me out on a date! He actually wanted me to start seeing him before he would offer me any money!"

Francheska burst into laughter. "Is that all? Mother, you're such a prude. Why didn't you say yes? All you have to do is have dinner with him a couple of times. Lead him on a little bit until he gives you the money. Besides, all you and Harold ever do is fight. Another man might do you some good."

Jeanette was speechless. She wasn't sure if she was more shocked by Pearson's suggestion or by her own daughter's words. She wanted to take ahold of Francheska and wash out her mouth or wash out her mind.

"I never taught you to think like this. Where do you get such attitudes? I would never compromise my self respect, no matter what I am after."

"Oh, Mother," Francheska said. "The world has changed. Don't be so old fashioned. This is the 60s and women walk the streets topless."

"Is it old fashioned to stick by what you believe in? Is it out of style to have principles?"

"Your principles are from a different world," Francheska said. "That world is dead."

Jeanette turned from her daughter and waved at an approaching taxi. Then she turned back and said, "It's not dead to me."

Chapter 13

It was the Germans themselves who took Yanina out of the madness of Auschwitz. Truckloads of prisoners were transferred across Poland and into Germany, to another concentration camp --Dachau, the once famous resort town where Germans came to enjoy mud baths, massages and other pursuits of health and relaxation, now a place of death as heinous as that of Auschwitz.

The heads of the camp were already well known for their cruelty and torture. Among the prisoners, even the barracks leaders were to be feared -- criminals, perverts, the insane. Hitler, it was rumored, had empied prisons in Germany and had even made some of the criminals soldiers, in charge of Dauchau. Exterminations and murders were rampant and the fear was just as thick as in the other camps of death.

Yanina's stay in Dachau was brief. On the third day she was chosen along with scores of other female prisoners, those still strong enough to work, for forced labor. They were taken to Nackenheim, a quaint German town on the Rhine. Yanina was assigned to a family -- a mother, father, two small boys and a grandfather. The Hartmanns. They were farmers and Germany gave them extra laborers to help increase food production for the war. A French soldier who had been taken prisoner was also assigned to the family.

The family took pity on Yanina from the start. They assigned her work duties, but were very lenient with her performance, and while

Yanina understood and could speak their language, there were very few words spoken. It was winter of 1944 and Yanina's job was to help with the slaughter of pigs and the making of sausages each Friday. She would work along side of the two boys, while their grandfather supervised. At first the boys obeyed their parents orders not to talk with Yanina. But as time went by they began to quietly exchange information and develop an affection for her.

"What is your name," asked Karl, at 11 years, the elder of the two. Yanina smiled but didn't answer. "Don't you have a name?" asked Hans, the younger brother. Still she said nothing.

"She looks wise but doesn't speak," said Karl. "She's just like an owl. Let's call her Owly.

The house was in town, but the farm was located outside of town. Around the house Yanina was given a list of regular chores -- darning socks, ironing, washing the cobblestone yard, picking old and rotten potatoes and apples out of the cellar to feed the pigs. She was given a room of her own, upstairs above a garage. It was a large room with a toilet and a big window. Yanina could hardly believe it. It seemed she had never seen such a big room, and so beautiful. She even had her own feather bed, large pillows and blankets. The comfort of lying in that bed at night was unbelievable. Yet, despite this new world of big beds, rich meals and the apparent kindness of the German family, Yanina was on her guard. She was suspicious of their nice words, their concern.

The French prisoner was kind to her too. Yanina stole chocolate from the war packages he sometimes received, but he was very understanding. He even began giving her all of his chocolates as soon as the packages arrived. He was staunch, silent and compassionate.

The father of the house had been forced into the army. On occasion he would come home in his uniform and complain about the government, about being forced to soldier. "I am a farmer," he complained to his wife. "I know nothing of this army business." He was a big man with thick fingers and a strong back from years of farming.

Yanina's work was not very good. She made mistakes, she forgot to complete her chores, but the family was patient and never punished her. One Sunday Frau Hartmann allowed Yanina to remove her prison clothes, marked with a large "P" for Polish prisoner. She gave Yanina a small blouse and skirt and a hat and took her with the family to church.

It was a Catholic church and Yanina did not want to go inside. "What is the matter with you child?" Frau Hartmann asked. "We know you are not a Jew. Come inside with us. Surely you haven't forgotten how to pray."

Yanina acquiesed, but inside she was filled with a rancor beyond words. Forgotten how to pray? She had learned to give up on prayer years ago. How could she explain to this woman what she had seen, the incredible pain and cruelty? How could she tell this holy woman what was going on inside of her? She had already been ordered never to speak of the camps, and the family, fearing reprisal, said nothing of the condition of the prisoner assigned to them. There was a silent understanding going on and no one dared to speak.

Sundays were Yanina's favorite. She was free to do as she pleased, and because the family liked her, she was also free to roam, so long as she didn't leave the town limits. The Gestapo in Nackenheim kept a close watch on all the prisoners in the village, even though they didn't realize it. With a huge "P" on her shirt, and her skeleton-like appearance, Yanina was very easy to spot.

On Sundays the family allowed Yanina and the Frenchman to eat at the table with them. In every way, with every gesture, the family tried to show them how sorry they were for what was happening. They felt as helpless as the prisoners.

Yanina's mind was weak and her memories blurred. She knew only her suspicion of kindness, the immediate gratification of eating and sleeping, and her ballet. On Sundays she would go out past the vineyards to the little shack in the middle of the potato fields. There she practiced her plies. She did bar work by holding onto a small shelf, and sharpened as best she could a few middle steps. She was still weak, but little by little was gaining strength and weight.

Food was an obsession. Yanina began hording it, filling her pockets with bread at the table and hiding it in a small hole she found in the shack. Whatever she could steal from the family would end up in that hole. Never realizing it would rot, she gathered and saved her crusts, turnips, half-eaten apples, cereals and bits of meat like a squirrel gathering nuts and seeds for the winter. When she ate, food was the most immediate escape. The richness of cooked meats, the flavors of fresh vegetables and thick warm breads, blotted everything from her mind. While her mouth was full she could remember nothing, none of the suffering and hunger that she had known before, none of the faces of those who died of starvation and thirst, none of the guilt at having survived while all those around you had suffered unimaginable horrors -- all of this was buried more deeply than the pit of her stomach, filled now with what must surely be the warmest and most wonderful meals in all of Europe. Perhaps it was the smells that affected her most. While Frau Hartmann prepared the dinner, Yanina sat at the table transfixed, breathing in vapors of a meal she never believed she would ever enjoy again -- the smell of a family gathered around the dinner table, the smell of love and care for those you love, the smell of foods that sent her to the edge of remembering her past, her own family and the thousands of meals they enjoyed together.

Karl and Hans watched her with great curiosity as she waited for her dinner, almost trembling, her eyes closed but moving behind her lids like frightened mice. And when she ate it was like watching the pigs in their pens, her face right down on the plate to inhale her dinner as quickly as possible.

"But Mother, she eats like a pig," Hans protested at first.

"Say nothing, child," she whispered gently. "Just let her be."

Yanina was aware of their patience, she appreciated the love and protection they showed to her, the help they gave her when she couldn't lift the bags of onions, their allowing her to waste time and forget her chores. It gave her hope that there was still love in the world. Winter was the easy season, but when spring came, Yanina, the children, even the old grandfather -- all left for the fields at five in the morning and did not return to the house until five at night. At first Yanina dug holes in the earth with a hoe, The Frenchman would drop a potato into the hole and the grandfather would cover it up. Later they planted cabbage and grafted trees. That was what Yanina enjoyed the most. She became very good at the grafting, and very fast. The family allowed her to work all by herself. For miles and miles she would graft peach and plum trees and no one watched her. At lunch, the old farmer would call out from far away and Yanina would go to the tool shed, stretch out and eat. Most of the time she was there all alone. At the end of the day, he would yodel that it was quitting time. Yanina would cross the field and join the others and they would all walk home together, sometimes whistling, sometimes singing German folk songs.

No words were ever exchanged, no good morning, no good night. When they got home, Frau Hartmann had dinner ready and they all ate.

Yanina had no household chores during the planting season.

After dinner she would go upstairs and look into the mirror and wonder who she was, what her name was. Then she would practice her ballet as quietly she could.

The bombings started in late spring. One night Yanina was sleeping in her room when a siren woke her. She heard the family scrambling from their beds and running for the cellar. They called for her to join them, warning her that her life was in danger, but Yanina wouldn't budge. When she knew they were safely locked in the cellar she went outside into the courtyard to watch the sky light up. The bombs fell everywhere and from the ground the Germans would use their flood lights to reveal the dozens of planes overhead. Yanina watched them shoot into the sky, sometimes hitting one of the planes which would burst into a spectacular show of sparks and colors and make the dark night seem like daytime. Then suddenly, it was all over. The bombs stopped falling, the planes disappeared and the siren ceased, leaving an eery silence.

The family came out of the cellar and saw Yanina in the courtyard. "You are going to get killed! Are you mad? Next time come with us to the cellar. It is safe there."

But Yanina just shook her head. She was thinking of the camps, she was thinking of returning to Dachau. "No, I don't want to go there. I don't. I never want to go there again."

The attacks from the sky increased. Yanina was milking the cows and the Frenchman was shoveling manure when they struck the next time. A plane roared down out of nowhere. It swept the farm and fired its guns in a spray of thunder and then disappeared. Yanina screamed for help. "Someone help me. I am pinned down by the cows, I will be trampled to death!"

The cows were in a state of panic. They were lined up from wall to wall and belly to belly. There was no space anywhere. Yanina was at their mercy, hoping someone would open the gate so they could run out. She did not have the strength to force her own way to the door and feared she would be crushed by the violent bucking animals. She tried to grab the cows' skin or any hair she could get a hold of, but kept slipping. Cows' hind legs were kicking and bucking in every direction. Finally Yanina got ahold of the ears of one of the cows and climbed on top of it to get away from the other hysterical animals. At last it became quiet outside and the cows began to calm down. Yanina could see that all of the milk had been spilled. When she opened the barn door she saw a body just outside. It was the Frenchman. He had heard her cries and was coming to help. His body was riddled with bullets and there was blood splattered everywhere.

Yanina ran back to the house, but there was no one there. Then she headed out towards the fields. On each side of the road, tall wheat was growing so neatly, swaying in the wind. People were working again in the fields as if nothing had happened. Children were playing on the road, and more people were doing their daily work. A mother was riding a bicycle with a tiny infant in the front basket, singing to it tenderly. No one said a word to Yanina. It was forbidden for German citizens to speak to prisoners. Most of them just smiled and nodded in silence. Others turned away. Yanina felt that these people cared nothing about the war. It was not their fight. They just wanted to plow their fields, grow the food, love and feed their families.

Suddenly the sky, so clear a moment ago, was filled with airplanes. They just dropped out of nowhere. There was no sound of warning, the people heard nothing. But there they were coming at everyone, lowering themselves so that Yanina felt she could almost touch them. The spray of bullets came with them, sending up clouds of dust. Yanina knew that there was something wrong. "Stop! Stop!" she cried. "These are not soldiers. They are just farmers!" She didn't know if she was screaming this or if it was just echoing in her heart and head.

The bullets flew everywhere, the people ran in all directions looking for cover. Yanina just stood frozen, looked up with her fist clenched at the airplanes, and cried out in German. The planes were a dull green and seemed like huge grasshoppers. Some of them came so low she could almost see the faces of the men inside. All around her people were being killed by their guns. Yanina stood astonished that she was unharmed while the bullets came down like rain, and the people who ran for safety were being killed.

The planes moved on to new targets and Yanina began walking back to the town. Once again she was surrounded by suffering and death. The mother and her child were dead on the roadside, their bicycle twisted and broken, with one wheel that spun endlessly, quietly. People wept and tried to help the wounded. Some held their dead companions in their arms. In town the doctors and medical people were already setting up facilities to help those who had been hurt. There was a great confusion in the town and a great weight of sorrow. By day's end Yanina made her way back to her German family. In the distance she could still hear the German artillery firing away into the night.

The attacks seemed to subside for awhile. The people went back to their fields and tried as best to put their grief behind them. At the end of summer Yanina began working in the vineyards. She was given a pair of clippers for cutting the grapes from the vines. When enough were gathered, the workers would bring down a wagonload of them to be crushed. Then she would go back up to cut more grapes. The grape harvest was busy, everyone had a specific chores and there was no time to waste if the wine was to be made properly.

Each day that passed without incident eased the tension in the town. The harvest was winding down and the grapes were pressed and coopered and the wineries were all cleaned. When the work was done a week of festivities began. The German villagers tried to forget the war so they celebrated even more intensely their harvest fest. They organized a parade, tables of food, wine, beer and dances. In every street there was singing and dancing, accordions playing and the men of the village in their leather pants and the women in their tyrolean dresses. Even the horses were decorated with beautiful flowers for the occasion.

When the celebrating ended, Yanina began to wander the fields. She looked forward to Sundays so she could walk along the banks of the Rhine River, staring at its moving waters, wondering how far they had come and how far they would travel. She wouldn't allow herself to think of her past. She would only stare at her surroundings and listen to the sounds of the birds and the flow of the river. There were German children playing along its banks and she wanted so to join them, but she knew she could not. So instead, she would hide in the brush and listen to their games.

The sirens had begun again just two days earlier, warning the villagers of more bombings. Still, the planes had not come for many weeks and already Yanina had forgotten which siren was a warning and which meant everything was safe. As she walked the narrow roads of the farms she saw a group of black people walking so slow, in a row of five, guarded by Nazis and their machine guns on each side. Yanina's fears sprang up and infected her. She saw the looks on their faces and knew the horrors they would face as prisoners of the Germans. The reality of the war was once again before her. In the wheat fields she saw hundreds of prisoners digging ditches for the German battle strategies. The Black Boots shouted and used their whips. The brief peace the village had known was disappearing again into the sounds and smells of war and killing -- something all too familiar to Yanina.

Sensing trouble, she began packing more food into her hiding place inside the barn, never noticing the stench of rotting fruit and meat that eminated from the hole. The smell did not matter, only the preparation needed to prevent starving. After she put away her most recent rations she would begin loosening up for her dance. Her joints were a little looser than when she first arrived, she could feel it. And although she still was barely more than a skeleton, she could feel the slightest progress in her strength. One Sunday morning she was headed out to the shack with a bit of sausage left from the morning meal. As she closed the door and stepped toward her hiding place the floor boards opened before her, and to her astonishment, out came the blackest face she had ever seen.

"Don't be scared, little girl. We won't hurt you," he said. Then Yanina saw that there was another man with him.

Yanina had learned English as a child, and was able to understand. "Don't shoot. I am Polish. A prisoner." She was trembling, not so much at the thought of being shot, but at the sight of this strange face-arising from the earth.

"We won't hurt you, I promise," the first one said. "We need something to eat," he motioned to his mouth. "You know, food." Yanina understood. She reached into her pocket and felt the piece of sausage with her fingers. She tried to remember the feeling of living without food, but could only go so far as the sense of panic she carried from the experience. Then she looked at the dark faces below her with the white hopeful eyes.

"This," she said, offering them the meat. They thanked her and stuffed the sausage into their mouths. "That was very good, little girl, but I'm going to need a bit more than that if I am to survive till we take over Germany. I am an American," he said, "You understand?"

Yanina nodded.

"Our plane was shot down. We've been in this hole for two days and need more food."

Yanina smiled at the Americans and turned to go back to the house. "Wine too. We need some wine," they shouted to her as she closed the door.

Yanina fed the American flyers for several weeks. They had a talking machine with them and when they learned that Yanina could speak German, they asked her to send messages to the German planes, directing them away from the American positions. Yanina shouted into the box, "Achtung, Achtung! and repeated the instructions the Americans had given her.

They told her that the American army would arrive soon to free all of the prisoners in Germany. The first flyer was especially polite to her and thanked her each time she brought then food. "When this whole mess is over, I'll see to it you get to America. Would you like that?"

Yanina lowered her head and smiled. Then she looked up at his face. "What is your name?" she asked him.

"You just call me Billy," he said.

"My name is Sugar Plum," Yanina told him.

"Sugar Plum, I like that," he said, smiling. "That's a real pretty name."

The air raids continued. Herr Hartmann was fighting in the war full time now and it was all Frau Hartmann could do to protect the children from the bombs. Grandfather Hartmann had fallen ill and spent most of the time in the cellar, so he wouldn't have to be moved when the planes came.

During the raids, Yanina always stayed outside. She knew no fear of death, and in fact in some ways hoped it would deliver her from the world she had come to live in. The family had given up trying to get her to seek safety, and when the bombings ceased Karl and Hans always rushed outside to find Yanina, or what was left of her. During the attacks she would watch the skies, sometimes standing against the barn, sometimes sitting on the cobblestones as the Germans shot down planes and the parachutes that escaped from them.

In between the raids, Yanina gathered food. For herself and for the Americans. One of the Nazi soldiers assigned to the village noticed Yanina's habits. "Kommen sie here!" he shouted, grabbing her by her prison shirt. "Why do you carry so much food? You are far too skinny to eat that much."

"It is for the workers," she said quickly. "The Hartmanns have put me in charge of bringing food for the workers in fields." The soldier grabbed Yanina's thin arm in his hand and squeezed it until she thought it would break. Then he pulled her close to his face. "I don't like you," he said. "I don't like having prisoners run freely in this town. I just want you to know I will be watching you closely."

The bombing was continuous now, and the Hartmanns spent most of their time in the cellar. It would make things easier for Yanina to bring food to the American flyers, but the Nazis were out in full force. They watched her every move, she could feel it. Yanina had to put the food between her thighs and walk very slowly, as if she had been hurt, so that she wouldn't drop anything in front of the soldiers.

The Hartmanns sent Yanina out into the fields one morning to bring in a bushel of potatoes when the sirens went off. The "alert" siren was crying loud and clear and she could hear the airplanes above her. The bombs began to fall and the earth shook with their thunder. Germans everywhere were running for cover. Yanina kept walking as if in a daze, holding the bushel of potatoes in her arms. She could see the little shack not a hundred meters away. She was thinking she ought to drop off a few potatoes for Billy and his friend when a bomb landed in front of her. She fell to the ground and could see nothing but dirt filling up the air. As the debris settled, the air opened up ahead of her. The shack was gone. Bits of wood and shrapnel were still landing all over the ground, falling in a kind of slow motion. Yanina just stared at the huge hole in the ground where the shack used to be. She expected Billy to just appear out of ground, but knew inside that he could not have survived.

Yanina got up and turned back to the fields. She wandered among the wheat, trying to stay out of sight. When night came, the attack was over and she found her way back to the Hartmann cellar.

War came to the village in full force. The Nazis were everywhere. They dug ditches day and night, and put their huge guns into them, covering the ditch with green cloth that looked like grass. There were prisoners of all nationalities being brought in to do the digging. The Nazis would shoot overworked Dachau prisoners and replace them with captured soldiers -- French, Americans, British. The Nazis didn't shoot these prisoners, just pushed them to work faster and faster. Rumors had it that the American army was very near, and leaflets fell from the sky telling all prisoners to hold on, because the end was near.

Two dozen Nazi motorcycles came up the hill early one morning, followed by a dusty black auto. Everyone in the fields were herded together and then the prisoners were separated from civilians. German farmers were pushed to one side and lined up, prisoners were moved further away under heavy guard. German soldiers with their machine guns also spread out in front of the farmers, standing at full alert. Yanina was in civilian clothes that morning, overlooked as a prisoner. She found herself standing with the German citizens. Everyone was ordered to be still, and not to move. Fear gripped Yanina when she heard the commands. Are we going to be eliminated? she thought. Not now, with the Americans so close. To her suprise, the Nazis turned their backs on the farmers and raised their arms, shouting "Sieg Heil!" Then they turned to the German people and ordered them to do the same.

A motorcade pulled to a stop in front of them and several men stepped out of the car. "Must be important people," said a peasant behind Yanina. "Here to inspect the front." Then the whispering rippled down the line as the farmers recognized who had emerged from the black auto. "The Fuehrer. It's the Fuehrer," someone said.

Everyone began shouting "Heil Hitler!" Yanina stood silent, right in the front line between two of the Black Boots, who were standing at attention, ready for action. She made a move forward and to her suprise, no one pushed her back. When she looked up she saw him, just a few feet away. She was face to face with Hitler, a stocky man that seemed to Yanina to have a very weak face. He took a step forward -- there was only one foot between them -- and looked into her eyes. Yanina slowly raised her arm so as not to appear defiant. She still looked thin and pale and would surely have been recognized as a prisoner were it not for the simple German dirndl dress that the Hartmanns had given her. As Hitler looked at her, Yanina painfully managed a smile and looked at his eyes, so strange, as if he were not there at all. The eyes were cold, such as the insane people had. His skin looked sallow and sick, his mouth thin and tight under a brush of mustache. He stood for what seemed an eternity but was only a brief moment, and Yanina wondered how this seemingly ordinary man could be responsible for all the tragedy in the world. She prayed to God to strike him dead on the spot, but knew that no such miracle would happen. Oh, if only I could find a long, very sharp stick, I could plunge it into his heart, she thought. No I can't reach his heart, but the stomach is right in front of me. Those buttons, they will be in the way, I have to aim precisely so I can stab him through all the way to his back, she thought. Pierce him from one end to the other. I'd have to use all of my strength to kill him instantly, otherwise he will not die and I will be shot for nothing. It must be a very long stick.

As she stood there dreaming, realizing there was no weapon at hand to fulfill her desire, Hitler moved on. Little German girls handed him flowers, the German farmers bowed their heads in respect, and the Gestapo guards marched closely behind him, in their strange goose step. Yanina knew she would never forget that face, a face of stone, a face of weakness, a face so dark -- not from lack of light but from lack of compassion, lack of humanity.

When the motorcade drove away, Yanina ran home as fast as she could. She entered through the door and saw Herr Hartmann sitting in the living room, his German uniform still buttoned to the chin.

"Please come in and have some tea with us," he said to her. It was the first time he ever spoke to her directly. Yanina sat down with Herr Hartman and the children, who were already at his feet. "It looks like the Allies are coming in full force," he said. "They are taking many cities and things are bad for Germany. The French, the British, the Americans -- they are all fighting against us. It is all mixed up, all around us. The destruction of our farms and our factories is unbelievable. I hope we will all survive this. I want you to know that I am just a farmer, not a soldier.

I don't want to kill anybody, especially you who have had to endure so much. I'm no Nazi. I had no choice. Please forgive me."

He looked at his children and nearly wept, and then he reached out and hugged his wife. He poured more tea, then turned to Yanina. "We have been good to you, have we not?"

"Yes," she said.

"This Hitler, he is a bad man. I have always thought so. I must apologize for his cruelty, for all of this killing." As she looked at his sad face she felt his wonderful human warmth and it stirred her heart deeply. She hugged him and answered, "I will never forget your kindness," she said. Yanina actually felt a part of this family, these people troubled by war and fearing that any day could be their last.

The sirens sounded and the family rushed to the cellar. But Yanina still did not join them. She stood in the courtyard and watched a sight she had come to love -- the sky lit up with enormous floodlights and airplanes bursting into every color of the rainbow.

The next Sunday morning Yanina joined the family for breakfast: coffee and delicious pastry that Frau Hartman had made the day before. Herr Hartmann had gone back to his army unit. After breakfast the family walked in silence up the hill to church. The sermon concerned the end of the war, the inevitable conclusion to the fighting, and a prayer that those in the village would be spared. Outside, the village was serene and beautiful. There was not a sound of the war anywhere. In Yanina's mind, the past no longer existed. No camps, no suffering, no smell of death. There was only the sun and the laughter of children playing. She felt secure, and all her hope for a return to loving people and trusting people seemed to have come true.

Frau Hartman walked along the Rhine with her children and Yanina dawdled behind them. As she watched the river she heard boys and girls her age playing along the banks of the river. Forgetting she was a Polish prisoner and was that morning wearing her insignia, she relaxed her caution and approached the children. She wanted so much to be a part of their playing. She walked up to them with a smile, and they smiled back. A sudden warmth spread throughout her body -- she felt so good at being accepted. They were coming close to her now, when one of the boys shouted, "Look who is here -- the Polish prisoner."

"Come here," shouted one of the other boys. A sense of panic overtook Yanina. She was frozen. "Come play with us," one of the girls pulled her by the arm, then raised it so everyone could see the camp number imbedded in her skin. "She is a Jew!" she shouted. "Let's drown her! Let's have some fun drowning a Jew!"

Yanina fought with all her strength, but it was very little compared to that of the healthy young farm children. "Leave me alone," she cried. "I am not a Jew, I am a Catholic. No, please let me go!" Now all the children were screaming filthy Jewish slurs and they dragged her to the river, pushing her in while one of the larger boys held her head under water. "I can't swim!" she screamed. "Let me out, I can't swim!" But the more she protested the more excited the young Germans became. Yanina splashed her way to the shore, but again they grabbed her by the arms. Then two of the children took her legs and they swung her back and forth, back and forth like a swing, letting her go flying far out into the river. Yanina managed to swim back toward them, but they only jumped in again and pushed her back out, all the time calling her a filthy Jew.

Yanina knew she could no longer fight them. She felt they would drown her for sure. She tried to swim to get away from them. She paddled her arms and kicked in panic to escape. As she did, she could hear them further and further away from her. She was escaping. The voices were fading. When she realized she was getting away from them she got a burst of energy and paddled that much harder. Finally she came to the shore and they were nowhere to be seen. She had swum to the other side of the Rhine. She looked behind her and there they were, the village behind them. Yanina was elated. Not only had she escaped the children, but she had swum a great distance when she didn't even know how to swim.

But her escape was illusory. When she looked up she saw the Black Boots. Soldiers were everywhere. A gun barrel was pointed at her head. "What have we here?" asked the Nazi. "Trying to escape, are we?"

"No, no," Yanina protested, but when she tried to explain she felt the barrel of that gun in the forehead. It knocked her to the ground.

"Look she has as number," she vaguely heard them saying. "It is a Jew trying to escape." Yanina was barely conscious, but realized she was in the grasp of the killers again. She was loaded onto a truck, but she was not alone. The truck was already filled with people. Jews. They were being taken to Dachau.

They were Dutch Jews. One of the woman spoke to her. "It does not look good child. The Nazis have gone mad. They are loosing the war and they know it. Some of the Nazis are killing themselves to escape capture, and that is good. But they are killing Jews with a rage that is unbelievable."

The blow to the head had disoriented Yanina completely. She faded in and out of consciousness. When her head finally began to clear she realized she was back in Dachau.

Chapter 14

Jeanette never knew exactly how to be a mother. That was something she finally realized, and it hurt.

It's not that she wanted to put the blame on herself. No, her ruined relationship with Francheska clearly fell in the lap of her husband, Harold Berman. It was just that she had never learned how to be a mother. Her own mother had been taken away from her so long ago she couldn't remember who the woman was, and her childhood was taken away too. How could she be expected to know how to be a mother when she had never had anyone to show her how?

Jeanette was only sixteen when she had Francheska. She didn't even know she was pregnant until she awoke in a hospital with the nurses holding up her baby -- that's how ignorant she had been about sex, and about life in general. Six years surviving the inescapable war in Europe, most of that time in concentration camps, had ill-prepared her for the rigors of motherhood. She had been stripped down to the barest form of human being, a minimal organism whose body was just strong enough to support her two remaining emotions -- hope and guilt. Her mind had long since retreated into the realm of fantasy.

Within a year of getting out of the camps, she was a mother. She had less than one year to adapt to the world outside the repression of the camps, one year to try to regain physical strength, to find an identity and a means of survival in a post-war Europe where nearly 60 million displaced persons wandered, each looking for an identity of his own.

But she had done her best. Francheska, after all, was the beginning of a new family. Jeanette's own family had been killed in the war. She could still not recall their names, their faces, the wisdom or sadness in their voices. But when Francheska came, Jeanette could finally love someone that existed before her own eyes, someone that she could touch, someone who needed her -- a family at last.

She cared for her infant as best she could, getting help from Frau Pager, who had been so good to her when she needed help. She watched Francheska when Jeanette went out to find work. Forming the ballet company demanded time, and travel and late hours, and Frau Pager had been there to care for her young daughter.

Later, as Jeanette traveled throughout Europe with Madame Karsavina and danced with the De Cuevas Ballet, Francheska was there with her. Often it was someone else who looked after her, who cleaned her and fed her -- even Jeanette and the other dancers had someone to dress them and feed them and fix their hair -- but at the end of the day little Francheska always ran for her mama, and hugged her and told her how much she loved her.

Jeanette and Francheska had been very close. Together they survived Jeanette's first marriage. They survived the separation and the ordeal of coming to America, when Francheska had been left behind because Jeanette's husband did not want her. It took her nearly two years to get Francheska into the country.

But, in spite of the hardships, they had still loved each other. Francheska was her only real family.

That's why it hurt so much to have lost her love, to have lost her respect, to have lost the ability to communicate with her. There was no way for Jeanette to realize that in the 1960s mothers and fathers all over America felt the same way about their children because their children had rejected them too.

Her husband was of no help. He seemed to feel nothing and explained nothing. But even if someone had explained it to Jeanette she would have known that her war with Francheska was more deeply rooted than being a part of adolescent rejection and cultural trends.

Jeanette thought back to how much Francheska had adored her. It was just after she had married Harold. She and Francheska were best of friends. They had moved to San Francisco with Harold, Jeanette's new husband, leaving behind her brief career in Hollywood where she had danced and taught dance and known many of the stars of the movie industry. Even though Jeanette devoted herself to being a wife and mother, she could not resist involvement with the world of dance. She soon began teaching ballet in their home.

Francheska was fascinated by her mother's ability to teach people. She was enthralled by the beauty of ballet and decided right then that she too would be a dancer, just like her beautiful mother.

When, soon after her marriage to Harold, she discovered that he waged an emotional cold war on her, it was only the love of Francheska and the dedication to ballet that saved her sanity.

Francheska began studying ballet with the other students who came to the house. She learned quickly and Jeanette could tell from her abilities, even as a ten-year-old, that she could become a very successful ballerina. Two of her best students were friends of Francheska's from school. They too showed they had talent, and began spending so much time at the house, they became like members of the family.

Jeanette's inspiration and ability to direct their talents made the girls idolize her. To them, Francheska was the luckiest girl in the world to be the daughter of a woman who was not only beautiful, but an outstanding ballerina as well.

As Jeanette's relationship with Harold became more difficult, she spent more and more time with Francheska and with her students. Her love for Francheska and ballet became more and more desparate as she suppressed the anger, the confusion and the guilt that Harold made her feel. The harder she worked to make her life a success and the prouder she became when it was successful, the more distant he became, withholding all emotion, punishing her with silence. Jeanette knew that her desire to live a full life and to experience that life with enthusiasm caused Harold to be unhappy, but she couldn't understand why.

During that first year of their marriage she had tried to get him to legally adopt Francheska so she could have a complete family and the proper roots on which to build her own life. But Harold refused. The more Jeanette pleaded, the more silent he became. For her, it was total frustration. She finally had the opportunity to build a life of her own, to become fulfilled and independent and successful. But her own husband squelched her hopes. She looked to him for understanding and support, and he gave her silence.

That's when the dreams began.

In the middle of the night Jeanette would find herself on her knees crying, holding onto the door knob of her bedroom door with both hands. "Mama, Mama," she cried, "why didn't you come back for me? Why did you leave me?"

In other dreams she saw a young blond girl by the name of Yanina, and a man and a woman with their arms reaching out from a enormous mound of ashes, crying for help. The young girl could do nothing to help. Jeanette awoke screaming and was overcome with guilt all day. She wished for her husband's arms around her, wished that he would talk to her, soothe and comfort her. But he withheld affection and remained silent, making her feel even more guilty.

The nighmares were followed by days of deep depression. Jeanette struggled to feel excitement about life. Exhausted on the inside, she forced herself to carry the appearance of happiness, to put on the front while dancing and teaching. And it worked. At school she was happy and whole, but as soon as classes ended, the depression settled like sudden nightfall.

She tried desperately to explain to Harold that she needed love and understanding. He could not give it to her. Francheska was the only one who gave her the love she so desparately needed.

But even that came to a bitter end. Francheska was only ten years old when it happened. Why Harold would have done such a cruel thing, Jeanette could not comprehend. She confronted him.

"Francheska just came to me in tears, telling me she knows how she was born, that she was a child of rape. She even showed me the dictionary to prove she knew what it meant!"

Jeanette turned to Francheska, who had followed her into the room. "Who told you this?" she asked the girl.

"Him," Francheska said, pointing to Harold.

Jeanette shook with anger. "Harold, how could you do such a thing? The child is only ten years old!"

"It's time she knew the truth," he answered coldly.

Jeanette could not believe it was all happening. She called one of Francheska's friends and arranged with her mother to have Francheska spend the night there. When she was gone, Jeanette went back to Harold.

"What have you done! She is completely confused! She cannot sort out rape, sex, pleasure, force. How could you tell her such a thing?"

"It's time she knew," Harold said again.

"Why do you make it sound like it's my fault I got raped, like I deserve to be punished? Why do you reject us? Why do you suddenly feel you have to do this? Are you jealous of our closeness?"

Jeanette stood in front of him, as he sat on the sofa.

"I think it's time -- why do you keep saying it's time? Time for what?" she screamed.

"Time for her to know you're no angel!" Harold snapped.

Jeanette burst into tears. "Why do you want to punish me, why? Once Francheska had grown to be a woman, once she had understood men and sex I could have explained to her what happened. But you make it seem as if I were dirty and guilty."

Francheska did not understand, and from that day on she turned against her mother. She fought Jeanette at every opportunity. She rejected her and gave her the silent treatment, imitating and siding with Harold.

That was nearly eight years ago. Since then, Jeanette's home life had been hell, a constant struggle for survival. From the beginning, she could not understand the rejection. Why had Francheska turned on her so fast? It wasn't her fault that she'd been raped. Why did her little girl turn from a loving child to a hateful one and why was that hate directed toward her mother?

By the time she was in high school, Francheska began lying about her activities, where she went after school, who she associated with. One day Jeanette received a call from one of her teachers.

"Is your daughter alright, or is she ill?" the teacher asked.

"Why, she is in school," Jeanette said, surprised.

"She has not been in school for one week," the teacher said.

Jeanette didn't know how to respond. When Francheska returned home in the afternoon, she confronted her.

"What in the world are you doing? Where have you been all day?"

"In school," Francheska said coldly.

"But your teacher said you haven't been in school for a week. What is going on here?"

Francheska didn't even flinch. "The teacher is lying," she said.

"Why would she lie? Why would she lie?" Jeanette asked desparately.

"Because she hates me."

Jeanette didn't know what to believe. She knew her daughter had deceived her on other matters, but she didn't what to lose her. She needed her daughter's love more than ever. Perhaps the teacher didn't like Francheska. Perhaps there was some kind of mistake. She took Francheska to the school to see the teacher.

As she approached the woman, she could not contain herself. "How dare you lie about my daughter?" she said to her.

The teacher reacted calmly, pulling out her attendence schedule and showing it to the angry mother.

Jeanette was completely torn. The teacher had shown her the schedule to prove her daughter was lying, but her daughter stood there accusing the teacher of lying. It was as if Jeanette's limbs were being torn off her body.

She said nothing. She took Francheska by the arm and hurried her out of the teacher's office. On the way home, her anger and frustration overflowed.

"Why are you doing this to me? Why?" she shouted at Francheska, who sat in the car across from her mother and stared back defiantly. Jeanette could no longer hold herself back. She struck Francheska across the mouth, and blood started running from her lip, where one of her teeth had cut her.

Francheska jumped out of the car at the next intersection. Jeanette was shocked. She followed her daughter as she ran, calling for her to get back into the car, but Francheska would not even look at her. Finally she darted between a couple of buildings and was gone.

Jeanette drove up and down the streets looking everywhere. Two hours later she found Francheska in a restaurant by the ocean. It was nearly dark. She got into the car without a struggle, but no words were spoken as the two of them drove home.

It was as if war had broken out between Jeanette and Francheska. Jeanette felt at a total loss. Once again she turned to Harold for help, but he did nothing. In her desperation to make her daughter behave, she resorted to spanking her with a belt. She tried to be a strong parent, she believed, in the only way she knew how. Nothing seemed to work.

She begged Harold to step in, to tell Francheska that she was wrong. She pleaded with him to spend time with her, to tell her she should stop lying and hating her mother. He was emotionless and immobile. He refused to participate.

Jeanette's nightmares increased. Her helplessness made her feel as if she were imprisoned again, fenced in by emotions and actions she did not understand. Her depression increased. During the day she might find herself sitting for hours, doing nothing, saying nothing. Other times she would find herself in a tirade, angry and violent and throwing dishes. She tried running away, disappearing for a few days, hoping that her husband and daughter would come to look for her. But they did not.

One day she started screaming and could not stop. Harold called a doctor, who came and sedated her with an injection.

For Jeanette, the loneliness was unbearable. She got no love or affection from Francheska or Harold. She was abandoned in her own home and began feeling that it was all her fault. Everything that had happened since she was a child had been her own fault -- the war, the death of her family, the tortures and beatings in the camp -- all of it. She had lost her roots and now had even failed to create a family of her own, a loving family that cared about each other.

Somehow through the years she had managed to keep her teaching career alive. It was the only thing that kept her mind off her desperation. It had helped her cope. Jeanette knew she had to keep dancing. She had to come up with the money to get Giselle produced and staged. Right now it was the most important thing in her life.

Chapter 15

Yanina knew it was just a matter of time before her turn would come. Dachau was madness. The Nazis were desperate, trying to kill as many people as they could, as quickly as possible. Yanina found herself with a familiar job -- piling the dead. The bodies were piled up behind the gas chambers. So many people were being gassed that the Germans did not have enough ovens to burn the remains, and not enough strong people to bury them either. Prisoners who refused to work were shot and thrown with the other dead. There were mountains of corpses. The Germans were confused and morale was low as the bodies became too much for even them to bear.

The chaos was beyond comprehension. There were male prisoners with female. There was no system, not even any food. Prisoners were on their own to stay alive. Death by gas, shooting or starvation seemed inevitable to everyone. People dropped dead everywhere. Yanina had grown weak in the two months she had been back in camp. She was diseased and her bones were protruding sharply beneath her skin. Her mind was going again, and the only feeling she knew was anger and a dim vision of a small girl dancing in the ballet.

One of the Nazi matrons tried to force Yanina to wear a placard, front and back, confessiong all sorts of crimes so all the inmates could see why she was being punished. She refused. Yanina knew she was finished. It was the end and she wanted to die, to be released. As the

Nazi matron pushed the placard at her, Yanina turned in a final burst of energy and bashed her fists into the Nazi's face. The Nazi was shocked. She grabbed her whip and started to beat Yanina. As the Nazi snapped the powerful whip, the end popped back and caught her in the face. Her fury became even more intense. Enraged, she came at Yanina, who had picked up a rock. All of her suffering and the memory of all her beatings gave her strength to hit back. The prisoners nearby whistled and shouted, and some even applauded. Astonishment ran through the crowd. Someone struck back! Frenzied with rage, the Nazi woman started to kick Yanina, and fighting desperately, Yanina grabbed onto her hair and pulled her to the ground. "Use your pistol! Shoot me! Come on you swine!" Yanina cried out. The crowd became silent, overcome by the emotional battle. Everyone was waiting for the outcome. Yanina watched as the Nazi pulled her pistol from its holster. This is it, she thought. After all these years to die by a bullet will be so easy. Much better than being gassed. The Nazi woman, looking to Yanina so well fed -- a heavy German woman with blond hair standing off to one side -- stood up, stiffened her body, and to Yanina's amazement, put the pistol into her own mouth and blew off the top of her head.

Yanina struggled to her feet. What had happened was too much to understand. She felt only a hollow disappointment at still being alive. She stood with the rest of the prisoners for a moment, then from nowhere, she heard herself begin to sing the Polish anthem. The words were her own, she no longer remembered the originals. "Yeshuze Pilsa niezginewa puky my zyjeme..." "Poland will not disappear, as long as we live. Some day Hitler will be hanging upside down. March, march to Hitler -- so the typhoid will destroy him. We will not be punished. We will live forever!"

The group of prisoners gathered there joined in as Yanina led them through the words again. "March, march to Hitler -- so the typhoid will destroy. We will not be punished. We will live forever!"

But the glory of that moment was brief. Nazi guards came and the prisoners scattered. Yanina tried to run, but before she could stir herself to move, she was grabbed by one of the Nazis and thrown into line with those to be gassed. The line progressed quickly. Yanina knew she was getting close when she heard the music of Chopin and Mozart being played on violins by some of the women prisoners. The only other sounds she could hear were the noises of the approaching war.

She was exhausted. I am finally finished, she thought. I no longer want to live. As she stood there in line, she could hear the cries of the children, the moaning of the half dead in piles of corpses. I don't want to be saved anymore, she thought. Let me die! God, let me die!

As she stood near the gas chamber door she realized that there really would no longer be a life for her. For so many years the life had equaled the hope she clung to. Now, she saw that hope as the most foolish of emotions. She had been tricked, seduced by it, led through the valley of death by its treacherous hand. The hope of rejoining her family, the hope of ballet, the hope of life — all of it was a betrayal. The hope that kept her alive in the end had led her to the place where she would die. I will never see a bird fly again, she thought. Never taste an apple, never be a mother or a wife to someone. My life will be extinguished. The world is so beautiful, the trees so beautifully shaped, the sky and the earth in all of its colors, so beautiful. I will never hear this beautiful music again.

The line moved forward and Yanina felt the urge to run and plead for her life. I want to live! she felt like shouting suddenly. But she knew the SS guards would not listen. She had seen that tragedy acted out too many times before. She began to take solace that she would never have to be naked in front of Nazi soldiers again, never have to get her head or body shaved, never have to stand in roll call for hours while the Nazis miscounted and counted over and over again. She would never have to be beaten again or have crabs and lice".

Suddenly she was pulled out of line. "Come you, at once!" the voice of a German Black Boot thundered as he pulled her away. "No, leave me alone!" Yanina wimpered in her confusion. "Not work anymore. I'm tired, I'm sick, I can't stand up anymore. Leave me alone." The girl in line behind her was also being dragged away. Yanina tried to go limp but the Black Boot jerked her to her feet. Finally, he pushed her up against a wall, took out a rag and blindfolded her. Yanina could hear the other girl being blindfolded next to her. There had been a number of other prisoners there too, about 30 in all, lined up against the stone wall which was blood soaked and red.

The girl next to her began crying and Yanina waited for the firing of the rifles, wondering if she would have enough time to recognize the sound before her life ended.

The last seconds seemed an eternity. What's keeping them? Yanina thought to herself. The waiting allowed the sounds around her to penetrate her fear. She could hear shooting from other areas of the camp, and a clangor of rattles and squeeks, a rusty sound she had never heard before. Yanina nudged the girl nearby. "Hey, I don't hear the sound of the Black Boots on the gravel, do you?"

"No," said the girl. Then she shouted out, "Hey swine, why don't you shoot?" But there was no response, only the sound of the iron scratching and squeaking, and shooting everywhere.

"Don't move," Yanina said to the girl defiantly. "They want us to run so they can shoot like we are trying to escape."

The gunfire was getting nearer, but nothing from the firing squad. It seemed the bullets were whistling in every direction. There were the sounds of people running and the prisoners knew there was a great commotion all around them. The squeeking sound grew louder and louder, so unbearable that Yanina wanted to cover her ears.

Suddenly, she felt someone reaching up to grab her blindfold. It didn't come all the way off at first, then the hands were there again, finally pulling it away. To Yanina's amazement, there was a small Japanese man in a green uniform standing before her. She thought at first he was going to shoot her. But he knelt down and bowed several times. Behind him was a tank with an American flag on it and several other Japanese soldiers.

Yanina wanted to call the man "Little Ceasar," but he looked so polite and sorrowful there bowing, that she didn't know what to say. When she finally realized that the soldiers were Americans, she was overjoyed. "We are free," she finally spoke. "They have come to save us."

It was too much to believe. Yanina walked outside of the gates, which were flung open, and back inside several times saying to herself, "We are free. We are free." As she looked into the camp from the gate, a Black Boot was running toward her to escape. Yanina prepared to block his way, but before he got to her the other prisoners were upon him. The skeleton-like prisoners, the living corpses of the camp, tore into the Nazi with a fury. They tore him apart limb from limb. The tore out his eyes, his legs, his arms -- like wild animals -- right before her eyes. Yanina stood there watching as the American soldiers tried to restrain the male prisoners.

The camp was utter chaos. Prisoners were attacking Germans wherever they found them. The Americans were working to calm the survivors of Dachau, speaking to them quietly, offering them cigarettes and candy bars. A number of prisoners died because their poor dried up stomachs burst trying to digest the candy. Yanina spent the night in camp with the other prisoners. American doctors took great care to help everyone they could. It was unbelievable, Yanina thought, to see the Germans being rounded up, arrested and marched out of the camp. Everyone was stunned by their sudden freedom. Yanina looked at the gate of death and there were no more trains coming in, no more corpses for her to pile, no more gas chambers or ovens with their horrible stench. In the next few days in Dachau, as she began to realize that she was truly free from the cruelty of the Nazis, she cried an ocean of tears for the ones that never made it. She could see faces flashing in front of her -- one minute alive, the next dead. She could hear the voices moaning. She could see the eyes staring as if to tell her they were still alive. She could see the arms stretching out toward her. Those many long years, those endless seasons that came and passed and Yanina could save no one but herself. Why should I be alive, why was I spared? she grieved inside. My guilt, will you ever let me forget, will you ever let me forget? As she cried, she felt a new life begin for her. But she didn't even know her name. Who is my family? Where will I go? Then she heard the voice of the gypsy ringing inside her head.

She flashed back to the scene, a memory from her childhood: She was with a huge gypsy woman. A little boy was there with her, though she could not remember how she knew him. She and the boy were in the gypsy's camp for many months and the gypsy treated them with special care. Yanina remembered she had been sad, that she moped around the gypsy's home wimpering and feeling helpless.

"Stand up straight," the old woman commanded. You are of noble blood. Never allow yourself to look like that! Straighten those shoulders. Walk with the pride befitting one of such noble background." Yanina dared not argue with the woman. "Your parents arc great people," the old woman said, "and when it is safe for you to return, they are going to be proud of how strong you are."

Yanina and the boy lived with the gypsy and her family in the depths of a great forest. The gypsy taught Yanina to be strong, to be proud, to spit in the face of adversity. In the gypsy camp, it was Yanina's old woman to whom the other gypsies came for advice. Yanina could still see her face -- broad smile and huge laugh, eyes of the darkest green, as deep and alive as the forest itself. She was the seer of the camp and had a secret elaborate system that surrounded her augury.

One day Yanina asked the old woman to divine her future. "Tell me what my life will be," she asked the old gypsy. "No no, child. You are too young. You don't need to know such things," she replied.

"But I do. I must know. I am old enough. I am of noble blood."

The old gypsy smiled. She walked up to Yanina and took her hand. "Come with me," she said. But when the old woman consulted her charts and books, she turned white. She became very angry. "I was right. You are too young to bother with such things." She stood up and slammed her books shut. "Go, child. And never ask me this again."

"What is it? Please, please tell me. What will be my life?" Yanina stood her ground. "You must tell me, I command it!"

The old woman sat back in her chair. She sat for a long time, just staring at the table between her and this strange little girl she had been asked to protect. "It is too horrible," she whispered.

"You must tell me. I insist." Yanina tried to look as brave and strong as she could. She sat up straight, then leaned across the table toward the old woman. "I must know," she said firmly.

The old gypsy looked up at Yanina. There were tears welling in the corners of her eyes. She was trembling ever so slightly. "You will lose all of your loved ones," she said. "You will suffer many deaths and many unspeakable hardships. Then you will cross a great water and you will find peace."

The Americans were shocked at the sight of the prisoners in Dachau. They brought in the German citizens from the neighboring towns and made them put the bodies in coffins and bury them with a prayer. They forced the Nazis to pile bodies in huge mass graves and bury them. They allowed the prisoners to jeer and accuse and curse them. The townspeople never looked at the prisoners. Their shame was all over them. They did not believe, they did not want to get involved, they did not ask questions. They bore the guilt of their country's atrocities.

Once more, it was time to be transferred to another camp. Yanina and the other prisoners were told they were going to a D.P. Camp for displaced persons. As they left Dachau, they walked at their own pace, gently guided by the soldiers, their rescuers. But the suspicion remained. The prisoners feared another camp, another gas chamber. When they arrived at the camp, they were examined, showered and given new clothes. Yanina received a G.I. outfit and looked lost inside it. There was food everywhere, and in the dispensary, the Americans tried to give Yanina an identity. She could remember nothing. For a brief time in Auschwitz there was a woman who called her Yanina, but for most of her memory the prisoners had called her Sugar Plum Nut. In Dachau, it was simply Polish Girl. The German family called her Owl. For years, it seemed, she had never really even carried on a conversation with another human being.

"You must have a name," the American soldier said to her. "What will we call you? We have to process papers for you."

Just then, one of the other soldiers came in complaining about his headache. He asked the soldier at his desk if he had any Bayers aspirin, got some and then left.

"That's it," she said to the American. "That's it -- Bayers. Johanna Bayers."

"Okay," the American said, writing quickly on his papers. "Johanna Bayers, it is."

It felt good to have a name, she thought. Yes, Johanna Bayers is a good name. One that is easy to remember. For the next few days, she told everyone she met what her name was. "Hello, I am Johanna Bayers. My name is Johanna Bayers." She would never again forget her name, she decided.

Around food, Johanna was an animal. She lunged at any food that was brought near her and even tried to stab a fellow prisoner who happened too close to her plate. Her system was still in shock. Every time a hand touched her, she jumped. And when the Americans told the prisoners they were going to be relocated, she ran away screaming, "Why don't you shoot us now. Why this lie? Kill us now, don't deceive us about relocation again."

The Americans took great patience with her and all the prisoners, gently reasoning with their fears and raw emotions. When Johanna had calmed down, she joined other prisoners in a march to the Ansbach D.P. camp. Once more the march took them a long way, across fields and ditches, the war-torn countryside. Their guides were French soldiers, mixed with a few Americans, with an American officer in charge.

The march seemed to last forever. The beauty of the country was overwhelming, in spite of the scars of war. They passed through forests where few men had ever been. It was virgin and wild. Trees bridged the streams -- old trees, broken monsters felled by age and weather. From beneath them, growing out along the grown, new branches shot up, bathed by sunlight through the gaps in the forest roof. They crossed wild canyons and steep slopes, crossed more streams and by daylight followed a faint cattle trail over a low rocky hill, through a winding forest of manzanitas. Their walk through the wilderness startled many birds that soared across open meadows, disappearing into the trees. Johanna took note of the powerful beauty surrounding her. She saw a butterfly drift through the sunshine and shadows along the trail. Bluejays flashed by in splashes of gorgeous color across the forest. Tiny birds everywhere hopped from bush to bush, imitating other birds. Her senses were bombarded by the beauty of the world she had forgetten ever existed. She saw a woodpecker stop in the middle of his pecking, cocking his head to survey the passing parade of humans. Flowers of blue and yellow seemed to carpet the way for her feet. She noticed the forest rising overhead and the clean joy of sweet forest air, seasoned with the aromas of flowers.

Drunk with the clean and beautiful country around her, Johanna realized there was no room for contempt and hatred there. She felt only respect for the world. It was like a church with its atmosphere of holy calm.

The prisoners came to a large farm and were given places to sleep. The farmers gave them sacks of bread, sausage, cheeses and fruits. That night, lying in the barn sorting out the cruel past, Johanna felt the passion of something new happening to her. She might one day have a life again, she thought. She clung to her new identity and would not allow herself to address the empty feeling inside when her mind turned briefly to the question of her real name.

Johanna walked outside the barn to look at the stars. A woman came close to her. She was older than Johanna, and though she had learned to understand a little French, Johanna could not figure out why the woman wanted her to follow. Johanna's feelings of freedom and excitement made her head spin. In that moment, she relaxed her guard and with innocent trust, followed. Lead by the French woman, she left the barn where the other prisoners were making their beds. She and the woman crossed a little farm road and started up the side of a hill on which huge trees stood like evening sentinals. As they walked, the French woman led her by the hand. Johanna could hear the cry of an owl, and with each step breathed in the aromas of the crushed grass beneath her feet.

They reached the top of the hill and Johanna didn't even look at the woman. She could not take her eyes off the huge moon and its milky light and the trees and their branches cutting bold silhouettes against the sky. When she did look for the woman, she was gone. Suddenly there were several soldiers approaching from the other side of the hill. Johanna was surprised she did not feel the immediate fear that men in uniform had come to cause her. The soldiers surrounded her and she stood undecided whether to offer a greeting or wait until she was spoken to. They were smiling and she was getting ready to smile back when, before she knew what happened, one of the men tied a handkerchief around her mouth, while another grabbed her arms and dragged her toward one of the trees. Johanna was panic stricken and struggled to free herself from her captors, but two other soldiers grabbed her legs while a third tied her arms over her head around the massive tree. Yanina could not believe what was happening. Her liberators had pinned her to the ground and one after the other mounted her. Their huge bodies crushed her chest and forced the air from her lungs, and their brutish hands covered her mouth as she tried to scream. The pain was unbearable -- the stinging and ripping of her womb as they penetrated her, the filthy soldiers pressing their gritty faces into her neck.

Johanna's eyes fixed on the sky and the pain came together in a cry to God for mercy. Then her eyes rolled back and gazed at the shadowed tree above her. There seemed to be something moving in that branch off to the left. Perhaps a bird. It seemed to hop from branch to branch, or lept rather, as if in dance. Johanna wondered if it were looking for its nest, or for its mate. While the soldiers acted out their fantasies and frustrations on her helpless body, Johanna lept to the branch and the wings of that bird. She felt its tiny heart beating so quickly, its chest heaving as it watched the human tragedy below. She felt the song in its breast and in its throat -- the most lovely of evening songs, she was certain. And when that bird fluttered and flew off into the air, she joined in that irresistible flight, like a never ending grand jeter that would take her above the trees, the hills and the barn where the prisoners slept, to a world far, far away from cruelty and pain.

Johanna found herself vomiting in the grass. One of the soldiers had untied her and now the whole group of them stood off to the side, panting like dogs. She could not get up. She tried to stand, but could only get onto her knees, which were covered with blood that still ran down her legs. As she tried to get to her feet she heard the soldiers speak in French to the woman. Suddenly there was a burst of laughter, and a voice in English that exclaimed, "You brought us a virgin!" someone said to the woman, handing her money. "The Nazis overlooked her for us," Then the laughter, the cruelest sound imaginable, exploded into the silent night.

Johanna could still hear their laughter as they walked over the hill, leaving her weeping against the tree. She felt the deepest betrayal and shame of her body. There was nowhere in the world that was safe, she knew that much. No God, no one that cared. All that she knew was guilt and shame, feelings more powerful and consuming than belief in a Father in Heaven.

Slowly, she made her way down the hill, falling, crawling in pain, hiding her secret. She felt it was all her fault. Outside the barn she found a wooden trough with water in it and tried through the darkness to wash away the blood from her legs. She told no one of her shame and spent the night against the barn, staring into the sky, afraid of everyone, feeling alone and insignificant.

When morning came, the DPs were gathered up and another day's march began. Johanna joined the tail end of the marchers, keeping to herself, wimpering and weeping as she walked. She saw the soldiers who had raped her, saw them point and laugh to each other about her. She tried to hide her face and kept her head down, watching the tears drip off the end of her nose into the dirt. She felt betrayed and violated and much much older. Nothing like this ever happened to me with the Nazis, she thought. Why with my liberators? The confusion was overwhelming and in her shame, she took another road, getting as far away from the others as possible.

Johanna's path led up to a main road, and as she stood there bewildered, two Americans in a jeep pulled up behind her. When she saw them she ran as fast as her weak legs would take her, but they quickly caught up to her.

"No, no, don't hurt me," she cried. "Please leave me alone."

"Come here, little girl, I want to help you," one of the soldiers said.

"No, no!" Johanna shouted, scratching and biting at him.

"You need medical care," he said. "You're very sick. Let us help you."

"She's like an animal," Johanna heard the American say to his companion. But she was too weak to fight anymore, so she gave in. She let them guide her to the jeep, still terrified.

The American, an officer, took her to a camp where the soldiers bathed her, examined her and gave her new clothes.

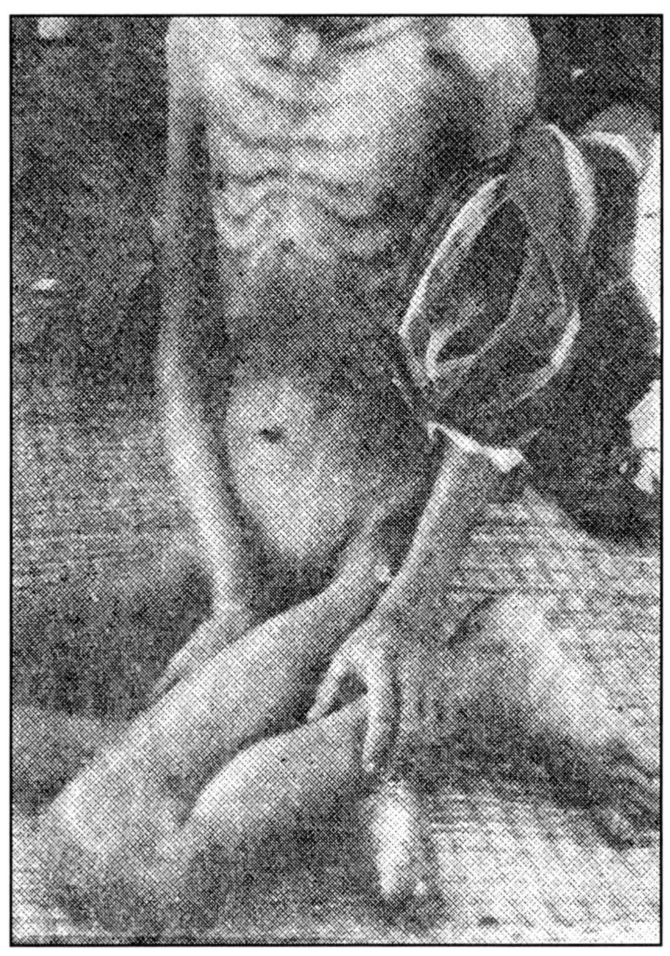

Liberation Day 1945

Yanina Cywinska

Chapter 16

"Hello. Hello, are you with us? Miss Bayers?" The voice was sing-song, exaggerating the words like people do to children. "Miss Bayers, wake uuu-up." It was a pleasant enough voice. Certainly there was kindness in it, perhaps affection too.

Johanna opened her eyes. When she saw the soldier she reacted with a jolt. Her body became rigid as she clutched the covers beneath her chin. Through her fear she could not see his face, only the uniform, and when he reached for her, she felt like she was going to snap. Suddenly she was screaming, like a cat under attack -- limbs thrashing and her teeth and claws aimed at the nearest bit of flesh.

"Whooaah!" The soldier was on his feet now, three steps back from the bed. "Miss Bayers, calm down. It's me, Lieutenant Drucker. Don't you recognize me?"

The voice sounded more familiar. Again that tone of kindness. Johanna still scratched at the air, but the face at the foot of her bed began to look more familiar. Did he say Drucker? she heard a voice inside ask.

"That's better," Drucker said when Johanna finally called off the attack. She was quiet again, clutching the covers under her chin. "Well, you certainly haven't lost your spirit," he said.

It was Drucker. Johanna felt better now that she recognized him. She even managed a faint smile.

Drucker had been so kind and patient with her during her recovery. He found her a special bed in the DP camp infirmary, closest to the officer's medical facilities. He visited her every day, and gently reassured her through his kindness that there were still people in the world who could be trusted. Her recovery from the rape had been slow. She was unconscious for two days in Drucker's camp, and weak and feverish since she arrived at Ansbach.

The first day she came to, there was a great deal of shouting in the room next door. It was Drucker. He was yelling at the man in charge of the platoon that had raped her. He was calling for the court marshal of all ten men, French and American. Drucker and another man shouted at each other. Johanna didn't hear the other man's name, but she knew they were fighting over her.

"You're feeling better now, aren't you?" Drucker had come a little closer to the bed. "You are going to be just fine. You're in good hands here."

He reached into his pocket and took out a chocolate bar. "Here. The doctors said I shouldn't give this to you, but what the hell. You only live once, right?" Drucker gave her a soft pat on the head, then turned and left the room.

Johanna was well enough to walk around the camp and after Drucker left she got up and dressed herself. She was to be moved out of the infirmary any day, back into the large dormitories with the other DPs, and already she was eating with them in the large dining hall.

Later that day she went to look for Drucker, but she could not find him. He didn't wake her up the next morning, or the morning after that. Johanna began to worry. She hadn't seen Drucker in days so she went to the front gate and waited for him. She spent the night and next day there before someone noticed her crying and staring out through the wire fence.

Johanna still had no real sense of time. She didn't know how long she had waited for Drucker. It seemed to her one continuous moment of concern. In fact, being inside a camp again made her wonder exactly where she was. The sounds of the American trucks thundered inside her head, and if any kind of siren went off she would find herself face down in the dirt when it ended. At the gate she stared at the soldiers moving freely inside and outside of the camp. She wondered where they were going with their guns and uniforms. She even wondered when the next trainload of Jews would arrive.

She stood and stared or she sat and stared, but Drucker never came. When she was finally discovered at the gate she was taken inside the processing building where an American officer told her Drucker was in America. He had been shipped back home. Johanna couldn't believe it. Drucker was the only person she felt she could trust. Now he was gone. But her disappointment was short lived. Her drained and emotionless soul would not allow her to feel anything -- no pain, no joy, no sadness. So Drucker's disappearance soon became another lifeless memory that she tossed onto the pile of her confused past. Besides, it seemed that all of a sudden there was another soldier checking up on her. He wasn't like Drucker. His eyes were not so friendly. But he was there. She couldn't actually remember when it all began. There were many days when she had no memory at all. Gradually, she began to notice his face every day, and one day learned through his own confession that he was the sergeant in charge of the platoon that had attacked her. Sergeant James Seabolt.

Sergeant Seabolt arranged for Johanna to work in the dispensary. When he had her alone, he would apologize over and over for the rape. Johanna still didn't know what that word meant, but she understood it had something to do with the attack.

Her work in the dispensary was easy work, and it filled up her time. It was many weeks before the Red Cross officially informed her that none of her family had survived the war. They were never certain of her real name, but they learned that she was indeed Polish, and that she had come from Warsaw. In fact, they informed her that they were planning to ship her back to Warsaw in a few days. When that day came, the DPs were lined up to be put in trucks and taken to a train station nearby.

American soldiers were everywhere with their large guns, guarding them and making sure they got off to Poland. Chaos nearly broke out when one of the DPs right in front of Johanna -- the memories of camps and Nazi trucks all too vivid, all too recent -- made a dash to escape. Those in line knew exactly what was happening. For many, the tempatation to try to escape was almost overwhelming. But they resisted. The American soldiers caught the panicked prisoner and held him to the ground. But to everyone's surprise, no guns were fired, no boots were kicked into his stomach or face. The soldiers held him down until a member of the Red Cross arrived, then he was taken back into the camp.

The thought of Poland horrified Johanna. Aunt Stasia's face leered at her through her memory, though she wasn't sure who the evil woman really was. So too did the suffering and dying in the ghetto, the shapes of dread from the death camps. No, she would never return to Poland.

Johanna boarded the train, but when it left the city and made its way slowly through the German countryside, she waited for it to slow to a crawl. And when it did, she simply walked to the door of the train car and jumped off.

How she finally got to Nuremburg she didn't really notice. A few days of walking, of standing outside of a local farmer's house until his wife offered food, of hiding from American soldiers. Then one day, on the edge of the city, she walked right up to a group of uniformed Americans in a jeep and asked where she was -- in perfect English.

When the Americans learned she could speak German, Polish, English and some Russian, they thought she was a gift from heaven. The trials of German war criminals were just beginning and interpreters were in great demand.

Johanna took the job with the Americans. During the following months she listened to the testimony of witness after witness, each telling his or her own tale of horror. She saw the German officers, too, trying to deny their knowledge of the abominable crimes committed by the Nazis against the peoples of Europe. Some days she spent interpreting their testimony for an American stenographer. On a few occassions, she was called to the witness stand herself to recount her own painful experiences. Like so many of the witnesses, she stood in sharp contrast to the Nazis on trial, who were robust and healthy. Johanna and the other survivors of the camps were hardly more than shadows, their bodies weak and pale -- delicate frames of bones held together by layers of translucent skin and thick clothes.

But the witnesses seemed to overpower the Nazis in mental strength. With each new testimony, it became evident the German officers were headed for conviction. The pressure became too much for many of them. Johanna watched their faces contort under the strain. The camp survivors were driven by their anger and the consuming desire for justice, for revenge. Though their bodies were weak, their minds became tenacious. The intensity of their recent experiences was so great that details of the horrid events were indelibly written in their memories. They remembered names, faces, exact conversations -- the guilty Nazis' defenses were no match. Johanna took it all in, listening to the details, reliving her own past, recounting testimonies to the American clerks.

As part of the payment for her services, the Americans gave Johanna room and board. She spent her meals with the occupying soldiers and officers, dining on what seemed like the most sumptous breakfasts, lunches and suppers. The food tasted so delicious going down, but most of the time she had difficulty digesting it. She suffered from cramps and nausea and occasional vomiting.

One of the American generals, David Clay, and his wife befriended Johanna. They realized her interpreting duties were valuable, but knew also that the teenage girl had serious medical problems. Johanna appreciated their kindness, but really didn't know how to show her appreciation. The last six years of her life had been so frenzied and violent that she had no way of knowing what was proper or how to make friends. She smiled and thanked people politely.

General Clay arranged for Johanna to fly to New York where she was put on a diet of liquids and baby food so that she could grow a new layer of stomach and become healthy enough to digest food again. When she regained her strength, she flew back to the trials to continue translating the testimony. But she was assigned a nurse to care for her and check her physical progress until she became healthy again and the trials came to an end.

Chapter 17

To the soldiers the voice was pure beauty -- a sound that cut through the thunder of the war that echoed still within them, a voice distilled from personal pain and the vapors of pain that rose above the burned and broken land that once was Germany. When they heard her sing, it made the thunder go away and it left each one of them limp, and somewhat empty, and longing for home.

The soldiers came back every night, and when a few were blessed with the news that they could go home, there were always more soldiers to take their places. Most were Americans. But there were the English and the French too. They all understood her. They all came to see the young blonde girl in the tight dress. And they all knew that she knew more about human loss and suffering than she probably even realized. Perhaps she had really lost her lover. Perhaps it was a brother, a father, a whole family. Perhaps much more.

Just say I love him
I've loved him from the start
And tell him how I'm yearning
To say what's in my heart

Just say I need him
As roses need the rain

And tell how I'm yearning
To have him back again

If you should chance to meet him
Any time, any place, anywhere
I was a fool to leave him
Tell him how much a fool can care

And if he should tell you
He's lonely now and then
Well tell him how I'm yearning
To have him back again.

To Johanna Bayers it was more than a song. She knew that. It was a window into her aching soul. It was an undressed wound described in phrases of romance that revealed as much about what she had never had, as it did about what she had lost. From the stage she could feel the heat of the spotlight. It froze her in one place, behind the microphone, and blinded the features of the young men in the club. They appeared like silhouettes, hot shadows giving off waves of smoke that drifted above their heads and hung in a haze where her eyes would focus as she sang. Sometimes she felt the melody and words of the song were the only things that kept her from evaporating, herself, from turning into a spire of smoke and drifting into a corner of the room.

She had been singing that same song for weeks. She had lost track of how long. Ever since the USO officer had discovered she spoke English and she could sing. Lieutenant Mahar. He dressed her up, had one of the American nurses fix her make-up. She had a powerful voice, and he hired her to MC the shows at the American Stork Club in Nuremberg, as well as sing in them. Over and over again she sang that simple song. And with it she became for a few months one of the main attractions for the soldiers still stationed in the cities of occupied Germany.

Johanna had met the lieutenant when she auditioned for the USO with her ballet company. Virtually helpless with the simplest daily proceedings, she was driven to dance. She could not understand money, simple arithmatic, but she had managed to contact the displaced dancers of Europe and form a ballet company. It was as if she were a sleepwalker, who by day was the broken, helpless Polish teenager, bereft of home, family, direction. But in her walking dream she possessed the singleminded power to bring dancing to the stage.

While still living in Nuremberg she had put ads in the local newspapers for dancers. Germany was swarming with the displaced and directionless. Johanna's dance company was a way for some of them to forget the horrors of the recent past. The company was small, but talented enough to get bookings in the local opera houses that the citizens of the cities of Germany, with the permission of the occupying armies, managed to reopen. It was their attempt to reform their culture from the ravages of war, to build a bridge with their past that was pure, that remained outside the shame their country had brought upon itself.

Johanna's company had performed for the USO, and that's when she had met Lt. Maher. For the weeks she performed with the USO as MC and singer, Johanna kept her ballet company in work. She booked the performances, she taught the dancers what she knew, she learned from the older dancers and found more talented ones to join the group.

In spite of her company's success, Johanna found she could not dance the way she was to. In fact, she did not even dance with her company, except when she was demonstrating choreography for the particular ballet -- the way it had been taught in Russia. She gained weight uncontrollably, it seemed. With her heavier hips and legs, she couldn't get off the ground with the grace that was needed. During one of her shows in Nuremburg Johanna met a woman who said she recognized her. Frau Pager. The woman said she had worked as a maid for Johanna's family in Warsaw. She told Johanna her real name, and stories of her mother and brother to convince her. But the words were without meaning to Johanna. While she told the stories, Frau Pager watched her face for some kind of reaction, but there was none. Johanna's impassivity frightened her, and compelled her to stay in contact with the seemingly helpless Polish girl.

Why people would want to be with her was a mystery to Johanna. Frau Pager. The USO lieutenant. Especially Sgt. Seabolt, the man who had been in charge of the platoon when Johanna was raped. He had tracked her down in Nuremberg and when he found her, he told her he planned to marry her. Johanna's awareness of men was very small and she could not see that he was driven by guilt, a consuming guilt far deeper than even he realized, a guilt that puffed his face with distress and promises of a new life for the girl his men had ruined.

Johanna took a leave of absence from her ballet company to stay with Frau Pager in her village outside of Nuremberg. But it was more than just a visit with a gentle German woman who said she would help her regain her health. To Johanna, it was an opportunity to escape the rapid change that had taken hold of her life. The dancing, the soldiers, the people who praised her or wanted to be near her. Johanna's mind was still that of a child. She could not pretend to understand what was happening to her. Nor could she understand how her body was changing and the turmoil she felt within her belly. She continued to gain weight and wore large baggy clothes to cover her changing body.

Johanna kept in contact with the ballet company, and quite often came into the city to check on their progress. From Frau Pager's home she would walk through the woods near the autobahn to catch the streetcar to the city. One day as she crossed the autobahn and walked toward the path to the streetcar, she felt a pain creep though her body. It seized and wrenched her belly until she screamed and screamed as people gathered around her. She fell to the ground and passed out.

When Johanna awoke she was in a hospital. She was told she had given birth to a little girl.

Johanna knew nothing about babies -- nothing about conceiving them and giving birth to them, nothing about caring for them. Frau Pager had not even realized her state because Johanna's body had remained small, and was hidden by Johanna's large clothing.

Put up at first in a U.S. Army hospital, Johanna was soon transferred to a German hospital, where she lay in total shock as the attending doctor explained to her that she had conceived the child through rape and that the government was putting the little girl up for adoption. Being accustomed to having people tell her what to do, Johanna did not know she had choices, only orders to be followed. She had been told what to do her whole life -- from her parents making decisions for her as a child to the Nazis directing her every move. Of course, she did as the doctor told her.

When she left the hospital a few days later, she went back to Frau Pager. The old German woman tried to explain to Johanna what had happened to her. She told her of her body. She told her about children and what it means to be a mother.

That night, as she lay in bed, Johanna thought about Frau Pager's words. She thought about how much she wanted a family of her own to replace the one she could not remember ever having. She could not recall from within her soul the slightest memory of her mother, but knew more than anything that she now wanted to be a mother, herself.

Johanna rose from her bed and dressed quickly. She left the house without sound, careful not to wake Frau Pager. In the dark of the night she found her way to the hospital and she entered through the large doorway without being noticed by the soldiers outside or the doctors inside. She went up the stairs to the second floor to the hallway where the babies were kept, hiding by the steps until the night nurse had checked on the sleeping infants and gone from sight. Then Johanna walked down the hall and opened the door to the nursery.

There she saw her little girl, her new family, stirring gently in her sleep, the name Bayers taped to her little wrist. Johanna took her in her arms and held her close.

"Francheska," she whispered. "My little Francheska, I will never let you go." Johanna cried softly and held the baby as tight and sure as she wanted to be held herself.

"I will never leave you alone," she said. "We have each other now. I will never leave you alone."

Chapter 18

The wedding was simple and beautiful. Frau Pager was especially taken with the romance of the affair. She found Johanna a magnificent white gown and made arrangements for the guests and the minister, and spread yellow mums on the ground where Johanna walked to take her groom.

Sgt. Seabolt was proud. He invited his closest friends and even his superior officer, and he stood next to his bride to be in his polished uniform of the United States Army. But he was most proud of his act of reparation for the horrid immoral deed his men had done. He was rescuing a young helpless victim of the war. He was making amends for his failure of responsibility and he knew in God's eyes, he was putting himself back on the road to salvation.

Johanna was all smiles. The whole affair was confusing -- the ominous line of soldiers on one side, Frau Pager's unbounded joy, the congratulations of her ballet dancers. She hardly even knew the man she was about to wed, but she knew one thing: his promise of marriage meant she could keep her baby. It meant that Francheska could become an American citizen and have a proper legal name.

Johanna's smile belied the fact that she knew nothing of men and marriage. Even the things Frau Pager had explained to her about having the baby had meant little. It was all so strange and unbelievable.

The wedding procession took them through the streets of Nuremberg, as was customary, in a public and symbolic display of the vows the two were about to exchange. And they were wed in a small chapel in a ceremony of English, Polish and German.

Johanna kept her ballet company. It was doing well, and Johanna's reputation from the Stork Club brought her many offers to sing. But after marriage, she discovered the man she had wed would not allow her to do anything.

"You take care of me and the child. And no show business," he told her. "You're my wife now, and that's that."

Johanna's desire to be on stage was stronger than her fear of disobeying the strange figure that had come into her life to give her more orders. Fortunately, he went away on maneuvers frequently so Johanna was able to secretly perform in shows and secretly teach choreography. When he was gone, she would teach. And when he was home, she would have an assistant conduct the classes.

Little by little, Johanna started practicing ballet. All along she had taught the classic ballet that poured suddently from her memory from the years of training in Leningrad. But since the war she had been too weak to dance. Now, she was finally regaining enough strength to get back to the one thing she was certain she loved. While she taught her company, she practiced right along with her students, and when they left, she stayed and practiced even more. She began to perform roles in some of the ballets, roles that required pantomime and acting and little dancing.

The changes in Johanna's life were so rapid, it seemed as if she were caught in a pirouette gone out of control, swirling, swirling. Sometimes the world around her appeared like beautiful scenery viewed during a drive through the countryside. More often, it was spinning madly, at odd angles, reflecting images both terrible and wonderful. Her health was improving steadily, but the American doctors whom she visited on occasion warned her not to overdo, not to try to progress too fast.

Their warnings fell on deaf ears. Johanna was grabbing life by any limb or lapel which she could hold, trying to make up for lost years.

Her new husband was never around -- always shipped away on maneuvers. When he was gone, she and Francheska stayed with Frau Pager, who took wonderful care of her little princess. Johanna's schedules were heavy with engagements and the ballet troupe was getting local recognition for its excellence.

One evening after rehearsal, Johanna returned to Frau Pager's house to learn that her husband had taken the child and all of their belongings to a new house provided by the American government. She taxied to the new house, located in a beautiful country setting.

Over dinner she sat with her new husband, amidst the wonderously furnished mansion that was her new home. Francheska was asleep and her husband asked the maid to leave the room. As the door closed behind her he began to tell Johanna his feelings on her career.

"There are so many things that you have started," he said. "This dancing, this singing business. I want you to quit it all. Soon we will leave for America, so transfer your obligations to someone else."

Johanna looked at the man who sat across the table from him. She realized she did not know him at all.

"I am studying to be a minister, a Methodist minister," he said, lifting his head proudly. "I have a vocation that is greater than either of us -- the service of God. You are my wife, and when I am a minister, you will be a minister's wife, you must not forget that. It is not proper for you to be in show business.

"Your duties will be to serve me and my congregation, do you understand?"

His voice was taking a more urgent tone and his face became stern and threatening, and to Johanna it seemed she was sitting across from a soldier who held her prisoner. Sgt. Seabolt angrily explained how important it was to obey the word of The Almighty and as he chanted on the glorification of The Lord, she realized that she had married a man whom she felt nothing for, who had arranged the ceremony and planned to control the rest of her life.

Inside, Johanna was numb. People making decisions about her life was the way it was supposed to be. There was no reason she should expect otherwise. Was it not the way all marriages are made? The man across the table might have been her father, or a teacher at school, or a guard in the camps -- what difference did it make? But to give up dancing -- how could he possibly expect her to do that? Even as he insisted that she would never again set her foot upon a stage, she had no thought of letting it go. Ballet was a world within her. Without it she would cease to exist. His commands of giving it up were the clamorous ravings of someone she did not understand. The words had no meaning.

Seabolt's moral order became even more confusing to Johanna. Love and affection were frowned upon by the Lord, he explained. They were sinful. Make-up, fancy clothes, jewelry and other personal indulgences were also sins. He ordered her to cover her chest with dresses that had high necklines and that revealed nothing above the ankle.

"But why should it matter what I wear? I will wear whatever I please," Johanna objected.

"You will obey me!" he shouted, slamming his fist on the table so that the glasses clanked together. "You are my wife and you will do as I say, do you understand! You are a raped woman, a sinner. You were raped because you tempted the devil. You women are whores. Cover up everything and never look a man in the eye."

Seabolt looked down at the table and straightened his silverware. "And there is something else. You will give up your foolish Papist beliefs. No more Roman Catholic for you. You are the wife of a Methodist minister, and you will abide by the real laws that The Lord has laid down for us."

"I will not," Johanna said proudly.

Seabolt lunged across the table and grabbed her by the arm. "You will do as I say, do you hear me!" Then, before Johanna knew what had happened, he had dragged her upstairs to a bedroom, her arm jammed behind her back the whole way. He pushed her onto the bed and as she turned she saw the fury in his eyes.

"You will not leave this house," he shouted. "You are my wife and you will do as you are told."

For three days, he kept her in the house, personally guarding it so she would not leave, while the maid served her and Francheska meals. Johanna did not even try to escape. She simply ate what she was served, and spoke to no one except the child, and on the third day when he opened the doors of the house to her, she said nothing.

"Now do you understand what I expect of you?" he questioned sharply, confident that she had learned her lesson. But she did not answer.

That night they shared their bedroom for the first time. It was Seabolt's decision again. Until then they had always slept in separate rooms. For the most part, he had been away, but when they had been together, even on their marriage night, he had treated her like a child, like a young guest he was not sure how to approach.

"I do not want to be with you," Johanna said when he came into the room. "Why are you so mean to me and my child, who you saved from adoption?"

Seabolt's face was pained, as if there was something inside of him, stretching his skin to escape. Then he smiled wryly. "It was all a lie," he said.

"What do you mean a lie?" Johanna asked.

"There was no one who wanted to adopt the child. There are thousands of homeless children in this country. Why would anyone want yours?"

Johanna could not believe it. She focused her eyes more intently on this strange man, trying to discern who he could be. "But you said tonight you are studying to be a minister. A man of God, you said. "Ministers don't lie," she said.

Seabolt had been standing by the doorway, but with Johanna's words he stepped carefully across the room toward the window. He spoke slowly at first and very softly. "I know God will forgive me. I wanted to marry you and I was afraid. I was afraid you would say no. You had so much going for you, so much that you were involved in. I know God will forgive me because it is his will that a man should have a wife."

Johanna was silent. She couldn't understand what she was hearing. It infuriated her to think that he had deliberately lied, that he had tricked her, and now was telling her what to do with her life -- a life that for the first time she was beginning to enjoy.

"I can't sleep with you," she spoke sharply. "I don't love you. I don't even know you!"

Seabolt's eyes filled with rage and he seemed to grow taller. Then he walked up to Johanna and spoke into her face. "You are my wife. You have no choice."

Johanna pushed him away and ran from the room. She ran down to the end of the hall and into one of the guest rooms, slamming and locking the door behind her. Then, she lay down on the bed and by the fading evening light she stared at the elaborate carving on the ceiling until she fell asleep.

It was in the middle of the night when she was awakened by the sound of her bedroom door being opened. By the glow of a small nightlight Johanna saw a shadow coming toward her. The figure crept silently through the doorway and then with a wild leap he jumped onto the bed and pushed a pillow over her face. She struggled for breath, but her husband was much too strong. Just as she felt she was going to pass out, he took the pillow away. Then, pinning her arms to her sides, he straddled her and held her legs tight with his feet.

Johanna let out a shriek as he tried to kiss her. Reason left her completely. She felt trapped and panic stricken -- it was as if she were still suffocating, even though he had taken away the pillow. Shocked and paralyzed with fright, she heard his unbelieveable words as if from far away: "I will kill you first, before I will ever let you go!" He had her shoulders and arms pinned beneath his knees and he tried to force his sex into her mouth. Johanna continued to struggle as he gratified himself on her, and it seemed to her that she was loosing all sense of herself, that her mind was leaving a helpless body to struggle all its own, once again imprisoned in a place where she knew no love or care or emotion other than fright.

Chapter 19

Morning came and Johanna was alone.

The thoughts that filled her head as she woke and fed Francheska were not of the previous night's events, but of the singing engagement she had been offered just two days before. She would sing with the USO in Rome, and then travel with the show to London. It was a short engagement -- only a few weeks -- and Johanna quickly got on the phone and accepted. She had to travel that very afternoon. While the sergeant was away, she quickly packed and took her little girl with her.

Johanna was an instant hit, mostly on the strength of her performance of "Just Say I Love Him" which was just about the only song she ever sang -- night after night. After Rome, she also hit it big with the soldier audiences in London, and a review praising her singing appeared in the American Star magazine. In all, she was on the road a month, getting friends or fellow performers to care for Francheska backstage during showtime, and doting on the child when she was out of the spotlight.

When she returned to her home outside of Nuremburg, her husband was not home. The maid explained that he had telephoned, and that he would be returning in a few days from maneuvers. Johanna spent her time in thought. What would become of her? She had a little girl whom she loved, and a madman whom she had married. The complete acceptance of her circumstances might have appeared unbelieveable to anyone who had grown up with a reasonable amount of independence.

But for Johanna, it was not a question of changing her life, just surviving it. That was all she had ever learned to do.

One thing she did realize was that she was no longer a woman without a family or a country. She was the wife of an American, and the sudden pride of being able to go to the American PX, the American clubs and hospitals, began to overwhelm her.

Johanna asked the maid to watch Francheska and set out to go shopping at the PX. It was an unbelievable experience. She could not get over the variety of things she saw in the store --fruits and breads, bottled drinks, things in cans in so many colors she could not keep her hands off of them: meats in cans, vegetables in cans, fruit in cans. Johanna could not believe that she found even pineapple in a can. The labels were so tempting and so colorfully designed, and it was all hers! Everything was hers just by reaching out and taking it off the shelf. By the time she got to the checkout counter she had accumlated five baskets of her heart's desire.

The checker saw her coming and smiled. He had seen it before, the young European wife of an American coming into a place of relative bounty after the years of deprivation during the war. Slowly and patiently he explained to Johanna how to shop, how to make a list of only what she needed, and then buy the things on the list.

Despite the minor setback, Johanna was floating on air as she packed the groceries she bought into the car. Caught up in the excitement of buying anything she wanted, Johanna went next to a deparment store. The sights of the wonderous clothes was almost more than she could bear. She found a dress and bought in instantly, and it was so soft and so beautiful she could not believe it was hers. The sales lady suggested a pair of shoes to go with it, and she bought them too. Then, with the aid of the lady, she made up her face for the first time in her life. Everything smelled so feminine and fine that Johanna was nearly swooning.

When she arrived at the house late that evening, she was still reeling with delight. She got out of the car, a bag of groceries in her arm, and opened the front door. On the other side was her husband, stern and larger than she had ever seen before. His face was like ice as he slowly eyed his young wife and her new appearance. Then a rage came over him.

"Look at you!" he bellowed. "You look like a whore!"

Before she could react, he grabbed ahold of her and knocked the groceries out of her hand. Johanna saw only his furious fists and then canned goods sprawling across the floor beneath her. He dragged her into the kitchen. She could hear him puffing like a train engine and could feel the madness in his grip as she struggled to free herself. Seabolt turned on the hot water and forced her face into it, burning her eyes and lips. He screamed madly.

"Never again! Do you understand me! Never again, you slut!

You are a preacher's wife, not a street-girl!"

Johanna escaped from his wrath for a moment and burst into tears from fear and confusion. As she cried terribly, leaning against the kitchen door, she heard Francheska crying too, and ran to protect her, to soothe her, and placate her fears. But when she looked up, she saw Seabolt coming at the two of them, still consumed with rage. He held a heavy piece of wood over his head.

"Please leave us alone," Johanna cried out. "You are supposed to be a good man and a preacher. You are supposed to be a man of love and compassion. Why are you so cruel? I am a good woman!"

Seabolt lowered his arms and his head and began weeping pitifully. He fell to his knees and cried into his hands, and while he was shedding his tears of guilt, Johanna took her child and left the house.

In the days that followed, Johanna lived in desparation. She asked Frau Pager to help her and Francheska, and Frau Pager agreed to do whatever she could. But Johanna could not make her believe the insanity she was living with.

"Not Sgt. Seabolt, Johanna," Frau Pager objected. "You are exaggerating. He is such a good man."

"You don't understand," Johanna said softly. But Frau Pager's objections confused her. It was true, her husband presented himself so well to the outside world. He was respected by everyone who knew him. He was going to be a preacher. Even when she went to the American authorities for help after Seabolt went into his rages on other occasions, she ran into a stone wall of disbelief.

Johanna began to assume the fault was her own. And like she had so many times in her life, she accepted the guilt, and wrapped herself in it, and made it a constant companion.

Dance and post war military operations again came to her rescue. Seabolt left with the Infantry on an assignment that lasted several months. While he was away, she threw herself into the world of dance once more.

She spent every day with the ballet company, and brought it to a level of success that she was able to sell it to a German couple from Mainz. Johanna continued to sing at the Stork Club, and practiced her ballet daily at home, hoping to be able to accept a new dance offer that was made to her. It was to dance in London. It had always been her dream to dance with a major company. Someday she might even get the chance to dance the role of the Sugar Plum Fairy, she thought. But the events her life had in store for her were outside of anything she could dream.

Offers to perform kept coming in, and Johanna accepted one as a guest dancer for a week in a ballet to be held in a little haven in Monte Carlo. It was not a major role, but the advance publicity built her as an ex-Auschwitz victim who had lived to dance, and tickets for the week's engagement sold fast.

In her dressing room on opening night Johanna was a nervous wreck. She feared she would not be able to dance or that she would forget the steps once she got on stage. To make things worse, her attendant spoke a dialect of French that Johanna could barely understand, and she hovered over her -- one moment jumping for joy at Johanna's success, and the next offering to help her prepare herself. Her own nervousness and the repeated opening and closing of doors made it almost impossible for Johanna to go over her routine. Finally she escorted the attendant to the door with a mighty push, and then went back to concentrating on her dance.

There was a knock at the door and as she said "Come in," Johanna hurled her make-up tray at the attendant. But to her amazement it was not the attendant coming back to pester her, but the Prince of Monaco, his chest and arms smeared with make-up, liquid eye shades running down his sleeve and dripping onto his shoes. He was stunned and silent. Johanna burst into tears.

The Prince ordered his people to hold up the performance for a few minutes. He came back to the dressing room and closed the door behind him. Then he bowed, took Johanna's hand into his own and kissed it.

"Welcome to Monaco," he said nobly. "I especially want to tell you I am proud of your accomplishments. After what you went through during the war, you too should be proud."

Johanna was unable to speak. She could not believe that this fine Prince stood before her, still holding her hand.

"I will see you at the Hotel de Paris for the ball," he said. Then he turned and left the room.

Johanna felt she was dancing for him that night, and for what he had said. The performance went well. The critics were critical but kind, and at least she had been mentioned in their reviews, she was proud of that.

The ball at the Hotel de Paris was magnificent. It brought back images of her past life and the beauty of fantastic balls she vaguely remembered attending. The ballroom was white and gold with enormous sparkling chandeliers. Red carpets and red roses seemed to be everywhere. The buffet table was exquisite. Johanna stood fascinated before the food that seemed works of art. Each ice sculpture, each pastry, each caviar dish was almost too fantastic for her to comprehend. The seafood was displayed so impeccably and the colors of the whole affair blazed with beauty.

As the orchestra began the Vienna Waltz, Johanna was still fixed upon every piece of wood, every piece of art work, the silk napkins, the lustrous silver. She saw the Prince of Monaco across the room, but could not keep her gaze away from table. Before she realized it, he was standing again right in front of her. He bowed and asked her to dance. Johanna graciously accepted, and when he escorted her to the dance floor, she felt she was floating on air and that the world was her very own.

Johanna and the Prince danced around and around in the elegant steps of the waltz, till she felt dizzy from the magnificence of the evening, the glitter from the chandeliers, the whole room that seemed to be spinning and spinning.

The Prince looked into her face and said, "I hope your life will be better now. If there is anything I can do for you, please let me know."

Johanna said nothing. She danced silently, snuggling up to this man, dressed so beautifully in his uniform, full of medals and a sword at his side. Was she dreaming? Was she home with her father? The feelings were overwhelming and Johanna knew this night marked a new beginning. She would practice and dance until she was famous all over the world.

The next day the Prince invited Johanna and the company directors for the tour of the castle, and then to the casinos for some gambling. Life in Monte Carlo revolved around three things -- the Hotel de Paris, the casino, and the Cafe de Pari. At all hours of the night and day the mechanical clacking and ringing of the gambling machines could be heard, and from time to time the laughing cascade of money falling as a prize to some lucky gambler.

The Cafe de Pari was a meeting place for all visitors to Monaco, many of them among the world's most famous people. One night the Prince of Wales enjoyed his crepes suzette at the table next to Johanna and her company. And as they were leaving the Aga Khan came in, another patron attracted to the cafe's gastronomical creations.

The last day of their stay, the company went on a yacht that cruised around Monte Carlo and the surrounding areas of the Mediterranean. The day ended with another wondrous dance and a champagne dinner. For the whole week, Johanna's clothes were provided for her by the local dress shops, using Johanna as a public model and enjoying the publicity that was showered upon her and the group and the beautiful gowns.

Then came the final morning. The ballet troup enjoyed breakfast at the cafe for the last time, and with their gifts and flowers that rained upon them during their week long performance, they all left for their homes.

Chapter 20

Johanna's life continued to jump between tragedy and opulence. Dancing took her all over Europe, from city to city, never staying long enough to explore or enjoy the sights -- just the stage and the travel, the travel and the stage.

When her husband returned from his assignments again, Johanna had to return home. She felt like she was living with a stranger. She still could not comprehend the irrational violent monster that lurked beneath the seemingly charming and composed person who was studying to be a minister.

One night she arrived home with food for dinner and when she saw him sitting in the kitchen she knew there was going to be trouble. His face had that dark blue color that meant something horrible was brewing inside. As Johanna set the plates on the table he lept with a pantherlike spring and grabbed her tightly by the shoulders. She pulled away, but he swung his hand towards her, and before she could protect herself she felt the searing sting of his palm across the side of her face.

"Don't you dare touch me again," she screamed, but he was coming toward her and his face that awful color it took on when he became violent.

"I'll not only touch you," he shouted. "I'll give you the beating of your life."

Johanna's thoughts flashed to Auschwitz and automatically, her hands went up to her face to shield herself. She feared his constant haranguing about how it was a sin for her to have such a sensous face would mean he might try to destroy it so other men can't look at it. He grabbed her, spinning her around. He hit her hard this time, knocking her down. She staggered momentarily and then slid to the floor. He yanked her up and began hitting her with his fists. The force of his blows sent her flying across the room, glasses and plates scattering to the floor around her.

He punched and slapped her again and again, and finally slammed her against the closet door. The back of her head hit the door, and through the groggy mist that closed around her cut the knife of an even deeper dread.

Is he going to kill me? she thought. This minister, this man devoted to God, this man who felt unbearable guilt for her rape -- was he going to kill her? As she hit her head again, her knees began to sag, and he grabbed her by the shoulders and hit her in the stomach with his fist. Johanna crumpled to the floor, gasping for breath. He leapt on top of her, crouching over her like an animal, a string of vile names spewing from his lips. All Johanna could do was shake and mumble.

"No, no please don't. Don't hit me anymore. Stop it, stop! What do you want from me?"

But he would not let go of her; she could feel his hot breath as he shouted: "You're mine, all mine! No one can have you! Now do you understand, do you?"

He shook her violently, screaming, "You will never leave me!

Never!"

"Leave me alone," Johanna managed to cry.

He burst out laughing and slowly released his grip. Johanna somehow got to her feet and staggered into the bathroom. She looked at her bleeding face. There were welts all over and the beginning of terrible bruises. Thank God her eyes were okay, she thought. Every slap she had received caused her teeth to cut into her cheeks and tongue. Her chin was red and swollen from the blows. Her breasts and every part of her body throbbed. After she washed herself, she felt anger, guilt and confusion. Why would he do this to me? After her beautiful trip to Monte Carlo and all the glitter and the glory, the incredible contrast of her trip -- the exhiliration of her performance, the love and admiration she felt there, the encouragement she felt from everyone -- to this evening in the hands of a madman, her husband. Shame came over her, deep rooted guilt and shame, as if it were her own fault.

She climbed into bed, the pain cutting her every movement, and huddled up against the pillows. She shivered, feeling numb and sick inside. All of her spirit seemed to die as she realized no one would believe her if she told them what had happened. She lay there for a while, then Seabolt came towards her. She flinched as he climbed into the bed next to her.

All night long she never got warm. She just lay there frozen inside till the gray light of dawn broke outside the window and she heard him get up. He walked around to her side of the bed; she could feel his eyes on her. Then he bent over and kissed her on the cheek. Johanna kept her eyes closed tightly as he walked out of the room and closed the door.

She wondered who the man could be, the man that threatened her so often, who said he wanted to destroy her, who said he would kill her or disfigure her face, carve it up with a knife so that no man could ever want her again. "You will be destroyed when I get through with you. You will have to depend on me," he would scream.

Johanna curled into herself as tightly as she could. I'll never dance again or sing again or be able to earn a living again, she thought.

She was still lost in thought when Gertrude, the maid, came into the bedroom. When she saw Johanna, she burst into tears. She tried to help Johanna sit up, she got a towel and cloth to wash her swollen face, and the tears kept coming. Then she collapsed to her knees and put her face into the bed.

"I am so sorry, Frau Seabolt," she cried. "I am so sorry, but I must leave. My mother has insisted I leave your house this very day." She put her face back down onto the bedding. "It is your husband, Frau Seabolt. I am pregnant. He forces me to sleep with him. He threatens me. He said he would kill me if I did not do as he wanted."

Even through all her pain, Johanna was shocked. She burst into tears too. "Oh my God. I am so sorry," she said.

"I am scared," Gertrude said. "I told my mother and she said she would help me. She would go to the American army and complain."

"Yes, you must do that. You must." Johanna felt a glimmer of hope. "I have told them, but they don't believe me. They think he is intelligent and charming. You must go and tell them what he is really like."

The complaint was filed, but little came of it. Seabolt was questioned and reprimanded and told to stay away from the girl. Johanna gained nothing. In fact, she was more frightened and confused than ever. Her spirit was nearly destroyed. She hid in her home and did not answer the telephone. Fellow dancers came to her house to see if she was ill, but she would not answer the door. All the while, her little Francheska clung to her, stroked her hair and her back, knowing that something was wrong with her mother. She would look up with sad eyes and hold her mother's hand in silence.

Johanna felt as if she were being smothered. Seabolt's love for her was so bizarre and twisted that she lived in constant terror. He was like a puppetmaster, pulling all of her strings, demonstrating total control of everything she did and felt. He wanted to break her will entirely, she realized.

His fear of losing her was demented. He would take her to church and pull her to the alter and insist that she confess her sins, asking for God's forgiveness. Johanna found herself kneeling while he cried out to God to forgive this sinner. Forgive her for having a sensual face and body. Make her cover her sins. Forgive her, for she is a whore and a slut and she bore a child of rape!

Sometimes at church, Seabolt was allowed to lead the congregation from the pulpit, preaching the "Word of God."

"Love each other," he would say. "Love thy fellow man because the meaning of God is love! Come, sinners, kneel in front of me and yee shall be forgiven!"

Listening to the unbelievable oratory, Johanna for the first time realized he was totally insane. Until then, she just was not sure. She did not know what to think. She did not question her condition or even think to run away. Life, it seemed, had always meant suffering, beatings, outrageous human cruelty. She did not even wonder if she had the right to be free of it.

In time she began hiding her neck, her ankles. She looked only at the ground for fear of being beaten or dragged to church.

Charges were finally brought against him and he was ordered to pay all medical expenses for the young girl. But for Johanna, it meant that they might finally believe what she had said about him all along.

Seabolt's captain came to the house one day and sat down with her. He explained that her husband was suffering from paranoid schizophrenia. He had gone AWOL while on recent maneuvers, the captain said. He had beat himself to a pulp with a rock, and then returned to his company claiming he was attacked. But people had seen him do the deed himself. Sgt. Seabolt was hospitalized for the condition, the captain explained. His family history worried the doctors: his mother showed signs of madness, his sister had already been committed for the same condition. Someone in the family had attempted suicide.

But time passed quickly, and the army soon decided Seabolt was as well off at home as in the hospital. It only meant more terror for Johanna.

One night, over dinner, he became frantic because Francheska wet her pants. He grabbed the child and took her to the shower, dousing her with hot and cold water to teach her a lesson. Johanna fought desparately to get Francheska free.

"She is only a child!" she screamed. But Seabolt pushed her away.

"The girl needs lessons, hard lessons!" he shouted.

Johanna made another attempt to pull her screaming child away from her husband and burned her own body in the water. He pushed her away again and her arm crashed through the glass in the door, cutting her hand. Francheska saw the man go after her mother and ran out of the room. Suddenly Seabolt just stopped, and sat down on the bathroom floor, wimpering.

Johanna ran to the telephone and called an ambulance for help. Then she found Francheska and hid beneath the stairs. Seabolt was just coming down the stairs when the ambulance drivers arrived at the door. Before she spoke to them, Johanna turned to look at him. He stared at her with that dark color on his face.

"If you tell them anything, I will kill you," he whispered.

Johanna was petrified. She was torn between her little Francheska's safety and fear for her own. But when she got to the hospital, she did not answer any questions about the cuts and burns. She just sat huddled in the corner while they attended to the child.

A woman from the hopsital came to talk to Johanna after the doctor had treated her wounds.

"Can I help you in some way?" the woman asked.

Johanna did not even look up at her. "You would not believe me if I told you. No one else does," she said.

"Well, try," the woman answered. "I know something is going on in your household. Won't you tell us so we can help you?"

Before Johanna could answer, Seabolt walked into the room. She did not even know he had been following the ambulance all the way from home. She froze with fear and anger. There was no way to tell. No way to explain to the woman that she was living with a total madman.

Johanna said nothing. She picked up Francheska and went to the car with the one person in the world she feared the most.

On the way home, neither of them spoke. And when they got inside the house, she comforted Francheska on the couch while Seabolt paced, forth and back again. When the little girl finally fell asleep, Johanna left her on the sofa and went upstairs to prepare her bed. But when she got to the top of the stairs, she heard Francheska scream desparately. Johanna turned and ran down the steps and could not believe what she saw: her husband had the little girl pinned on the sofa. He had his pants down and was preparing to force his sex upon her.

Johanna lunged at the man and grabbed him by the collar, pulling him away from Francheska. Seabolt knocked her down and she took an umbrella from the umbrella stand and began beating on his back and neck. He overpowered her again and grabbed her by the throat. As his grip tightened around her neck, she managed to scream for her life. Then suddenly, someone was banging at the door.

The banging stopped them both for an instant, and Johanna recognized the voice of Frau Hofman, the maid's mother. Johanna escaped from Seabolt and as she ran toward the door, he threw a flower vase that bounced off her shoulder and crashed onto the floor.

"Get away from that door!" he bellowed.

On the other side, Frau Hofman shouted, "I am here to help you. Please open the door!" She was banging as loudly as she could.

Johanna flung open the door. "Please take us out of here, Frau Hofman," she pleaded. "Please help us!"

Turning to gather Francheska in her arms, Johanna heard Seabolt shout, "Stop, or I will shoot."

She stood frozen, but was surprised at the words that suddenly issued from her mouth. She might have been thinking them, she might have been screaming, Johanna could no longer tell.

"Go ahead and shoot! It should have been done long ago. Nothing ever improves in this life; we'd be better off if you shoot us."

As the bullets discharged, Frau Hofman pushed Johanna and the child down the steps. Johanna tumbled, protecting Francheska's head from the concrete. Then she heard a scream and Seabolt began to cry.

When she looked up, she saw him bending over Frau Hofman, who was shot and had fainted.

Slowly, she stood up and walked into the foyer of the house. Her husband raised his eyes to her, begging for forgiveness. He looked like a helpless boy, and Johanna felt her heart going out to him. The poor confused soul looked so pitiful -- his personality completely changed. He was on his knees kissing Johanna's feet, begging for forgiveness, crying ever so softly. She could not help but feel sorry for him, despite all that he had done. He was sick and helpless and pitiful.

Johanna went to help Frau Hofman, who was moaning by the front step. She was conscious again, and Johanna could see that the bullet had only nicked her arm. She was hardly even bleeding. By the time she was back on her feet, the police had arrived because of reported gunfire.

When they asked for an explanation, Johanna was speechless. Her little girl was asleep on the sofa -- too frightened to even cry anymore. Frau Hofman was tending to her own wound, and Johanna sat on the floor, comforting a grown man in her arms as if he were a little child -- the very grown man who just moments before had tried to kill them all. To Johanna, the scene was so pathetic, so strange. Her emotions could not handle the confusion.

Frau Hofman spoke to the police.

"It was an accident," she said. "So please go. Leave these people alone."

"But you have been shot," the officer objected.

"It is only a very small wound," she said.

"Just the same, it was a shooting."

"It was an accident, I tell you," Frau Hofman raised her voice. "Just an accident. Now please go away."

The policemen were eventually pursuaded to leave. With no one pressing any charges, there was little they could do.

After Frau Hofman had bandaged her arm, she too prepared to leave.

"Don't go," Johanna pleaded. "Thank you for saving our lives. Please take my little girl with you; she is not safe here," she said.

Frau Hofman realized that she was right. Though what was right and what was wrong had become all tangled at this household, she knew that the little Francheska should not remain with such a confused and dangerous man.

Johanna stayed with Seabolt. She did not know what else to do. With no family or relatives, and virtually no friends to turn to for advice or help, it was the only choice that she had. She was still a lost soul. Unaware of her rights and unexposed to normal relationships, she could not imagine that life was anything other than fights and beatings and torture. She was still a prisoner of the camps, of the imprint that heinous experience had left upon the very core of her being.

But the outside world had not forgotten about her. In the mail one day she received specially delivered contract to do a musical film. It came from a German agency that said she would be perfect for the part.

Johanna read the contract, with a promise of excellent pay, and trembled at the thought of performing again. There was nothing she wanted more. Despite her limited understanding of day to day living in the rebuilt civilization that was post-war Germany, despite her emotional confusion, she knew that she wanted to grow. She wanted to make up for her lost years and become the world famous dancer she had always longed to be.

Still, she didn't dare accept. Seabolt would kill her. In fact, she was so frightened that she hid the contract in the bottom drawer of the dresser in Francheska's bedroom.

The nightmare that was her life with Seabolt was a bad dream that kept repeating itself, over again and over. She never knew when he was going to snap, but she was as sure of it happening again as she was of her desire to dance.

It was at dinner time again that he flew into another rage. Johanna could see it coming. The horrible blue blood filled his neck and face.

"So you think you are real hot stuff, don't you?"

Could he have found the contract? she wondered.

"No, I don't," Johanna said. "On the contrary, my every thought is that somehow all this madness is my fault. What have I done? Why are you so cruel?"

Seabolt spat onto the table. "I don't want that bastard child of yours around here anymore!" he shouted. "You are never going to see her again!"

In his hand, he held the butcher knife he had been using to carve the meat. But by the time he raised it above his head, Johanna was running away from the table as fast as she could. She ran throughout the house, crying out for help from someone, anyone. There was no one else in the house but her husband, who was always behind her, screaming madly. She could not understand the words. Johanna ran wild, hysterical, and everywhere she ran he was right there with the butcher knife, charging at her. She ran for the door, but it was locked. She turned to get away and tripped over the rug and fell against the sofa.

Seabolt caught up to her and stood above her, raising his arm it seemed to the ceiling, as if to get enough distance and the power he needed to put the knife right through her. As he came down, Johanna rolled off the sofa and fell between his legs. He hit the sofa, burying the knife into the springs with his powerful thrust. The momentum carried him over the top of the sofa and he banged his head against the wall. Then he let out that pathetic whine that frightened Johanna almost as much as his cries of hate and murder.

"Oh what have I done?" he wimpered. "Have I hurt you? Why do I do this, I love you so much. I am sorry. I am sorry."

Before Johanna could even respond, he changed back again -- back to the raging monster. He had pulled the knife from the sofa and was coming after her. Johanna ran down the hallway and was stopped by the sound of an explosion in one of the bathrooms. Seabolt stopped, and as if nothing unusual had been happening, he calmly and sanely looked into the bathroom, announcing to Johanna:

"A tank blew up. Water is running everywhere. We need a plumber. Please call a plumber, Dear."

His calm was so sudden and so genuine, that Johanna stopped her flight and walked over to the telephone. She picked up the phone and dialed for a plumber, realizing that it might be her only opportunity to get someone to come and help her.

She called public services and told them who she was and the man who answered said he would get a plumber to the phone. Seabolt went back to the bathroom to look at the leaking water tank. As Johanna waited she thought out her plans to tell the plumber to send someone to help her. Her hope grew stronger and stronger and finally he came to the phone, but before she could speak she heard her husband call out: "It's okay! I've fixed it. We don't need a plumber."

"Sir, please come and help me," Johanna spoke quickly into the phone. "I beg you. He is trying to kill me. I am all alone and I need your help!"

Seabolt suddenly came at her again and Johanna ran for the door. She unlocked it, but could not get it open because of snow that had drifted against the outside of the house. Finally her fear gave her strength and she forced the door open with a powerful shove. She ran into the snow, not even realizing that she was nearly naked. Her husband had torn away almost all of her clothes. All she was left wearing was her underpants and her bra.

Johanna found herself knee-deep in snow. She ran for the road but could not find it. She ran across a field and fell into a pit of snow that went above her waist. Seabolt was still in pursuit, puffing, calling her name.

The night was pitch black and there was not even moonlight to brighten the snow. Johanna could not see where she was going -- no trees, no bushes, just land and space and snow ahead of her. She heard his breathing behind her and the crunch of the snow from his combat boots sharpened her fear and sent her running faster, faster. She heard him calling from a distance, a faint call, and she kept running. Her eyelashes were frozen and her hair was beaded with snow. She thought that somewhere there must be people who care, people who would help her. Up ahead she saw a tiny light flickering. She headed toward it, hope carrying her forward through the freezing snow.

Then she recognized the house, and like Seabolt's knife, the realization went through her heart -- it was her own house. She had run in a complete circle.

Johanna pleaded to God to let her die, to let it all end. Then she saw the Military Police come out of her house with her husband in handcuffs. He was clean and dry, as if he had never left the house, had never chased after her through the black night and deep snow, calling her name, coming to get her.

Johanna learned later, after she had been admitted into the hospital and treated for exposure, that the plumber had called the police, and that Seabolt had shot at the M.P.s when they came to investigate. And through the daze of her physical illness that ensued, she learned, there in that hospital, that Seabolt was going to be locked up for good, and that she was going to be reunited with her daughter, her little princess, her dear little Francheska.

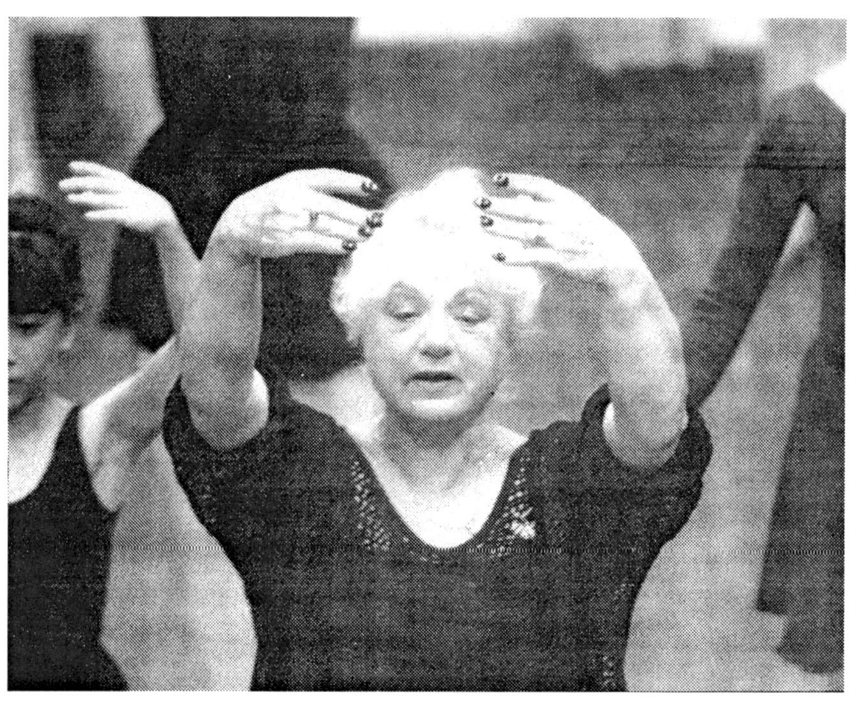

Yanina Cywinska at 65 characteristically jumps in to demonstrate a difficult step. She urges her students to set their goals high, then attain them

Chapter 21

Johanna was afraid she might have to cancel Giselle. Hopes for coming up with enough money to stage it were getting dim. Worst of all, her personal life was ruining her. Her struggle with Harold and Francheska was draining all of her strength. Some days she was so depressed she could not get out of bed to go to the school and teach ballet, leaving the responsibility or rehearsals solely to Kirsten. But the more she felt Giselle slipping away, the more determined she became to see it performed. She owed it to the dancers who had worked so hard to master their parts. She owed it to herself. Giselle had become a symbol of her struggle for independence, for freedom from betrayal and unhappiness. There had been times in her life when, like Giselle, she found herself dancing, drunken with happiness from life's beauty. Lately she had felt more like Giselle's ghost, defiantly trying to dance her own message of hope under the nose of the oppressive Myrtha, Queen of the Wilis.

The oppression was the guilt she carried with her every day -- the guilt of not being able to make her own husband and daughter happy, and the guilt of having been a survivor of the camps and the war and the devastation that had ended the lives of so many loved ones.

The dreams reminded her of that second guilt. Lately, they had been getting worse. More powerful, more vivid and more horrifying, they left her weak and defenseless and wanting to hide.

In her most recent dream two faces had appeared. She knew they were her mother and father. The faces were not distinct, but they were recognizable. Far from her home, the incinerators were spewing out human fat. It ran from the ovens, out through the iron gates of the camp, hot and steaming and smelling so sweet and disgusting. It ran through the cracks of the buildings and down into her town in Poland like lava from a volcano. It ran right up to her house, nearly touching its beautifully sculpted doors. Johanna was a young girl and knew the steaming suet was about to engulf the house. She ran across the red Kishan carpet and flung open the huge front doors. There were the two faces -- her mother and father.

They were drowning in the flowing suet, sinking into it as if it were quicksand, their arms reached out for her, their fingers spread in ten directions, blood running down their arms. Her father called out to her, called his favorite name for her:

"Ninochka, my little Katchka! Save me! Help me!" he cried.

But she could not help. She could not move. Her feet were glued to the Kishan carpet. Her hands were stuck to the sculpted doors and she could not pry them loose. As she helplessly watched her parents drown in the human fat -- the color of yellow, the smell of sweetness -- her ears filled with the sound of speeding trains, their wheels screeching against the railroad tracks, the cars rattling and rumbling like her bed that shook as she awoke screaming.

The incident had convinced Harold that his wife needed to see a psychiatrist. He convinced her.

The thought frightened Johanna. What would the psychiatrist do? What would he ask her? She really didn't want to see him, but she knew that she needed someone to help her deal with the rejection she got from her own family.

When she arrived at the phsyciatrist's office he asked her to tell him about her past.

"I am not troubled by my past, Doctor," she said. "I know it was tragic, but I am interested in the present. I need answers for right now. I need to know how to cope with everyday life. I know nothing of normal everyday life."

The psychiatrist leaned back in his chair. "Well," he mused, "brief me on your past anyway."

Johanna described her life. She started with Auschwitz and then the rape and the cruel husband. She told him everything she could remember.

The doctor was overwhelmed. He stood up and looked at her. "You tell me your past does not bother you? Johanna, there are people who have experienced only one tragedy in their lives -- broken romance, rape, infidelity -- and their whole life is ruined by it. These are people who may have had loving parents, good education, family and friends to help them cope. But they cannot cope. They drink, take dope and become totally self destructive. And you think your past does not bother you?"

"Yes, Doctor, I can cope with my past. I only need to be loved and needed. How do I make my family love me? I don't need blame and rejection. Doctor, just help me with my daily living. I know nothing about normal everyday living."

The doctor tried to explain how the past affects everyday life, how unresolved problems create inner turmoil. Johanna insisted that it wasn't the past that was troubling her, it was the present.

"If I had warmth and acceptance and fairness at home, I could handle anything," she said.

Johanna explained some of the battles she had with her daughter and her husband. He listened patiently and then suggested she take valium to help her cope.

"I will write up the perscription for you," he said.

"I don't want medicine, I want answers," she said.

"The valium will help you feel at ease. It is nothing to worry about."

"To me it is, Doctor. I don't want to be dependent on anything, not medicine, not drink, not religion. I want to depend only on myself. If I get used to taking medicine to help me cope, I'll just have to cope with that much more later on."

"But you are ill," the doctor said.

"Why do you say that I am ill?"

"Johanna, you don't know your real name. You don't remember your family and you are having nightmares. Those are not good signs."

The doctor's words angered her. "I know I have a lot to face, but I will not be labeled 'sick. ' I am not sick. You are putting this sick business into my head and I refuse to accept it!"

"Have it your way," the doctor said quietly.

Now it was Johanna who was standing. "I am functioning fine. I keep a fine house. I am a good mother and a successful ballet teacher. I want to grow, learn, and to be accepted by my husband and daughter. I need your help to cope with both of them."

The doctor edged his chair up to his desk and began calmly. "Johanna, it is the past that is affecting your present. You must realize this. I suggest you go to a mental hospital and we will help you understand your past. Then you can learn to cope with the present."

Johanna was angered and confused. "Doctor, something doesn't make sense to me," she said. "Why are you trying to label me 'sick' and put me in a hospital and make me take valium? That is going backward. I want someone to show me a way to go forward. I am paying you good money. I should be able to choose what I need. I have no time to be ill."

Johanna left the office more troubled than when she arrived. Her gut feeling was that she was okay, and she fought with all her might the suggestion that she was mentally ill. She felt she just needed to understand more, such as her husband's constant silence and indifference toward life, and Francheska's resentments toward her.

She had a few more sessions with the doctor, and each time she felt like she was fighting for her sanity. Sure she was depressed, just as a world would be if there were no sun, just as a flower would not grow without water, warmth and care, she thought. But she realized she was no closer to finding that care and warmth than when she went to the doctor for help. Harold and Francheska were worse than ever. They took up the notion that she was mentally sick and belittled everything she did. They made her feel that everyone in the world was normal except for her.

Francheska continued to deceive Johanna at every opportunity. She cut classes in high school. She took money from her mother's purse and denied it. She began missing ballet classes and when Johanna threatened to pull her from the performance, she laughed in her mother's face.

"What do I care? It was your idea that I become a ballerina in the first place." Johanna was frustrated and powerless.

One morning instead of going to her appointment with the psychiatrist, Johanna went for coffee to the Sheraton Palace Hotel. She sat by the window and watched the San Francisco traffic stream down Market Street. The cafe was very crowded that morning and a blonde woman came up to Johanna with her coffee and asked to share her table. She and the woman struck up a conversation. First they talked about the fog and traffic, then they began to talk about themselves. The woman's name was Frances Farmer. Johanna did not recognize her.

Johanna opened up to her. She told her about the doctor she had been seeing and the things he had recommended. As soon as Frances heard about the psychiatrist she became angry.

"Stay away from him," she urged. "He will mess you up."

Johanna was a bit surprised at the woman's sudden reaction, but as she listened to the things she said, Johanna realized she had been right to resist the doctor's conclusions.

"He will ruin you," Frances said. "Promise me you will not let them do this to you! They never believed me. I was okay, but they wanted me to conform to what they expected. I fought them. I argued, and the more I argued, the more they called me insane. They've ruined me. Don't let them do it to you."

Frances was still a beautiful woman, but Johanna could tell she was struggling with the ideas she wanted to express. She told Johanna that she had once been a famous actress. She explained that she always resisted meeting the expectations people had of her and that her resistance got her in trouble. It was her own mother, she said, who had her committed as mentally ill. Eventually the doctors lobotomized her.

"Promise me, you will not let them destroy you," she said to Johanna.

The two women shared stories for several hours. They met again for coffee two more times that week, then Frances disappeared completely. Johanna never saw her again.

A few days later, she made another appointment with her psychiatrist. When she came in, the doctor asked her to lie down on the sofa.

"Why?" Johanna asked. "I can talk much better standing."

"Lie down, please," the doctor said patiently. "You are not being very cooperative today."

Johanna stood in front of him and thought of all the things she and Frances had discussed. "Cooperative? Don't you mean subservient?" Johanna asked. "Don't try to make me feel bad because I won't help you. I will not pay you all this money to lie on a sofa and tell you anything that comes into my mind, because on my mind is the fact that you are trying to talk me into something, trying to convince me that I am sick. I am not sick, and I don't need you to tell me that I am."

It was the last time she ever saw a psychiatrist. But it was not the end of her therapy. During their conversations Frances has suggested that Johanna do some volunteer work with a local mental institution. Johanna volunteered at a local institution and began to work four hours a week helping groom the patients. She was surprised to learn that many of the women patients were admitted for what seemed like minor events. To Johanna, it was as if the women had just given up.

Her second day on the job she was working with a woman named Margarite. Johanna was told Margarite went insane because her husband left her for another woman. While she tried to comb Margarite's hair and fix her nails, the woman had a fit and started to attack her. She kicked and clawed at Johanna until she became angry too, and took Margarite by the hair, spinning her around. Then she forced her down on a chair.

The woman was suddenly motionless. Johanna stood before her and started to yell. "You are really something! You lazy wench! You are rich. You have your parents, lovely chidren, and look at you. You are beautiful. One dumb thing happens to you and you go insane. You are so stupid. You could be living a beautiful life. But no, look at you! Why don't you wash that face, put on a smile and live! Why don't you just live!"

Then Johanna stormed out of the room, leaving the woman stunned in her seat.

When she came back to work the next day, Johanna was called to the volunteer supervisor's office. She was afraid she was going to be reprimanded. She knew she should not have behaved to a patient the way she did. But to her surprise, Johanna was being commended for her help. Margarite had immediately improved. She said she wanted to get out of the institution. She took complete command of herself and worked with her doctor to get released as soon as possible.

But not all of the women Johanna saw in the institution were so easily cured. Many of them were totally broken. Johanna saw one sad creature talking to a doll as if it were her child who had been killed in an auto accident. Others were guilt ridden and fear infested and broken beyond hope, she could tell. Johanna made a silent vow that she would never let anyone break her will. Her chance encounter with Frances Farmer, so well timed in her life, made her feel that perhaps there was a God somewhere, watching out for her.

Chapter 22

It was the impulse to dance that pulled Johanna from the hospital bed and back to the USO shows, where she could make her own money and get back on stage. She quickly lost herself in her work. It forced from her mind the physical and emotional damage that Seabolt had inflicted upon her. When she was dancing, there was no room left for anything else.

Johanna traveled with the USO in Germany and France. Mostly, she sang, but when she wasn't performing, she was practicing her ballet, or cooing over Francheska. It was in Paris that she learned that one of the teachers from her ballet school in Leningrad -- and one of the world's great ballerinas -- was living very close by. Tamara Karsavina, in her prime, had been one of the most successful and popular ballerinas on the world stage. To find her in person in Paris was more than Johanna could resist. When she was given word of where Karsavina lived, she went to the address the next morning. It never occured to Johanna that Madame Karsavina might have more important things to do with her time than to teach a young survivor of the concentration camps how to dance again. But when Johanna showed up at her doorstep in the morning, that's exactly what she requested.

"Please teach me," Johanna said to the somewhat startled woman. "I must learn fast. You see, I must be good enough to dance the Sugar Plum Fairy this year."

"What, this bag of bones?" Madame Karsavina laughed. "No, no, I would ruin you."

"I am strong, Madam, I will show you," Johanna said as she took a preparation for a double pirouette.

Karsavina stopped her. "Yes, yes, I see there are some things you could do, but I just don't know." She was familiar with Johanna. She had read accounts of the young camp victim who delighted audiences in Monte Carlo. But she hadn't realized how weak the young woman still was until she saw her in person. To try to make her into a real ballerina might kill her.

"Please take me," Johanna pleaded. "Just teach me. I can learn anything."

"I don't know," Karsavina said thoughtfully. "I might break you. "

Madame Karsavina was suprised that this Johanna Bayers was so persuasive. Certainly the girl had a strong will, that was important for any dancer. "We try," she said finally. "But you will have to live with me so I can feed you and watch you and bring your health back."

Johanna could hardly believe it. "Oh I would love it here, but how could I? I do not have such money."

"Never mind that," Madame Karsavina said. "You will be my Cherie, and we will work."

To Johanna it was like a fairy tale. She left the USO behind and quickly moved into her new paradise. Madame Karsavina had a magnificent estate and was married to a nobleman. Johanna lived in opulence and worked hard. She could not join a class at first; Karsavina trained her privately, sharing her fantastic knowledge of ballet. She understood every movement, and why and how and when to use each limb, each muscle. Johanna learned quickly, because Karsavina made her understand the mechanics, and had short cuts to each step.

The most difficult part of Johanna's new life was learning the ways of the exotic and eccentric super rich whose lives revolved around the Madame. From the moment that the family arranged for Johanna's suite, she realized she had entered a world that was beyond anything she could have imagined. She had her own bedroom and a sitting room of incredible beauty. She was surrounded by silks and satins. The first morning after she moved in with Madame, Johanna was told to come to breakfast on the balcony. When she arrived she saw the table was filled with guests from every country, waiting to meet her. As she sat down, Madame introduced Johanna as her "Ninochka". There was unusual silence and curiosity as the guests seemed to wonder who this young woman could be, and how had she charmed her way into Karsavina's heart.

In the tension of that elite company, Johanna, not knowing herself why she did it, suddenly flicked her fingers up in the air and a servant quickly appeared behind her.

"I would like my coffee now. And please remove the dish in front of me. I will not be eating anything just yet."

To Johanna's astonishment, Madame stood up and said to the table, "You see. She is one of us!"

With that the silence was broken and the chattering began. From that moment on, Johanna truly was one of them. The realization hit her immediately -- she had passed the test. And from then on she also realized that she must demand, not ask, that her every need be met. She must expect only the very best, as if she were of the same noble blood and in possession of the same wealth and stature as any of Madame's guests. She realized she must never even let it enter her mind, or let it slip from her mouth, that the food at Cafe Rue de Lopey was more reasonable than Maxim's -- otherwise she would never again fit in with the torrent of nobility and royalty and politicians and prominent people that stormed through Karsavina's life.

These were people, Johanna was soon to find out, whose wealth and position was so great that they didn't even know how to take care of themselves. They had grown up with maids and servants and were nearly too helpless to even feed themselves. They could not, or would not even turn on the radio by themselves.

Johanna was fascinated by everything she saw -- Madame and her husband who had unimaginable possessions and money, so much that they often appeared bored. But Johanna's fascination rubbed off on them. She embraced their world, and they wanted to show it to her in all its extravagant detail. They quickly became caught up in Johanna's excitement and suprise, and began calling her their "Bird of Paradise".

To Johanna, Karsavina was the most beautiful and powerful woman she had ever seen. She stood tall and slender with an aura of nobility that people felt as soon as she came into a room. Her face was a beautiful oval shape with delicate nose and large eyes, always framed with a stylish hat. She was the essence of Paris, Johanna thought, the total picture of a great artist. She carried herself like an aristocratic ballerina, but never hid her characteristic Russian gloom.

In Johanna's young eyes, Karsavina was fascination itself. She was the embodiment of what Johanna wished to be. She had lived through the last days of imperial Russia. She had so much to tell and she loved to tell it to Johanna.

"Ninochka, you have a need for me," Madame would say. "And I have a need for you. You are like a daughter to me. With you I can share my past, shop for clothes and jewelry, eat at Maxim's and share your young and innocent mind."

To Karsavina, theater was a holy place, and every day she acted as if she were on stage. Manners were of the utmost importance, she told Johanna. "A ballerina is a world ambassador, a refined diplomat," she said. "We as human beings owe each other every courtesy and kindness to make life pleasant on this tragic planet Earth," she said.

This philosophy hit home with Johanna. She felt as if Madame were talking about her own tragic past, and worked even harder to mold herself in the great ballerina's image.

One evening during her first week at the estate there was a cocktail party at which Johanna was to be introduced to Madame's society. She was dressed in a white Simonetta gown with jewelry that had been delivered especially to her by courier. Johanna was caught up in the excitement of the grand affair and as she took her place next to Madame she couldn't take her eyes off the gentleman in colorful make up sitting on her other side.

After a moment the guest turned and remarked suddenly, "What, my dear, are you staring at?"

Johanna caught herself and replied graciously, "I love your shade of pink rouge. It goes so well with the soft green eye shadow you are wearing. You are a man who has exquisite taste in colors."

Johanna instantly won his heart. For the rest of the evening he devoted himself to taking care of her every wish. She learned later that she had been sitting next to a bit of history. The gentleman was Felix Yusopov, the Russian prince and the assassin of Rasputin. After the Revolution of 1917 he had escaped to France and supported himself as a couturier. His house of fashion was one of the favorite haunts of the super rich. There gathered the deposed nobility of old Europe, the wealthy princes and princesses of Russia and other nations that had been forever changed by the last thirty years of upheaval and war.

The little Bird of Paradise had innocently landed in the royal gardens of a society whose members desparately struggled to recreate the gaiety and excesses that they had been reared to believe would be their heritage. In the Europe after the Second World War, it was only among themselves that they could make believe that world still existed. Johanna was their colorful pet, and she flew among them with a wide eyed energy that gladdened all their hearts.

Johanna never told Madame Karsavina about her marriage. She never had the time. Before she even called on the famed Russian ballerina, Johanna had arranged for Frau Hofman to watch Francheska, and now that she was in Madame's keep, her every waking hour was devoted to either studying ballet or mingling with high society. With dance, Madame concentrated on Johanna's lightness and beauty. The two worked hardest on her technique. Johanna's brain took the messages, but her body took longer to put them into operation. Madame wanted her to know the choreography so well that the steps would become second nature to her body, freeing her mind to interpret the roles.

Johanna was greatly encouraged by her progress -- the diligent hours of practice were beginning to pay off. And when she performed in public, Madame told Johanna she had a rapport with the audience that was unique. "You touch them, my Ninochka," she said. "That is so important."

When she wasn't studying ballet, Johanna was moving in the social circles of Paris and London. She practiced ballet early in the morning and had to be ready for "appearances" at lunches and dinners at the finest restaurants in Europe. Life moved at a startlingly rapid pace and Johanna reached out to touch and taste it all- Madame's schedule had her visiting designers, or having designers come to her home where they would fit her and Johanna for the beautiful gowns that they would wear to social engagements. The days were a whirlwind of masseuses and facials and hair dressers, then off to two hour lunches in restaurants of Paris. Then the limousine would take them back to Madame's for an afternoon nap.

Johanna would take two hours of ballet again in the late afternoon -- the same practice routine as in the morning. Then, after she had cooled down from her workout, she would begin the daily ritual of preparing for dinner at 9 p.m., or the parties and dancing that might be scheduled.

To Johanna it seemed that everyone in this world was always eating and drinking and attending parties so that jewelers and designers and caterers could stay in business. She had personal maids that kept ledgers, recording the days and the clothes that she wore -- the gowns, the jewelry, the accessories. Another maid would bring in selections of outfits with matching shoes and gloves and hats. Then a courier would arrive twice daily for her to select appropriate jewelry and a furier would stand by with two dozen coats to choose from, depending on the occasion.

Johanna felt as if she were backstage, preparing herself for a daily performance, with attendents adjusting her costume and her make up. The schedule was relentless and many times she was so tired that the manicurist and pedicurist would do her hands and feet while she slept.

If she had a moment to herself, which was rare, Johanna would begin to feel guilty that so much of her life was going into constant preparation for some social appearance, and not to studying ballet and working her body even harder. But quickly she would be brought back to earth with schedules and expectations and the constant reminding from Madame that she could not rush her progress. Her body was still very fragile from the earlier years of abuse.

So she continued to move all over the world, from party to party. She practiced still for two hours in the morning and two in the late afternoon, nearly every day. But she also made trips to Monte Carlo and St. Moritz and even to New York and Palm Beach, traveling in private planes with no need for money or passport. Johanna had not handled money as a child, nor in the camps, nor now in whirlwind of oppulence. In this new life all she had to do was walk into a jeweler or designer house and walk out with the outfits and jewelry. She never gave a thought about who was paying for it all. But she could see that she was bringing joy to Madame Karsavina's life, that she was a curiousity in her world and as such was in demand for any party.

One day the whirlwind set Johanna down in Ireland. The occasion was a fox hunt. Johanna was attired in a riding habit and they all stayed with a family that lived in a castle with stables and fine horses. The other house guests also were from a number of countries -- counts and countesses and nobility from all over the world, it seemed.

On the morning of the hunt it dawned on Johanna that she could not even ride a horse, but before she could say anything, Madame had introduced her to the the other guests, so proud, as if Johanna were her own daughter, showing her off to everyone, never giving a thought to Johanna's tragic childhood and the things she had missed. Madame always acted as though the young girl had lived a normal life, even a spoiled one.

Johanna decided to do her best and studied how to mount a horse by watching the others who had mounted and were now riding ahead of her. But when she got onto her horse she found herself on the back of a wild animal. The horse took off like lightning. Johanna was petrified, but she could see that Madame was watching her with her chin in the air, as if to say: You see, this is my elegant protege. She is a very fine horsewoman. Johanna realized she had to put on a good show, but it was very difficult. The horse either stood up on its hind legs or galloped at full speed, nothing inbetween.

Just when she felt she could take no more, a distinguished gentleman rode up beside her and took control of her horse. "Madame is proud of you," he said, "and you are not going to let her down. The rest of them are too full of whisky to notice you cannot ride, so I shall show you a few pointers. Do you mind?"

"I welcome it, sir," she said.

"First of all, your horse thinks you want her to stand up by the way you are holding her. So we solve that. Next, you are so full of fear, you are holding the reins too tight and squeezing with your legs. You are giving her a signal to jump. So now let's learn."

The gentleman was an excellent horseman. He rode with her across the countryside in pursuit of the foxes. He never left her side. It made her feel so secure. The horse, it turned out, was well trained and responded to his constant commands. He and Johanna cantered and trotted and galloped, totally under control. As they approached a large ditch, he instructed her to lean forward, pull up the horse and prepare for a jump.

Among this group that took its riding so seriously, Johanna could not be more grateful that she had him by her side to help her. It was the hunt of the year and Madame was the proudest person there.

Johanna and the gentleman stopped on a small hill and he offered her brandy from his flask. As they sipped the brandy and admired the beauty of the country, he told her his name: Count Cedrik de Guille of Spain. He had never married, he explained, because he had never found anyone suitable to his needs and lifestyle, or someone for whom he could truly feel attraction and love. They vowed to be close friends and keep in touch with each other. Then he asked her permission to escort her exclusively to all of the events that were to follow on the trip. Johanna agreed.

Soon she was swept away again into the social life of Madame Karsavina. Event after event took her to New York, Rome, Switzerland -- it did not matter, because everywhere Madame had important friends. Johanna met actors, politicians, counts and countesses from countries she did not know, even the President of the United States -- Harry Truman and his daughter, Margarite -- and Queen Elizabeth, too.

The Shitov in Paris and England were gathering places for this exclusive group and Johanna waltzed her way through the body guards and police and pomp as if it was the only life she had ever known. As each month passed she and Madame Karsavina grew closer. Madame told her that she brought her a great deal of pleasure and that she was grateful that they could share so much together.

"I don't want you to dance," she told Johanna one day. "I want you to marry someone who is rich and will take care of you, rather than have you work so hard in the world of ballet. It is an empty, lonely life, full of hard work and tears."

But Johanna would have nothing of it. She was obsessed with ballet. It was as if she had nothing -- no country, no schooling, no roots. Ballet filled the gap of all that was missing.

Still she enjoyed the life that developed with Madame. She became part of the family. Madame was like a mother, and her husband was like her father. The closeness they shared resembled something in the past which Johanna had forgotten, but felt very, very deeply.

Count de Guille followed Johanna everywhere and escorted her to the finest events. She received roses every week, no matter where she was. He showered her with diamonds, emeralds, and pearls that were a family heirloom. Johanna had to refuse much for fear of becoming obliged to him.

One day Madame and Johanna were enjoying lunch at Maxims in Paris and she opened the subject of Cedrik, who had confessed to her that he was interested in building a future with Johanna. He had gone so far as to mention marriage, she said.

"I would advise you to accept his invitation to Spain. Go there and meet his family, size up the situation and perhaps make a good life for yourself and make an old lady like me very, very happy."

As she continued, Johanna's thoughts flashed to her own marriage and the ugliness that word had come to mean for her.

"Madame, you do not know my past. You have not wanted to know so I have not told you. But now, I feel I must explain myself so that you don't think I am deceiving you."

"Say nothing, child," Madame said softly. "I know all about it and I am prepared to have your tragic marriage annulled."

"It is not for you to do," Johanna objected. Inside, she felt that even Madame should not control the important decisions of her life. Someone always had. Now it was time to make her own decisions. Johanna knew she wanted to make those choices, but she had no idea what choices to make.

"Besides," she said finally, "I, myself, just want to dance. That is all I want out of life, Madame."

Madame turned to her and gently placed her hand against Johanna's cheek. "We shall see, my Ninochka. We shall see."

Chapter 23

When the dancer performs the pirouette, she turns the body on one foot. The turns pick up speed as she completes another and yet another -- two, three, four turns -- ever faster, her one foot rooted to the stage and the other lifted slightly and bent at the knee. As she spins, she focuses her eye on one imaginary spot, and lets her body nearly complete a full turn before it whips her head in a tighter, faster circle and brings her eyes back to the same imaginary spot. Each time her body turns, her head waits until the last possible moment and then, in an instant, spins and catches up with the body again -- five turns, six turns, seven -- so that the vivid world of the ballet going on around her, and the dim reflection of stage lights off the foreheads of those in the front row of the audience, become a blur. The momentum carries the ballerina's body faster and faster and her eyes are always focused on the imaginary spot.

Johanna's life was this -- a pirouette spinning ever faster, her body carried by the momentum of the dance, and the dim and vivid world around her a blaze of people and images and feelings. At times she could not tell it if was her own body spinning, or the world around her, and the motion was so quick that she thought she might leave the ground in a tours en l'air of unbelievable finesse.

In one turn she was at an intimate dinner party in Madame Karsavina's home, sitting next to Salvadore and Gala Dali, Maria Callas, and being introduced to Marquis De Cuevas, whose ballet company toured the world. In the next turn, she was in the studio, practicing her technique over again and over, falling and getting up and falling, trying to make herself into one of the world's great ballerinas in the world's shortest period of time. As she turned again she would find herself gently stroking Francheska -- whom Madame had insisted join Johanna in Paris --as the little girl imitated her mother's every move, and then the pirouette would take her back into the whirl of late night social engagements and Francheska into the caring arms of her nanny.

Madame and her Cherie continued to shop in the most lavish salons of France, where they were greeted with formality and courtesy and treated to champagne while waiting for the models to show them their gowns and furs. Madame decided they should have identical outfits for one engagement -- pale lavender silk gowns that seemed to float as they moved, the bodice covered with rhinestones and pearls. With it they wore white ermine capes, trailing to the floor. Next they went to a Fabergé jeweler who supplied them with diamond bracelets, chokers, earrings and rings.

The same day they met Helena Rubenstein and had their makeup analysis done while Madame Rubenstein ordered the hairdresser to coif their hair accordingly. Madame Rubenstein was Polish and quickly took a liking to Johanna.

On the way home they stopped at a hotel for dinner. To Johanna, it seemed they could never eat in peace. Someone always recognized Madame and came to the table to greet them or ask them to dance. That evening she met Onassis and his beautiful wife, and Greta Garbo, whom Madame despised, but was civil to.

David Niven and his wife, Primula, were guests often at Madame's house. Johanna met Elizabeth Taylor in a coffee house on Champs Elyssee. Cary Grant, Peter Lorie, Gloria Swanson, Madame's great friend Elsa Maxwell, the world renown hostess, and many others were constant visitors at her fabulous home that dazzled with life of the rich, the noble, the stars and the politicians.

The couple Johanna enjoyed most was the Nivens, and also the Duke and Duchess of Windsor. The Duchess touched her heart. Johanna felt they were soulmates. Their friendship was instantaneous and Johanna told her the first time they met how happy she was that both of them were on the earth at the same time. The Duchess made her promise to always keep in touch, no matter where life took them, to keep their friendship living.

To Johanna she seemed so dainty, and as she spoke to the woman for whom the King of England had forsaken his throne, the Duchess would look at her so directly, with her large, luminous, violet blue eyes, piercing and intense. They were eyes that focused, drilled and rooted Johanna in attention. When the Duchess talked to her, Johanna felt that she was interested in her and her alone. She was alive and exciting and Johanna understood how she had so completely captivated the Duke.

One night the Duchess asked Johanna to come and play poker with her. She would teach her, she said, and it would be her pleasure, and then they would both go to Monte Carlo and really test her teaching. She told Johanna she had been a happy child and had very gay parents.

Once Johanna even had lunch in her home. A perfect hostess, Johanna marveled at this vibrant woman whose eyes were watchful of every move around her.

As they sat in the living room, the Duchess touched Johanna's hand and held it.

"You have lost so much, my dear one. You must consider us your family."

Madame was so pleased that Johanna got on so well with the Duchess. She told her that until Johanna befriended the Duchess, she had never invited Madame to join her at their vacation home in the Bahamas.

"An invitation has arrived and we are leaving Thursday. It is because of your charms that we have finally been invited," Madame said. She also told Johanna that her Cedrik, the Count, would join them on the islands.

"Cedrik is a close and dear friend of the Duke's. Besides, he wants to be wherever you are."

Johanna's dancing abilities improved and Madame used her influence in the world of art and dance to land Johanna a position with the De Cuevas Ballet. At first she got small parts -- a walking part, a mother part, a gliding part -- but slowly she made her way into the corps de ballet, the dancing chorus. Later she was to dance the Pade Quatre in Swan Lake, the cat and the waltz in Sleeping Beauty, the waltz of the flowers, snow flakes, and many other roles in the Nutcracker. She danced even in Giselle and learned by heart the entire repertoire.

George De Cuevas was a Chilean who had married an American lady of wealth. Margaret Strong was her name and she was the cousin of the Rockefeller family. It was rumored that De Cuevas had been a man of no particular noble standing until he bought a title for himself from the king of Spain. Margaret was totally enamored with the Chilean, married him, financed his purchase of the ballet company and kept it operating with her personal wealth. She was deeply in love with George, as all the dancers called him, and he became the force that moved her life from the intellectual quarters of the American East into the exotic new world of European art and dance.

Marquis De Cuevas Grand Ballet de Monte Carlo traveled across Europe and to America. Johanna worked hard and learned fast and began to feel her life was changing, that she was gaining independence even from Madame. With the company she became friends with the De Cuevas' daughter, Bessie, who was her own age. As their friendship developed, Johanna realized how different were their pasts. Bessie had known nothing but wealth her whole life. Johanna had lived through hell on earth and had been forced to grow up too soon. There was a distance there that Johanna knew in her heart could never truly be crossed. She could never be the young girl that Bessie was, even though they were the same age. Johanna always felt more comfortable with older people.

Still the two girls spent much time together, and it was because of Bessie that Johanna became like a member of the De Cuevas family. Once again, Johanna found herself spinning through the world of the super wealthy, the haute boheme whose lives revolved around ballet and art, and who never even carried money.

Dancing and socializing with the De Cuevas family took her to their country house in Saint-Germain where Bessie and her brother were born. Next, Johanna found herself on East 68th Street in New York or in a mansion in Palm Beach, a weekend house in New Jersey or even in New Mexico. It seemed the world was spinning still -- private planes to Mexico, to Europe, to Hong Kong and the U.S., then back to Europe again.

The Grand Ballet toured the world beginning in 1947, and George devoted himself to making it one of the finest ballets in the world. To choreograph the company, De Cuevas hired the legendary Serge Lifar, one of Europe's great choreographers. Lifar liked Johanna and told her often that one day he would plan a ballet just for her.

The costume designer was Raymundo De La Royne, another Chilean, whose aristocratic heritage was unquestioned. Coming from one of Chile's wealthiest families he looked upon De Cuevas with disdain because of his store bought nobility, but his artistic brilliance was vital to the ballet, despite the constant clashes he had with the company's director.

Equally important was his romantic connection with one of the Grand Ballet's principal patrons, Viscountess Jacqueline De Ribes, one of the grandest ladies in Paris society, whom the dancers considered the "godmother of the ballet." In the heat of the intense and frequent clashes between De Cuevas and De La Royne, it became the opinon of many that De La Royne was using the Viscountess as a stepping stone into Europe's high society, and that he had designs on taking over the ballet.

Life with the company was a world within a world. The practice and the performance of ballet involved hard work and sweat. Around that dance spun the politics and antics of its directors. George and Raymundo continued to fight. So too did George and Serge. In fact, after De Cuevas slapped Lifar during a heated rehearsal, the choreographer challenged him to a duel. The two men met the next day in the remote woods of France, and after each fired his pistol over the head of the other, they broke down in tears and hugged each other and pledged eternal friendship.

Stories circulated in the dressing rooms that George bankrolled all of Raymundo's extravagent parties, at the same time angrily blasting him for spending the ballet's money without caution. Often it seemed as if George and Raymundo were the married couple, instead of George and Margaret, who the dancers referred to as their "aunt", their "Tonde" Rockefeller.

There were fears among the dancers that De Cuevas, in his middle 60s, might overwork himself. Without him the Grand Ballet would fall apart, for certainly Tonde would disperse it if anything happened to her

George. Even Tonde, reclusive by nature, developed excentricities that amazed the people around her. She began wearing her face powdered in the purest white, and when she went out to restaurants, she would cover her expensive jewelry with handkerchiefs so that no one would be tempted to steal them from her.

In the midst of this whirling world of ballet, Johanna continued to dedicate herself to dance. She got more solos during the tour and wanted desparately to make herself into a prima ballerina. Audiences were receiving her well, the applause was longer with every performance. Madame Karsavina was told that something special happens when Ninochka goes on stage. She has the magic, they said, the musicality. She just needs more time to polish her technique.

Despite the successes, Johanna felt inferior to the dancers in the company. So many of them were already famous. Most had studied and trained since they were small children, without interruption, while Johanna felt too much of her life had been stolen by the tragedies she had been forced to endure. How could she ever compete with them?

One of the dancers, Maria Shear, had even made a film, "The Red Shoes." Johanna felt so far behind Maria that she increased her training and took private lessons from Lifar. She later made visits to England to see Madame Karsavina who was staying there. They spent many hours on the mechanics of ballet, sitting by Madame's huge fireplace. Madame told her that she wanted Johanna to learn everything she knew. She wanted to transfer all of her life's ballet knowledge to her so it wouldn't be forgotten after she died.

Her knowledge was vast and detailed. She explained the importance of the connecting steps, the lost steps, the soul of the dance and the drama and portrayal of character -- how to emotionally identify with each role a dancer performs. She explained phrasing of the dance sequence, putting accent where it is needed and subduing the small links.

"It is," she said, "like writing a sentence without puncutation if you don't learn where to put the accents. Ballet is like painting. Dancers must have the ability to dance the delicate steps, like delicate shading. These delicate steps increase the value of the main step, like an artist's delicate shading increases the master stroke. All steps cannot be of equal calibre or they will diminish the total effect of the dance."

Once, while the Grand Ballet was in London, Johanna got the opportunity to dance an important solo. She was nervous for days before the performance. It was a large theater and the Royal family would be attending. Madame had invited countless guests to show Johanna off, as if to say: "This is my work. This is what I have done with my Cherie. Come and see for yourselves!"

With so much to live up to, Johanna was a wreck. "What if I slip? What if I forget everything? What if I miss my cue?" she asked herself.

Johanna thought of her past and felt physically different from everyone else -- weak, dizzy and hot. She wanted to make everyone proud, especially Madame. "Is she kidding herself or is she right about me?" Johanna questioned. "Am I good or is it that she loves me so much she thinks I am good?"

As she sat in the dressing room before the performance the flowers kept arriving till the room looked like a furneral parlor. Her usual four dozen roses from Count Cedrik were on her dressing table with a boxed gift he had also sent, to be opened after the performance. Of course, the other dancers could not contain themselves and opened the gift before. It was a pair of diamond earrings each the size of a thumb tack. The girls envied Johanna, teasing her about her secret admirer.

Then came the knock at the door: "Three minutes till curtain time."

"Oh God," Johanna thought. "I wished for this in the camps, each time that death stared me in the eye, and now the moment is here and I am frozen with fear. Now I must produce, not just dream."

It was a small part, she reminded herself, and would be over soon. No need for so much fear. But as she stood in the wings with her male partner, waiting for the moment, she could not remember one single step, "If only I knew no one. If only the house was full of strangers, then I wouldn't be so nervous."

The curtain opened and she felt like running. She role required she give the illusion that she was a spirit. It demanded that in her steps she convey to the audience the feeling of flight. All of Karsavina's lessons had to be put to use.

"I can't do it," Johanna whispered to her partner.

There was silence around her. Then she heard her music. Suddenly it was if something carried her out onto the stage. As her part played, the orchestra seemed to excell in its beauty. She responded to every note, her body light and easy beneath her. Her grand jetes just jumped for her as the audience applauded with delight. The violins played and she took her piques and chained diagonally down the stage. Graceful flight brought her into the arms of her partner who lifted her into the air so high she felt her nose was going to scrape the scenery. Then she felt the sudden drop into a fish pose, as the dancers were once more applauded. With each step she felt assurance and more confidence. He held her hand in his as she developped into al la second, her leg nearly reaching her ear, then to spin and penchee arabesque. Johanna ran across the stange, finishing her dance with a series of entrechat quatre, passer saute tombee and step, step, grand jete out.

It was not herself who had danced, she realized. It was her spirit. Someone else inside of her moved her body, formed it into dance.

As she lept into the wings, a wave of relief came over her.

It was over. Whatever happens now, it was over. But the attendent pushed her back toward the stage. The audience was applauding for her to come out. Another push and there she was, back on the stage, totally out of breath, bowing left and right, looking into a vast darkness, knowing there were people there who had liked her dancing.

Johanna left the stage in tears -- tears of joy and sadness -- hearing voices from the past calling her.

"Here comes the Sugar Plum Nut. Let's applaud everyone! Here she comes!" as the laughter rang throughout the barracks at Auschwitz.

Johanna screamed at them, "I am a prima ballerina! You cannot treat me this way! I am dancing for you!"

But the prisoners hissed, laughed and spit at her, the Sugar Plum Nut. That's who she was.

Johanna's world was spinning again. She was getting dizzy, for she could not keep her eyes on the imaginary spot, she could not focus as her body turned and turned again, the world a blur around her -- faces through her tears congratulating her, smiles as wide as sickles, then more faces, those from the past, the people for whom she wept, the thousands of camp victims who could not see her triumphant dance that night.

Chapter 24

Madame Karsavina was ecstatic. She stormed into the dressing room.

"You are right, my little Cherie! You would be wasted in marriage. You have a sparkle, a charisma, a contact with the audience. You are in charge on the stage. It was wonderful!"

Johanna, exhausted, looked up from her mirror.

"You light up and you wake up the audience," Madame said. Her head and her hands were in constant motion. "They loved you. They would forgive you anything. They loved you so much, you made a mistake and they did not know. You were the music. You have it! From now on we will work even harder."

As she took Johanna into her arms, she was shocked at how hot she was. Madame put her hand to Johanna's head. "You feel too hot," she said softly. "This is not normal, What is wrong?"

"Just the excitement, I suppose," Johanna answered meekly.

"Okay. You have to go for the finale yet. Then we go home and you rest. They want to put you on contract and the company manager wants it signed now -- right after the performance. But I will have the chauffeur drive you home and then bring the manager there.

"Now prepare yourself. They want you back on stage."

Waiting in the wings for the finale, Johanna's head throbbed with excitement. The clapping of the crowds and the weeping ghosts of her past and Madame's outpouring of encouragement made her head spin as she tried to remember her part in the final dance. And as she moved closer to the stage she suddenly had to grab onto the backstage scaffolding to keep from falling over. Her legs had gone completely numb; she could not even feel her feet beneath her.

Waves of heat and chills swept through her and then they passed. Before she knew what happened she was back on stage in the performance's grand finale, dancing by instinct and desire. The numbness faded from her muscles, but the first shots in another battle Johanna would have to fight had already been fired.

On the way home in the limousine, Madame told Johanna that after the next night's performance, they were invited to Buckingham Palace to meet Britain's royal family. Johanna was feeling better but Madame was still concerned about her health, and planned to arrange an appointment with a London physician as soon as they returned home.

The next night's performance was a success, but it was physically draining for Johanna. Madame, trying to sooth Johanna's concern explained that it is quite normal for her to be so nervous.

"After all, you are not completely trained yet," she said. "But you are dancing already and you sell well. The audience is impressed with you, but it wears you out."

Madame stroked Johanna's hair gently. "It is your tragic life in the past that makes you so good, so fast. But it is also what drains your body."

After the performance, Johanna and Madame changed into their gowns and Madame's hairdresser did their hair. Their jewelry was delivered from the hotel's bank vault. Cedrik arrived as Johanna's escort and off they went to the palace.

Caught up in the activity of Madame's society again, Johanna was awestruck by the engagement at the royal palace. First there were the security guards checking everyone who entered. Then, the ornate beauty of the palace itself -- the elaborate furnishings and artwork and architecture. The dinner, accompanied by the deep humming strings of a chamber orchestra, was a wondrous delight of the senses that Johanna wished would never end. She wanted to drink up everything around her -- the lights, the sophisticated nobility, the tastes and sounds and pulsing energy of the entire affair.

After dinner, Madame and Johanna were presented to the Royal Family. When it was her turn to curtsy in front of the Queen, Johanna offered her hand and lowered her body to the floor. But as she did, without realizing it, the heel of her shoe caught in the tulle of her gown, so that when she started to stand up again, it pulled her foot and she fell flat on her face.

The hot flash of embarrassment scorched Johanna's cheeks, but the Queen took her hand and smiled directly into her eyes, helping her up and telling her how much the Royal Family had enjoyed the ballet's performance. The Queen was so tender and warm and sincere that she put Johanna at ease, at least until she could make her exit.

GRACEFUL BALLERINA FALLS FLAT ON
HER FACE BEFORE THE QUEEN

the morning newspapers read. Johanna became the talk of London, and felt totally humiliated. She spent hours crying over the incident, but everyone around her found it terribly amusing and great tea time entertainment.

Madame tried to allay Johanna's feelings with an explanation: "My Cherie, wherever you go, you create interest and publicity. That is good, not something to be ashamed of."

The publicity did follow, faithfully. Johanna received several offers for commercial work. London advertisers stormed her door to capitalize on her popularity. She appeared on a cookie box, and posed as a ballerina for companies that sold cherries and strawberries in spring. She began to relax and learned how to laugh at herself.

Johanna did her commercial work during the day, but at night, the De Cuevas company still had a show to perform. On the final day in London, one of the main dancers sprained her ankle warming up and Lifar ran panic-stricken backstage, trying to find a replacement who knew the girl's long repertoire: that of the Black Swan in Swan Lake.

Johanna ran behind Lefar and grabbed him by the sleeve. "I know the part," she said confidently.

"You? You know it all?"

"Every step."

"But your technique is weak."

"I can do it."

Lefar hugged her and kissed her on the cheek. "The part is yours," he shouted. "Now quickly, prepare yourself."

As Johanna was changing her costume for the role she realized that she could not even remember the name of the girl who had been hurt, a fellow dancer she had known for months. Yet, she knew her every step, every note of music and how each step played off of each note.

On stage during the matinee, Johanna performed beautifully. She became the Black Swan, a demanding role that requires an understanding of drama and an ability to communicate the character's complex emotions. The applause was loud and long, and after the solo finale, the applause brought her back on stage for two bows.

The day was a long one for Johanna, she was nearly swooning over her success and the dream of becoming a prima ballerina. She was worried about Francheska whom she saw less and less frequently, but who she knew was in good hands with the nanny Madame Karsavina had hired for her. She was also concentrating on the role of the Black Swan. The spells of weakness came again in waves but quickly passed. The excitement kept her from resting after the matinee, and she even forgot to eat.

All of her attention was on the dance. She wanted more than anything to dance her finest performance for the final show.

In no time, it seemed, the evening performance was beginning. Johanna waited in the wings for her cue and her anticipation made her think again of her past. She realized that she had not yet danced the Sugar Plum Fairy. Soon, I hope, I must dance for all the people that called me the Sugar Plum Nut, she thought to herself. I must prove to them that I meant what I said.

As the orchestra brought Johanna closer to the moment for her entrance, she felt a surge of assurance. Then she balanced out, feeling strong and confident in the role, teasing and flirting with her prince, pretending she was the girl he was in love with, drawing him closer and closer to her. She danced impeccably and hurried off stage to prepare for her return later in the ballet. But in the wings, the air was thick and Johanna felt a wave of heat that seemed to envelope her. Her legs weakened and she fell back against the wall to catch herself. Johanna saw the stage attendant coming, coming closer with a new crown for her to wear in the second act. He came closer still, moving so slowly, and suddenly became very clear. Then she saw nothing at all.

Johanna's legs gave out and she crumpled to the floor. The fire in her body raged uncontrollably, and through the confusion of dancers and managers crowding around her, the constrained whispers of concern, and the shuffling footsteps of the ambulence medics, she heard Madame's tears and felt Cedrik leaning over her, kissing her fingertips to comfort her.

Johanna was rushed to the hospital and recalled nothing of what happened to her until she awoke the next evening in a stark white room with silhouettes looming around her. When she finally focused her eyes, she saw Madame crying, holding little Francheska, assuring her that her mother would be just fine.

Then she heard words that almost made her heart stop:

"It's no doubt. She is paralyzed," the doctor said.

Madame burst into tears, and sensing her distress, Francheska began to cry too. Cedrik comforted Madame and the doctor spoke again.

"It is best to be open about these things. She has polio. She is fortunate that it is a mild case and she is not disfigured in the face. But she will never walk again."

Hearing this, Johanna tried to sit up. She could only lift her head. "But will I dance?" she asked.

The doctor took her hand and looked into her face. "No, I'm afraid not," he said.

It was as if the hospital had collapsed on her, suffocating her. Johanna broke into hysterics.

"It's not fair!" she cried. "It's not fair! I have to dance. Don't take that away from me! Please. I must have that! Don't take it away. Not now. I want to live. The ballet is mine!"

Johanna's body would not move. She could only throw her head back and forth in protest. Back and forth and back until she felt her strength leave her as the doctor administered a sedative.

Physically, she became helplessly imprisoned, but her mind continued to operate at full force. Unable to move, Johanna had much time to think and she went into deep retreat. As she waited in London for a decision as to what was to be done for her, Madame and Cedrik argued about which one would take care of her. The Count insisted that Johanna get an annulment from the American soldier and marry him right away.

"You need a home and someone to provide for you and your child," he implored. But Johanna would give no response.

It was finally decided that Francheska go back to live with Frau Hofman. She had been very happy with the German woman and asked for her frequently. Johanna and Madame decided she must be around warm and loving people and that Frau Hofman would give her the proper environment, and Johanna knew Frau Hofman would never let Francheska forget about her mother.

Before she was even released from the hospital, Johanna received a letter from the U.S. Army notifying her that her husband was under psychiatric care in the United States. The Army argued that she should realize she is the wife of an American citizen, and that her responsibilities were in America with her husband. Johanna did not answer the request, nor did she inform them of her own crippling condition.

It was concluded by the London doctors that Johanna had overworked herself. That she had tried to accomplish too much, too soon. She had never given herself a chance to recover her health. From the concentration camps and her years of near starvation, she had gone out into the world to work, without proper rest, care, food -- and her body had not had the chance to build up its immunities.

The doctors were undecided what treatment would be best for Johanna, and she was in no condition to determine her own future. Cedrik finally convinced Madame that she should travel with him to his castle in Switzerland. The Count's family, anticipating his long awaited marriage to the young ballerina, was greatly pleased that the two came to visit them in the Swiss mountains. Even in her stricken condition, Johanna brought Cedrik great comfort.

But marriage would never come, despite Cedrik's confessions about how much he needed her, and his efforts to convince her how much she needed him. Within her heart, Johanna felt truly sorry for him. He was the gentlest and most sincere of men, and she knew he loved her desperately, but she just could not respond. She had traveled with him to his homes all over the world it seemed, but she realized she could never open herself to him.

When Johanna returned to Paris, Madame showered her with affection, trying to show her that she was loved, that she had a family who cared for her, and a future despite her confinement to a wheelchair. But Johanna's response was cool, even to Madame Karsavina, whom she loved so deeply. Without knowing it, she was already shielding herself and her shattered hopes with an impregnable indifference. Johanna's friends and fellow dancers and the people she had come to know during the past few years came to try to cheer her, console her. But her depression deepened.

Johanna's physical condition had improved somewhat since the initial attack -- she was only paralyzed on her left side. The doctors who were treating her decided that she should be sent to a special clinic in Switzerland where she would be put on a strict vegetarian and natural food diet. The hope was that the pure food and pure air would strengthen her body and mind. Then they would see what could be done to rehabilitate her arm and leg, if anything.

As the days neared for her departure to the clinic, Johanna suddenly began to see the world around her in a brilliance she had never anticipated. She looked through her tears at Madame Karsavina's fabulous home that had become home to her, a place that brought her so much good, so much education, and opportunities she had never dreamed were possible. She thought of Madame, her dear lovely Madame, who became her admirer and her parent, giving her wealth and warmth and unending emotional support. Now, Johanna realized, she would have to leave it all behind.

Once more her anger with God surfaced. How could he be so unfair? Why would he punish one person so much? Believe in me and get heaven as a reward -- what rubbish! If he is almighty and sees everything, then he should realize how good I am. I know I don't deserve this, she thought.

The final days were counting down and they took Johanna to Cedrik's villa while he and Karsavina continued their discussion about what would become of her. As Johanna wheeled herself around the villa, she could hardly believe the world she was about to leave behind. She looked first at the fantastic entrance -- the black iron gate with gold sculptures like stately sentinals along the walkway, surrounded by gardens of roses and roses and roses, varieties from all over the world.

There were gardens of seasonal flowers, blazing with color, so many that it took a staff of twenty to care for the grounds, and the vegetable and fruit gardens as well.

The villa was the purest white with delicate pink trimmings, and so many carpets inside, all so intricately designed. The entrance was pure marble, and a large black and gold curved staircase led to guest rooms, all decorated by different designers, each with its own theme: one American, one French, one Italian. There were twenty bedrooms and ten full bathrooms with marble, white and gold showers, step-in tubs surrounded by plants and small gardens. Every detail suddenly became so important, so vivid. The bathroom fixtures were made of real gold, and the faucets were swans and the knobs the tails of the swans, against the backdrop of elaborate wall paper, reflected again and again in a series of mirrors.

In the dining room, the lower part of the walls were lined with Italian marble panels, while at the top a cornice with gilded cabinets and small trophies ran along the full length of the room, just below the ceiling. In the corners of the room were large golden trophies, surrounded with Cupids. The central ceiling was painted by Claude Vignon. In fact, each room had a magnificent painting on its ceiling, the living room, even the library entrance. Johanna was awestruck by the beauty that had surrounded her. She had lived with these many months, but had never noted it in detail, not until it was time to leave it all behind. It was a magnificence that, as she wheeled herself around the villa, she wanted never to forget.

Perhaps the most wonderous of all of the rooms at the villa was the ballroom. The count had collected many treasures for many years, historical pieces that had been used to help restore the villa to its original design with its period furnishings from 1770 -- the time of Marie Antoinette and Dauphin. The ballroom was all mirrors and the ceiling was also painted with beautiful shades of blue, red, yellow -- strong colors telling stories of a wedding, children, love and prosperity. Sixteen huge chandeliers hung from that gorgeous ceiling, chandeliers of silver and bronze, adorned with Bohemian crystal, twenty candelabra with human figures, almost lifesize figures holding up sprays of crystal. The windows stood tall from floor to ceiling. They were draped with curtains of white damask, embroidered with Cedrik's monogram in gold, and on the sides of the room, several enormous carpets, matching the colors of the ceiling.

Johanna's heart and mind were too numb from the crushing blow of polio to feel the tears that wanted to come as she thought about the ballroom, where she had danced with Madame and her friends. The room was like a fairytale. The ceiling paintings seemed more beautiful than Michelangelo's. The French doors opened to a huge balcony overlooking the gardens and the swimming pool.

In her bedroom, Johanna looked for the last time upon the blue satin, embroidered drapes. The matching bedspread and chaise longue. Looking up to the ceiling she saw the four monochrome medallions depicting charity, plenty, fidelity and prudence that she had seen each night before she slipped into sleep. The overdoors in her room portrayed the youth and virtue and the glory of the children of France. Next to the huge marble and bronze fireplace in the room, stood the large bronze candelabra with cupids warming their hands before a fire.

Madame was hurt deeply by Johanna's withdrawal into herself. She offered to adopt Johanna legally so that she could care for her. She tried everything to make her go back to her home with her, but Johanna argued that her home was a place of life and gaiety, and no one needed a cripple around to sour the happiness.

Through the tears of hurt and frustration, Madame heard Johanna explain: "I must be alone, completely alone, without feelings of being a burden, without feeling guilt, without feeling other people's pity at the sight of me.

"I will return," she told Madame earnestly. "But you must allow me time to grieve over the loss of my limbs, so it would be best if no one bothered me from this life. It will only confuse me. And I have a dream, a dream to dance here once again in our ballroom."

Madame was heartbroken when Johanna finally left for the Swiss clinic. Especially because she had cut herself off completely from the life in Paris and the villa in the country. Johanna knew she could not take the pressure of someone else's ideas, someone else's schedules and influence. She had to face this battle on her own, a battle that if she won, would find her back on her feet again -- dancing — despite what the doctors had said.

Chapter 25

Johanna began building the wall the moment she passed through the gates of the clinic. The isolation was needed, she knew, not to keep from feeling sorry for herself, but to keep others from feeling sorry for her. The wall was also needed to keep out the voiceless woe that pervaded the clinic. Johanna recognized it almost immediately -- the painful resignation of the patients, and the detached methodical treatment by the staff. One more crippled woman, whose dreams were more damaged than her body, meant very little to the staff who had spent so much time preparing patients for life without hope.

The day Johanna arrived she was introduced to doctors and nurses and shown to her room, so small and sterile. It was comfortable enough, but lifeless. The other patients, too, she could sense, surrounded themselves in fear and despondency. In the pit of her stomach she abhorred their despair, and knew that at all costs, they must be avoided.

The contrast of the clinic, high in the northern Alps, with Johanna's life in Paris -- so full of wonder, beauty, gaiety and life -- was too much to think about. Johanna closed herself to everything. She refused to see Madame Karsavina and her husband, even though they came regularly. She refused their gifts and slowly they stopped coming to see her. She turned away other friends from Paris as well. It was only Frau Hofman and Francheska that she wanted to see, but even they interfered with her ability to concentrate on getting well. After a few months she even stopped seeing them.

She was not going to let anyone's pity destroy her plan and her determination. In her brain, like an endless recording, played the message: "I will dance again, I will, I will." Johanna knew somehow that what she needed first was the right attitude. That she had to force her body to move. Most of all, it was essential to keep away the negative influences, the self-pity and the well-meaning friends filled with tears and condolences, whose love had the power to make her totally helpless.

In the world that Johanna built for herself, sealed off from the seeming human blight surrounding her and from the fantastic memory of Paris, there was only one thought -- to dance. Despite the paralytic condition of her body, Johanna knew her spirit was strong and alive. She filled her mind with powerful, positive thoughts. She repeated again and again the belief that she would walk again, and dance again. Every day, in the privacy of her room, she tried to walk. She pushed herself up from the wheelchair or from her bed with the strength of her right arm and mentally forced her legs to a standing position. Then she would fall. The clinic's staff wondered why she was always on the floor, but Johanna would admit nothing.

She lived for her dream: the ballroom in Paris, the Sugar Plum Fairy, starring at last in the role she had never danced. Her mastery of the role would be apparent to everyone in the audience -- her glisades, her arabesques, the pas de deux -- the applause would be deafening.

Johanna's concentration moved between the dream and her determination to walk again, interrupted only by the daily routines of the clinic. Nutrition was the heart of the treatment: whole grains, fresh fruits and vegetables, clean mountain water, all designed to help Johanna's depleted body regain the strengh it had lost during the past years of physical abuse. Mineral baths and regular massages kept her muscles from deteriorating beyond the point of recovery.

To the staff, Johanna was impossible. The nurses were a negative lot, haunting the halls and therapy rooms with their moods of impending doom. While Johanna's mind was clutching to the vision of walking again, the nurses were telling her it was impossible. It would take a miracle, they said.

Okay, fine, then a miracle I shall create, Johanna thought defiantly.

But the nurses were insistent. Johanna had constant bruises, cut lips, and bumps on the head from falling, and the nurses would chastise her for being careless. She fought them at every turn. Johanna wanted to use her paralyzed left arm to eat, but the nurses insisted on feeding her. They did not want to clean up the mess she made, they did not want to take the time.

"To eat by youself will take two hours," they complained. "We have many patients to care for here. You are not the only one."

Johanna could see that the nurses had convinced the other patients to resign themselves to their conditions. It would not happen to her. She would not become subservient to their conviction of defeat. Johanna did not even try to make them realize the extent of her will, or what she was really trying to do -- to wake up her useless muscles with messages from her brain. Somewhere she got the idea that if she kept thinking "Arm, wake up!" the message would reach her withered muscles and eventually her body would work again. She was obsessed with the theory. She knew her polio was a mild case, affecting only one side, but to function again on her own she would have to try and try again to make her whole body work. So she imagined herself in a role in Giselle, and in her mind, used her muscles to dance.

In time, the nurses became angry and impatient with Johanna's stubborness. They pushed her back into the wheelchair when she tried to stand. She fought their every touch. One day, her attending nurse became so infuriated that she slapped Johanna across the face, shouting, "Stop this! You are a cripple for life. You will never walk again!"

The paralysis had affected Johanna's speech, so she did not even try to answer. She just spoke with her eyes. And what those eyes said was so fiercely defiant that the nurses began calling her "Bitch", "the Defiant One", "the Duchess". It was the latter that finally stuck.

"Have you checked in on the Duchess?" the nurses would ask each other.

"That bitch is probably sprawled out on the floor again."

"Time to tell the Duchess to face facts."

The nurses were always giving Johana the "facts" and she was forever staring at them with hatred and noble, Polish defiance.

Johanna made little progress at first, despite her determination. The limbs would just not respond. But she held her dream tight, out of fear that if even the slightest ray of doubt were allowed to enter, the dream would fall to her feet in pieces, like a shattered mirror.

To fill the endless stream of time, she began painting. At first the nurses resisted, arguing that even with one hand, Johanna would probably accomplish nothing but make a mess. But they eventually gave in to her requests and supplied her with paper and watercolor paints.

Johanna began by sketching ballerinas. Her strong and sensitive lines helped her produce evocative pictures. She became fairly adept at the watercolors too, letting all her pent up passion flow out of her fingers, through the brush and onto the paper. The painting was a release, another attempt to deflect the fear and frustration from having only half a living body.

It was after many months in the clinic that a Dr. Knauer began visiting her. She noticed him at first, consulting with the nurses in the hallway, exchanging whispers as he glanced at her through the half opened door to her room. The nurses tightened their lips and passed judgement on her, while the doctor nodded and looked and nodded again.

"Good afternoon, Miss Bayers," he said to her moments later, pulling up a chair next to hers. "I am Dr. Knauer. I want to help you get well."

He never smiled, and to Johanna he seemed nearly as sterile and hopeless as the nurses. In fact, his greeting was to be the nicest thing he was to say to her, for months to come.

Dr. Knauer began to spend every day with Johanna. At first he just watched her with the nurses -- the feedings, the fights, the smeared food and broken dishes, the fallen Miss Bayers with bruised elbows as they entered her room in the morning. He directed the therapy sessions and worked her worthless muscles in new ways, stretching and challenging the tissues, massaging them harder and more deeply. Johanna at times thought she detected a smile on the doctor's face, but if she brought her eyes to his own, she became certain again that it was only an illusion. The doctor was just the same as the others, she concluded.

Before long, even he was telling her that she would never walk again. Every hour, it seemed, he was on her, scooting his chair as close as he could get, bringing his nose right up to her nose. "You will never walk again!" he shouted. "Do you understand me? Never! You may learn to speak some day, but you will never walk again!"

With his finger swaying in front of her, he kept repeating that one sentence. "You will never walk again."

You would think he might have something nice to say like "Good morning. It's a lovely day," Johanna thought to herself. But no, he said only one thing, over and over again, with his tone more obnoxious than she imagined any voice could be, nose to nose and finger swaying. He just kept barking the same message.

Anger bubbled within her till Johanna thought she would explode. She bit his finger. She spit in his face. If he came too close, she kicked him in the groin so hard that he doubled-up in pain. It seemed the only reason he had come was to drive her crazy. And she fought back with all of her might. One day the nurse came in and tried to calm Johanna, but the doctor told her to leave the room. It was just the two of them, doctor and patient, locked in some kind of battle that Johanna could not understand. There would be long silent moments when the doctor would say nothing, and Johanna would only stare. Then he would burst out with his sentence: "You will never walk again! And go ahead, bite my finger!"

When he was gone, Johanna found herself hating him so intensely that the only escape was to try to make herself stand up, to dream about ballet and try somehow to make her muscles move into the proper positions. When no one was near she would wheel herself to the bannister at the head of the long staircase. The bannister looked like a ballet bar and Johanna approached it humming the music from Tchaikovsky's Nutcracker Suite, the part for the Sugar Plum Fairy -- working herself into a trance. As she hummed madly she tried to get up and practice her plies and do her bar work. Johanna's vision of the ballet was so clear, and her humming so intent that she did not even know if her muscles were responding, or if it was only the image of the little girl dancing that she was experiencing.

Dr. Knauer came daily. It was always the same pattern, the same words, the sentence, like a judgement handed down in court: "You will never walk again!"

No "Hello," no "Good-bye," -- just those same words: "You will never walk again!"

With each visit, her anger boiled within her, and anger that screamed: "I'll show you, you bastard! I'll show you that I will not only walk again, but dance!"

The cycle repeated itself as the days passed into months: the confrontations, the silent stares, Johanna glued to the bannister late at night, gripping it desperately with her good arm as she hummed the Nutcracker Suite. During the day she continued to try to use her left hand to eat and to try to stand up.

One day, one of the nurses became so infuriated with Johanna's defiance that she tied her to the wheelchair to keep her from trying to lift herself. When he learned what had happened, Dr. Knauer became infuriated. Untying the knots himself, he reprimanded the nurse harshly, in front of several members of the medical staff.

"Never do this again," he scolded. "This woman was a concentration camp victim. She must never be made to feel trapped or imprisoned. Do you understand? It could destroy her.

I need her will, not her surrender!"

"But Doctor," the nurse objected, "she is a thorn in the side. She is more work than twenty patients."

"It's your job to care for her," he snapped. "Just do as I tell you."

The nurse bit her lip and turned her glance to Johanna, her eyes filled with such loathing that it sent a chill up Johanna's spine.

"Okay, Duchess," the nurse said softly, "have it your way."

But the nurse soon had her opportunity for revenge. Dr. Knauer stopped coming. At first, Johanna was relieved. The doctor had finally stopped harrassing her. But when he didn't come the second day, she was confused. She went to the bannister as usual, but just stared, looking to the lobby below to see if Dr. Knauer was making his rounds. On the morning of the third day, the nurse appeared.

"Hello Duchess," she said. "How is Your Highness this morning?"

Johanna lay in her bed, waiting.

"We have a little something special for you this morning," the nurse said. Then she walked over to the bed and pulled a hypodermic needle from behind her back. Johanna fought her like an animal. She spit, she screamed. The nurse grabbed her wrist and overpowered her and began to tie her to the bed.

"If you won't cooperate, we'll just have to take more drastic measures," she said in Johanna's face.

Johanna spit at her again, and began calling her names --her speech getting clearer with each curse. Finally, the nurse injected her and Johanna felt her strength dissolve.

The nurse left her like that all day. She tried to spoon feed her meals, but Johanna still had enough fight left to turn her head. The next morning, she injected her again, and each and every morning after that.

Drugged and delirious, Johanna called out for Dr. Knauer. She mumbled his name to the nurse, who responded, "You won't have him to save you anymore. He's gone to America and he's not coming back."

Johanna was crushed. For the first time since she had entered the clinic, she felt like giving up. She stopped resisting the shots. She lost her appetite and stopped eating. For days she lay facing the wall of her tiny room, wimpering and crying. She did not know how many days passed or how many began again with the nurse administering the injection and the world washing by in slow, thick waves. She didn't really care.

Then as suddenly as he disappeared, Dr. Knauer returned. Johanna felt his presence in the room, but through the sedative, she could not be sure if it was really him. He checked her eyes closely. Johanna could feel the thumbs holding up her eyelids, but still could not make out the face. Then he left the room. Later that day, Johanna's head began to clear. She was certain it had been Dr. Knauer. But where was he now? What was happening?

The door opened, and the doctor walked into the room.

"How are you feeling?" he asked, sitting on the edge of her bed. "I am very sorry about what has happened. That woman has been dismissed. Are you feeling any better?"

Dr. Knauer did not wait for a response. Johanna could sense the anger in his voice. "She disobeyed everything I had instructed her to do. She tied you up, she doped you, she lied about when I would return. I explained to her very clearly that I would return once each month to tell you that you will never walk again."

As Johanna heard the words her own anger welled up within her -- anger that Dr. Knauer had left her alone, anger that he so freely spoke about his harrassing threats of never walking again. She was so outraged that she lifted her arm to strike him -- her left arm.

Dr. Knauer looked at her with amazement.

"Look, you moved your arm."

"I did?" Johanna whispered.

"Yes, you did. You are angry enough to move mountains."

Johanna smiled weakly as the tears filled her eyes.

Over the next few months the therapists began trying to teach Johanna to walk with a leg brace. The progress was very slow. She had been fitted with the proper brace and they worked her leg to try to strengthen it, but she had yet to even stand up, let alone attempt a first step. When she was alone in her room, Johanna would wheel herself out to the bannister. Again she would imagine herself on the stage at the LaScala, dancing the Sugar Plum Fairy, She would visualize every detail, every step.

One day she found herself at the bannister, her emotions jumping from "Yes, I can do it. I can dance," to "No, they are right. I will never walk again." Sitting there in her wheelchair staring at the bannister, that beautiful ballet bar, she reached out and took hold of it with her left arm. The arm worked. Then she grabbed it with her right hand. Behind her she could hear Dr. Knauer whispering. "Leave her alone."

"But she will fall," one of the nurses said. "She is very close to the stairs.

"Let her," Dr. Knauer insisted. "Let her fall." "But she could be killed. The stairway is so steep." Johanna could hear the whispers, but she was also already lost in the Nutcracker Suite. Tchaikovsky's dynamic chords and melodies consumed her, as she pulled her body out of the wheelchair. Johanna's mind was on the stage, whirling amidst the most beautiful scenery in the world -- the Kingdom of Sweets, the brightly colored candies: Chocolate and Coffee Sweets, Candy Canes, Marzipan, Polichinelles. All the dancing creatures of the ballet's candy kingdom. She saw too the Prince seated on his enormous candy throne. Suddenly the ballet was interrupted by more whispers and the sound of her wheelchair crashing down the stairs. I am standing, she realized. I am up and my chair just fell down the stairs. I must be standing!

"Look, look everyone. She is standing on her own."

"Unbelievable," shouted one of the nurses.

Johanna went back to the melody. She hummed it with all her might and then dared to take a step. She took that step and took another and formed a first position, humming louder and louder. Then she felt her legs make the slightest move down into first position.

"Look, look, Dr. Knauer. I told you I would dance," she said, tears rolling down her cheeks. "I can stand and move my legs. I did it! I did it!"

"It's about time," the doctor said. "I was getting very tired of making you so mad at me. Now my shins can heal again."

As Johanna turned to face him, the tears kept coming. For the first time she realized he had been challenging her for so many months, hoping she would defy him and fight to prove him wrong. The strategy had worked, she could hardly believe it herself. But before she could look him in the face, she collapsed to the floor.

Dr. Knauer rushed to her side.

"Don't be afraid," he said, rubbing her head. "The first step has happened. Now it is just a matter of time and exercise, and you will walk again."

"Dance, Dr. Knauer. Dance."

"Yes, I hear you. I hear and I believe it too."

Chapter 26

Eighteen months after she took her first step, Johanna Bayers was released from the clinic.

She had recovered full use of her left arm, and was able to walk with little difficulty on her left leg, even though it was now a little shorter than the right. To correct that, she was given a brace to wear while she slept that stretched the muscles and joints.

Before she even left the clinic the American government reminded her that her deranged husband was in the United States under treatment. She was told to get in touch with his superiors in the U.S. Army, for it was required that the man's family join him in the U.S. Johanna was thrust back into the reality of her marriage. It was a condition she had been able to put out of her mind for the years. Now the thought of her husband made her tremble. The Army had diagnosed him as having serious paranoia and sent him to a mental hospital in Texas. To maintain her relationship would mean to renew the fears, the beatings and the mental anguish, she knew.

What Johanna wanted most, now that she had conquered her own physical illness, was to be rejoined with Francheska. But to bring her daughter back into the home of that madman was a horrifying thought.

Johanna was afraid for her child and for herself, but a memory of something her father once said made her resolve to do what the Army requested. Once you marry, you stay married, her father had said. No matter what difficulties you face, your duty is to keep the marriage going, to be loyal to your commitment. Johanna was confused by the realization she was remembering her father. She still could not put the pieces of her past back together to determine her true identity, her name and her history, but the memory of this man -- it was her father, she was certain of that -- gave her the strength to do what her duty demanded.

It was Cedrik who took Johanna to the American authorities, who helped her arrange passage to New York and all the way across the country. He had paid all of her medical bills in Switzerland, and it was he who took her to the ship that would bring her to America. Johanna had not spoken with Madame Karsavina for more than a year. It had been a painful break, painful for both of them. Karsavina still regarded Johanna as a daughter, but Johanna had needed the isolation to rebuild her strength. She only hoped that Madame would understand and someday forgive her.

The Count was with Johanna at the port where she waited for the boat to America. He came to say good-bye with a last hope that he might persuade her to stay with him in Europe.

"Your life, your home is with us, Cherie," he said.

"No," Johanna countered. "I realize now I must go." Johanna told him about the gypsy woman in the Ukraine, the one who had predicted that she would lose everything, that her parents would be killed and that she would suffer unbearably.

"She said that one day I would cross big waters and that happiness would be mine," Johanna explained. "Don't you see? These are the waters I must cross, this ship on that ocean, going to America. In America my life will be different. It will be better."

The aging Count held back his disappointment. He knew she would never change her mind. He knew that once this unusual woman decided something, there was no way to alter the course she set for herself.

"I understand, Cherie," he said. "But I will come to see you in America and I will love you until my death. And I will tell Madame that you will come to visit her, yes?"

Johanna smiled broadly. "Yes, someday I will come back and I will pay all of you back for everything you have done."

Cedrik moved closer to Johanna and took ahold of her shoulders. "We talked in Paris, Madame and I. We decided that if you send us money to pay back, we will return it. You owe us nothing, Cherie. What we have done for you we did because each of us had a need that you fulfilled. You filled in the missing puzzles in our lives. You brought us great happiness and joy. You are very special, my Cherie.

"You did not dwell on your past, you did not become bitter. You sparkled like this diamond," he said, holding up her hand and placing a beautiful diamond ring on her finger. "You are a woman of many facets, but you also stayed innocent and curious, inspite of your suffering. We learned a great deal from you, so remember, we needed you and you let us share your life."

Johanna fought to hold back the tears, and so did the Count. Then he took her in his arms and kissed.her forehead sweetly.

"Adieu, My Love, until we meet again. Please keep the ring to remember us by, and don't insult us by returning it."

The ship arrived and Johanna went to wait in line to be processed. With the Count gone, she began to wonder where her Francheska was. She looked in all directions but didn't see her anywhere. It occured to her that Francheska must already be on board the ship, but still she had not heard a word from Frau Hofman. At the processing station she asked about her daughter, but the people in charge said they knew nothing about her.

She must be on board, she told herself, and as Johanna walked up the ramp to the boat, she convinced herself that she would soon see her daughter again. Johanna quickly approached one of the ship's officers.

"I am supposed to meet my little girl here, my child," she said.

The officer took her to the ship captain's office, and he got on the telephone to begin the search for the missing child. But after several hours and a thorough search of the ship and the processing papers for all passengers, he told her the grim news.

"Your child is not on board."

Johanna could feel her heart racing out of control "Well, I can't leave without her. I won't leave without her."

"Please stay calm," the captain said. "I have one more phone call to make."

But as he was telephoning, Johanna became hysterical. She ran out of his office calling Francheska's name. She ran along the deck screaming at the top of her lungs, and then she noticed that the ship was moving, that it had already left port without Francheska. Johanna was still crying out her daughter's name when she lept from the ship into the water below. She began swimming with all of her strength, but to her surprise, the land was very far away. In seconds, sailors from the ship were in the water to rescue her and life preservers and ropes were lowered to bring all of them back on board.

Before she knew what had happened, Johanna was back on the ship, wrapped in a blanket and being taken to the captain's office.

The look on the captain's face was one of amazement as members of the crew brought in this strange woman, still dripping, with wild desparation in her eyes. The captain stood up and began pacing behind his desk. Then he stopped and turned to her.

"Please remain calm, Madame. And don't ever jump from this ship again! It might not be so easy to save you." The captain was clearly angered that he had nearly lost one of his passengers before the ship ever really left the harbor.

"I have called the authorities and there were no papers processed for your child. There was no way she could accompany you. In fact, your husband, Sgt. Seabolt, left specific orders not to bring the child to America."

Johanna was crushed and broke down in tears. "I must go back. I must. Please let me off this ship."

She begged and argued, but there was nothing they could do. The pain of leaving without Francheska was unbearable. At the captain's suggestion, Johanna wired Frau Hofman to explain what happened, and received a response from her within a matter of days. Frau Hofman said she understood the situation and urged Johanna to be calm, to get to America, and then work to bring Francheska there with her.

Upon receiving Frau Hofman's wire, Johanna radio-phoned her, lamenting: "Francheska will think I don't love her. She will be hurt and afraid. We are flesh and blood, I can't lose her. I'd rather die. I'll jump ship and get back to you."

"You listen to me," Frau Hofman said. "If you are dead then your little girl has no one. You get to America and everything will be fine.

You need America. Too much has happened to you. You know, your child does not understand what is going on. She is so little. She is very happy here and I will keep you alive in her mind always, until you two can be together again."

Frau Hofman's words began to make Johanna feel better.

"Be brave, my child," the woman told her. "Be strong and everything will be yours. You are going into a new phase of your life, a new country. You and Francheska will be together soon. Trust me."

The conversation finally calmed Johanna. Her heart was breaking for her little girl. She was lonely and without a friend on the ship, but pulled together her strength and told herself that she was going to prevail over these hardships, just as she had done with the polio.

The trip was a long one and afforded her much time to think. America -- the sound of it made her heart pound, A land where people are free, where there are no wars. As she stood on the upper deck watching the flying fish sparkle in and out of the ocean she thought of the American soldier she had helped in Germany. "Someday I will bring you to America," he had promised. "You will love it."

At night her heart pounded so loud she could not sleep. I am on the big waters and things will be better, she thought. I am crossing the big waters, Gypsy. I am coming to America, fellow Americans.

But for every moment of hope there was a moment of doubt as well. Totally alone, Johanna faced the realization that she really had no idea what was to become of her. She didn't have a relative in the world except Francheska, who was still in Germany. She knew no one in America. She had left her few friends behind and now there was no one who cared, no one to take care of her. It did not matter how she felt or if she cried or even if she disappeared from the ship. No one would miss her or look for her, she thought. The guilt from her years in the camps began to well up and she decided that her terrible loneliness was her own fault. Why did she have to be the one to survive? Why did she have to witness the helpless looks on their faces, all those who suffered the beatings and torture and killings? She must have done something to deserve it. Certainly she had been a bad girl when she was young to have her parents taken away and shot. Certainly it had been her fault that her husband was always so mean to her.

The prospect of returning to that man and to his beatings frightened her horribly. But it was her duty to stay married, she knew that. Even though her husband treated her no better than the Nazis. That's the way life was. That's the way men are, and once married, a woman has to take it and keep loyal and keep quiet about it.

Yet, Johanna had met a gentler, better people. She thought of Cedrik, who was so good and so gentle with her. His whole life depended on her happiness. He had been so proud of her and had once told her: "Men love and admire that which is self-respecting, and you are that."

The Count never got anything back from me except my company, and a few hugs and kisses, as if I were his daughter, Johanna thought. Why am I going back to this man who is so cruel?

But she knew the answer: Because I am an American and the Army dictates my moves, and because once married, it is forever.

As the days passed, Johanna attempted practicing ballet. Her slightly shorter left leg made the ballet practice difficult, and when she moved around the ship her body seemed crippled and weak as she hobbled around on one good leg.

Johanna also went back to painting, as she had done in the clinic. She used to say to herself at the clinic that if she could not dance with her legs, she would dance on canvas, painting the great scenes of ballet -- especially the Sugar Plum Fairy pas de deux.

The captain kept a close eye on the woman who had jumped from his ship, checking in on her from time to time. When he saw that she was a painter, he offered her $50 for one of her pieces, and spread the word among his crew and some of the passengers that Johanna was a fine artist. Suddenly it seemed, she was in great demand. People wanted sketches, water colors or oils of themselves and their children. Johanna became very busy and time passed quickly.

One day the captain announced that the boat would arrive in New York the next morning. There would be a farewell dinner that night and afterwards, passengers were welcomed to go up on the deck and watch the lights in the distance.

Johanna was so excited. They were approaching a new world. She could barely sleep that night, staying up late into the morning to pack her belongings. She could not wait to get to a telephone and call

Francheska. She did not care how much it cost. Besides, she had made a good amount of money selling her paintings on the journey.

Earlier, when she had stood out on the deck with all of the other passengers she felt the loneliness again, imagining that everyone there on the ship had someone with them who loved them, who was making the journey with them. Johanna did not even have her little girl.

When morning came all of the passengers were back on the deck again staring out toward New York harbor and the Statue of Liberty. The glory of the sight was overwhelming. At first, the Statue looked so small, but slowly as the big ship approached New York, the Statue grew larger and larger until the boat was right next to it and the Lady became so tall Johanna had to look straight up into the sky to see it at all. It was a beautiful sight. It promised opportunities of whatever anyone could want, she thought. It promised freedom from war, freedom from struggling for your sanity, freedom to choose and to prosper.

Johanna felt a commitment growing inside of her to make the Lady proud, to be a fine American. For this opportunity she was devoting her life. To be a fine American citizen and not a burden to society or the government. She felt so proud, and chills went up and down her spine -- just being there, in that great country. The emotions were overpowering. Like many of the passengers around her, Johanna found herself weeping at the sight of that Lady holding her arm so high, her face full of expectation, standing so tall to greet them all.

As the boat approached the dock, Johanna heard a military band playing the American national anthem and she looked up to the sky, the simple white clouds in the blue, and suddenly she realized that she was free, free forever. For the first time she felt she was free to make her own decisions, her own choices. She was free to speak and free to learn. She realized she had spent so much of her life praying to God, angry at Him for not helping the suffering people in the camps or in the ghetto. She had been so angry with God over other people's tragedies that she never realized till she was standing there on that ship that God had kept her alive through so many close calls, when death was ready to take her.

"Thank you, God, for saving me," she whispered. "And thank you for America, for here I shall be free enough to think for myself and to make this country proud of me."

As she prayed, all of her past flashed before her, all of the pain and suffering, the smell of the dead, the moaning, the crying, the arms reaching to let her know they were still alive. All of it passed before her as on a movie screen.

The boat finally stopped and the passengers began filing down the ramp. It was then that Johanna was struck again by her loneliness. Her emotions were pouring over her -- pride, then joy, then fear, then loneliness -- like the waves she had been riding on for so many weeks. When she looked around it seemed like everyone else had someone waiting for them -- an uncle, an aunt, a father and mother, sisters or cousins. Everyone was hugging someone and Johanna stood there alone. No one glad to see her, no one to hug or welcome her.

She walked down the ramp and into a new world. But there was no one to show her the way. She did not know what to do.

She walked to the right, then to the left, then back to the ship, which by now stood silent and empty. She scurried around in total confusion realizing that she had never had to think for herself. There was always someone else -- her parents, the Nazis, her husband, Madame. The freedom to make her own choices suddenly frightened her terribly.

Johanna took the letter from her bag that her husband had written to her. The instructions were to take a train for Chicago, and then change trains there for one to El Paso, Texas, where she would be further instructed what to do.

New York was overwhelming. But its appeal was powerful too. The thought occured to Johanna that maybe she should at least spend a few days there before she trained across the country. The first thing she would have to do is find a hotel room. And that she did, getting a modest room on the Lower East Side. Johanna was awestruck by the city. When she ventured out into the streets, she stayed near the hotel, afraid she would get lost in the incredible tumult of New York. As she walked along the streets, she could not understand how she had no need for official identification. Just money. In Europe, every corner you turned, you had to identify yourself, she remembered. Here no one bothered her. She was dazed by it all -- her past and the confusing present bounding back and forth in her senses, her head and her heart.

Once a fire siren went off and she ran for a nearby cellar, grabbing people in the street, urging them to follow.

"The bombing is going to start right now!" she screamed, every fiber of her emotions pulled tight with fear. She finally ran for the cellar herself, exhausted, confused that no one had followed. The people on the street just stared at her.

"Is she nuts?" one woman asked.

"Maybe drunk," said another.

"Hey, you," a man poked his head over the railing. "We don't have any bomb shelters here. Stop running! There are no bombs, so you can come out now."

A policeman, noticing the activity, helped Johanna from the cellar and sat her down on a nearby bus bench.

"Don't be afraid," he said calmly. "That was not a bomb siren you heard, it was a fire siren. Calm down and let me buy you a cup of coffee."

His kindness brought Johanna back to her senses. She realized that she was in America where they don't have wars. Still she had to muster all of her reasoning and all of her courage every time she saw a man in uniform, or heard a sudden siren. She had to reason with her automatic reaction to run, to hide or defend herself.

During her days in New York she came to realize the purpose of all the Nazi torture. It was meant to destroy a person, to leave that person with nothing but chronic anxiety, unable to function or ever become a leader in society. When she looked at a policeman's gun she rememberd the time a Nazi inserted a bullet in his pistol, placed the pistol to her head, and pulled the trigger three times. After he pulled the trigger, she could barely cope with the realization that she was still alive. It was unacceptable, almost more frightening than death. The repeated beatings she had had flashed back in waves and she would lose the strength in her legs and have difficulty walking. Fatigue, anxiety, nighmares, depression, headaches followed normal incidents on the streets of New York. Normal for normal people, yes, but to Johanna, grim reminders of her horrible history.

One day she passed a ditch where repairmen were working and she fainted right there as her mind flashed back to the Nazis raping a young girl and forcing her father and mother to watch. Then they forced her to watch as they beheaded her parents.

Walking the streets alone, full of fear and yet realizing that she was safe here in America, drained her emotions. Johanna found that for her another war began, a war of accepting the normal everyday life in America. A war of memories and nightmares. She found herself babbling emotionally and bouncing between the present and the past.

Slowly gaining strength each day, Johanna decided to visit the studio of George Balanchine. He was Russian and Johanna knew she could speak to him in his own language. She remembered that she had been introduced to him once at a restaurant with Madame. His ballet school was gaining noteriety and Johanna felt her love for ballet pulling her toward dancers. Feeling ashamed of her ruined body, hiding behind full skirts, aware that she was not yet able to dance again, Johanna still wanted to be near ballet, to look at a few classes, to hear the music.

She knew it would be a long road to dance again and she had to muster all of her courage to go and watch accomplished dancers with normal lives, dancers who had studied ballet since they were children and who now were Johanna's own age, dancers who never had any interruptions in their studies, who were emotionally pampered, loved and free from nightmares and memories. Johanna felt sorry for herself but still managed to work up the courage to walk through the door to Balanchine's school, where she knew everyone had such a headstart.

Johanna introduced herself to Balanchine and told him of her years with Karsavina and the De Cuevas Ballet, and she told him of her polio.

"Yes, Madame wrote me a letter and asked me to look out for you," Balanchine said. He sat on a tall stool and asked her to watch the class to the end.

"I don't know if I will ever dance again," she said to him, "but I want to so much."

Balanchine asked her about how she came to America, and told her about his own arrival. He also invited her to come back very soon.

Johanna came back three more times and each time he insisted that she stay through the entire class. He watched her staring at the dancers. At times she could feel the music so intensely that she would get out of her chair and try to make the moves, while Balanchine supported her with an approving grin.

The third time she came, Johanna arrived just as Balanchine was getting ready to conduct a company class. He saw her as she came in and pulled her aside.

"What you need is confidence in your ability. You are beaten down and exhausted from trying and losing. Confidence," he said and then walked into his private dressing room.

Johanna stood by the wall, watching the few dancers who had arrived early to warm up their limbs. Suddenly Balanchine was at her side again. He handed her the instruction stick and said, "You teach. I have to be in my lawyer's office in ten minutes." Then he bowed out of the room.

Johanna was aghast. "I cannot teach," she shouted at him. But Balanchine was already entering the elevator.

"Tough," he called back as the doors began to close.

Johanna turned to the nearly empty classroom She looked back toward the elevator. She was terrified. Fear opened up the emotion floodgates and she was awash in a confusion and doubt. She felt complete shame about the appearance of her body. Without even the slightest confidence in herself, she was helpless.

She knew she had to escape and ran toward the elevator, but when the door opened, a man stepped out and took her by the arm.

"So you are the substitute teacher. Let's go to the piano and work out a few pieces." The man spoke gently, but without doubt. "I ran into Mr. Balanchine downstairs and he told me the girl in the lavender outfit would be teaching. You are wearing lavender, so it must be you."

The man directed her toward the piano, but Yanina kept glancing to each side and over her shoulder, desperately looking for a way out.

"Mr. Balanchine tells me you are here five days in America. From Russia, yes?"

Johanna did not answer the man. She stood frozen.

"What do I call you?" he asked.

Finally she looked into his face. She struggled for a moment and then said, "Just call me Duchess."

"Okay, Duchess, let's get to work."

Johanna knew there was no escape. She had to think fast. The classroom was filling up rapidly. Dancers stretched at the bar and practiced their art in seemingly slow motion. Johanna thought back to the classes she had taught in Nuremburg, and also of her classes with Karsavina. How did Madame begin? Johanna thought to herself. She recalled her saying, "Cherie, always give one low step, one high, jumps, and then adagio, so the muscles have a change."

Oh Lord, here comes Tolehiff, Johanna said to herself. And there's Janet Reed. All these professionals who perform daily, rehearse daily -- what can I say to them? How can I teach them?

But when it was time to start, and the voice at the piano said, "Ready, Duchess."

As the plie music began, Johanna found herself directing, "...and two demi plies, and one grand releves and balance, four counts..."

To her amazement, all forty-nine dancers in the class were following. Johanna was in the spotlight and moved her body to her own directions. She wanted so badly to look professional that she plied harder, jumped softer and helf her chin high and back straight. She kept up the cadence, the direction, and the dancers worked hard, sweating as they followed. Johanna ordered a broad waltz and demonstrated what she meant, walking the combination through. "...glissage, assemble, piroueete, and here finish fifth upstage, fifth upstage corner, balance, balance, step, step, jete, grand jete, enterene, saute tombee, pas de bouree, step saut de basque, step saut de basque, step, step, jete..."

"Madame," one of the students called from the back, "do you want step, saut de basque downstage?"

The question startled Johanna, and made her realize that everyone was actually following her, trying to figure out the combination. She had been concentrating on the steps so intently that she had blocked out the fact that she was giving instruction to forty-nine dancers.

"No, that is not it," she forced herself to say. And with that, the spell was broken. She began to relax and allowed herself to get lost again in the dance. She ran the dancers through routines she remembered from Karsavina, and created new ones for them too. In no time, it seemed, the class was over. Johanna found herself surrounded by the dancers. They were clapping and clapping, shaking her hands and thanking her for the wonderful class.

"The steps -- I have not seen them since Europe," one of them said.

"Marvelous class, Madame," said another.

Being called "Madame" made Johanna's heart soar. She could not believe it -- professional dancers were thanking her for a class.

The pianist walked up to her and bowed. "Madame, it was a delight to be with you in class. It was an experience I shall never forget."

Johanna could not hold back her excitement. "Was it good?" she asked him.

"Not good, Madame. Excellent." Then he took her hand and kissed it.

Johanna's mind raced with exhilaration. She immediately began formulating plans in her head to begin teaching right away. She was totally lost in the daydream of it when she heard Balanchine's voice.

"You see, you can do it. And the more you try, the more your muscles will respond and give back to you."

Johanna took his hand to thank him and as she did, she realized what a dramatic gesture he had made, allowing her to teach his class, to rescue her from her own fear and self pity.

She knew then that she could teach, create choreography, and eventually dance.

"You did not have to see your lawyer, did you?" she asked.

"No," the smiling Balanchine answered.

"You did this deliberately!"

"Yes," he admitted. "I knew that between your will and your love for ballet, you would be good,"

Johanna's gratitude was beyond words. All she could do was smile.

"You will stay with us, won't you?" Balanchine asked.

"No, I must leave tomorrow," she said.

"Then come, let us have a bite together."

The taxi brought them to the Russian Tea Room for a glass of champagne and caviar. The music was Russian with the walls humming the balalikas and violins of Rachmananoff. Johanna could not contain her joy. "Mr. Balanchine, if I had to die, I would like it to be tonight! I am so gloriously happy!"

His answer was quick.

"But you have not lived yet, Madame."

Chapter 27

Johanna had already received papers from the U.S. Army reprimanding her for staying in New York for so long. Her husband had asked for her and the army said if she did not come soon, it would send military police to guide her to El Paso, where her husband was institutionalized. The military reminded her that she was in their charge until her husband was considered healthy again and released.

She boarded the train in New York with great anxiety. The thought of a train -- its oily smells and rhythmic racket -- made her think of the train to Auschwitz. She had to force herself to overcome her fears and step up into the passenger car. Inside, the seats were simple and comfortable. She put her belongings up overhead and sat alone in the farthest seat.

Outside her window she could see the people of New York. They moved with such urgency, and seemed to always know exactly where they were going. Johanna felt as if she were adrift, with no one to tell her what was the right thing to do. She realized that she had no friends in America, and certainly no family. She had never really learned to make friends. Since she was ten years old she had been forced to learn only how to survive. She had lived in the present for so long, concentrating on her immediate needs, that she accepted the circumstances, the people, the places and events that came before her as if there were no other possible reality. That's why she rarely learned people's names. She knew a face and a feeling it gave her, but the name never really seemed that important to her. And when it came time to move on, it never occurred to her that she should stay in contact with the people she had met. She simply moved on to the next set of circumstances.

Now that she was in America, she also wanted more than anything to do what was right, to be as good an American as she could be, to make the world around her perfect. This she knew was absolutely essential. Part of that goal, she also knew, meant she had to become independent. She had to make decisions for herself. She had to become free of all the people who seemed to want to control her life. But she had never learned how to make decisions. So the desire for independence, no matter how strong, frightened her at the same time.

To fit into this new country, she decided to give herself a more American name. Jeanette, she decided. It was similar to her name, but more appropriate, more American sounding, and she wanted so much to be a good American. Changing names was an easy decision for her. She had had so many names in her past -- Duchess, Ninochka, Johanna, and others she could not remember -- that changing her identity was no more difficult than changing her clothes.

The rocking of the train made her stomach tighten. Her thoughts turned away from America to her memories of the endless line of trains that slowly steamed into Auschwitz every day. Trains from all over Europe, trains packed with people of nearly every nationality. And when the doors opened, the people poured out -- little people shrunken by fear, people huddled in families, tall men, angry and proud, old grandmothers struggling to support their broken husbands. As this train churned across the country toward Chicago, she looked at the people around her. These people were just as diverse -- some were sophisticated and satisfied, some were quiet and alone, some looked just like the Europeans on the trains to Auschwitz. Certainly they had just arrived in America, as she had, and were anxious about a new life, still carrying the pains and scars of the war beneath their heavy coats and hats.

From within, she could feel her past welling. Faces began to appear before her, filling her with the terrible guilt of survival. Why did it happen? she asked herself. Will I ever be able to forget? Will I ever be able to be a normal person with good memories? Why can't I remember my name, my family? I only remember ballet.

Dance was a living thing for her, a goal that breathed and grew as she reached out for it. Throughout her life it had been like a membrane that stretched when she stretched but enclosed and protected her like an unborn child.

Jeanette had to change trains in Chicago. The city terrified her. She had heard so much about gangsters there that as she walked through Grand Central Station, she feared every man that walked toward her was a gangster with a gun beneath his coat. She ran wildly into the ladies room to hide, and waited until the last minute to board the train that would take her to Texas.

When she arrived in El Paso, a military person was waiting to take her to her quarters on the base. The escort explained to her that her husband's condition was not improving. Even the shock treatments he had been given had little positive effect. Jeanette sat alone in her room that night, listening to the wind and the sand whipping against the side of the building. In the morning when she went to take her clothes out of the closet, she noticed the floor was filled with beautiful soft white sand.

She had a new escort that morning, a woman named Dolores Green from the Red Cross. Jeanette explained to her that she wanted to process the papers immediately that would enable her to bring Francheska to the United States. She told the woman that if her daughter could not come, she would move back to Europe to be with her. The woman promised she would notify the military and do whatever she could to help.

When they arrived at the hospital, Jeanette was struck by how much it looked like a prison. Her husband, Sgt. Seabolt, had tried to commit suicide, she was informed. He was dangerous to himself and to her too, but she would be allowed to see him. She was brought into a tiny waiting room with iron bars dividing the room in half. Her husband walked through the opposite doorway and as he approached, Jeanette saw the dark detached look in his eyes, just like the eyes of Hitler. He moved slowly and silently toward the bars and fixed his gaze upon her. He was a complete stranger, Jeanette felt. Then he grabbed the bars and tried to shake them to pry them out of the floor.

"You bitch!" he screamed. "You put me here, didn't you? You are responsible for all this."

Jeanette stood up tall, shocked.

"I had nothing to do with it," she countered.

"It's your fault! It's your sensuous face, your innocent looks. They drove me here. You are a sinner! I will kill you for this. I promise, I will get you!"

The military took Seabolt back into his room, but the experience nearly crushed Jeanette. She was stricken with guilt, feeling, despite her husband's insanity, that it was somehow her fault. When she got back to her quarters she looked at herself in the mirror, detesting her face and her body, and wanting to destoy it all. In desperation, she flung her own fist at her face and her body and finally crashed her fist through the mirror.

Over the next several months, Seabolt showed a few signs of improvement. Sometimes he would be quiet, and seemingly normal, and the occasional tirades became less frequent. The military still needed his signature to process the papers that would bring Francheska to America. But Seabolt refused.

"You will never see her again," he shouted at Jeanette one visit. "The child is a bastard and I don't want it anywhere near me. "

"Then I will leave America," she shouted back. "I will not spend my life without her. I will not let her be forsaken. She is mine and mine alone. I love her and she is my responsibility."

To her surprise, Seabolt signed the papers later that week.

Then one afternoon the military police came to Jeanette and told her that her husband had escaped and left a note that he planned to "cut up" his wife. For three days the military police guarded her as the search for Sgt. Seabolt continued. At night they would stay outside of her locked bedroom door. Then in the middle of the third night, Jeanette awoke to see her insane husband leaping through the window onto her bed. She screamed, but the door was locked and the police could not get in. Seabolt brandished a huge knife but Jeanette managed to keep the bed between them. She tried to get to the door to let in the police, but Seabolt was too quick.

"I'll fix you. I'll mess up that face of yours," he shouted. "You put me in the nut house. I'll fix you!"

As he came toward her, Jeanette ran and avoided the swings of his knife. She tried to reason with him. "I had nothing to do with it," she said.

"Oh, yes you did. You're the one."

"I didn't even know you were committed till the army told me."

"Don't lie to me!"

Suddenly, an M.P. stood at the window, pionting a rifle at Seabolt.

"Drop it!" he shouted.

"Like hell!" Seabolt answered. "I'll slash my wrists before I let you take me to that dump.

"Drop the knife," the M.P. ordered.

Then Seabolt made a dash at Jeanette and forced her body between him and the M.P., pressing the blade of the knife against her throat.

"Let her go," the M.P. said. "I don't want to shoot you."

Seabolt edged toward the door, pushing the knife against her throat even harder.

The M.P. appealed for Jeanette's life. "She never did anything to hurt you. Let her go."

The door opened and there was another M.P. and a chaplain.

"Young man, God would not want you to spend your life in hell for this," he said. "Please let her go."

Then he opened the Bible and read "'Thou shalt not kill" over and over again. "You must remember, you are a man of God," he said. He laid his hand gently on Seabolt's shoulder and the madman collapsed to his knees, begging the chaplain for forgiveness.

Seabolt was recommitted. The doctors put him on new medication and almost unbelievably, he began to improve. In a matter of months he was released on a trial basis. The doctors felt it was better to send him home to his family, and after a few weeks, Jeanette gathered her things and boarded the train to join him.

She arrived in a small Texas town whose name she did not even know. The army had given her the tickets and she got off the train when the conductor told her to. She was the only person who got off in that town and there was someone waiting for her when she stepped off of the car. He nodded but did not say a word. The night was hot and dry and as she followed him to his car, she felt as if she was walking on a carpet of black crickets. He drove for miles through what seemed a vast empty land, never saying a word. Finally they arrived at an old wooden house. There stood her husband. Next to him was his mother, a short woman that must have weighed 300 pounds, and her father, a tall thin man. No one said a word.

They went into the house and sat down to eat dinner. No one spoke while they ate either. No one said her name. She wouldn't even have cared if they called her Johanna. In fact, she had not even told her husband that she was calling herself Jeanette.

After dinner, she asked to go to the bathroom, in hopes of taking a bath. But she was escorted outside with a flashlight. As they walked, Jeanette wondered what a bathtub was doing so far from the house. When she came to the outhouse, she understood.

All through the next day, no one spoke to each other. Jeanette could not understand it -- they seemed so strange. Finally in the evening she heard the mother outside talking. Jeanette looked out and saw the woman was alone, talking to herself, loud and clear. When the woman came back into the house, no one spoke.

Jeanette tried to adapt to living with these strange people, but could not feel comfortable. After several weeks she decided to bring up the subject of her daughter. Seabolt listened quietly as she asked if he had heard anything from the army about Francheska. He had. He told her that the army wanted them to go to Fort Ord near Los Angeles. She was to stay behind while he was issued a pass to go to Nuremberg, Germany to bring Francheska home again.

Jeanette was overjoyed but could tell that Seabolt was upset. He was angry that she had told the Red Cross about Francheska and that the Red Cross insisted she rejoin her mother. But there was nothing he could do. His commanding officer had learned of the matter and given him orders to go to Germany to bring back the child. Seabolt knew he had to obey or face being locked up again.

He went to Fort Ord a few days ahead of Jeanette to get his orders and arrange his travel to Europe. When Jeanette arrived in California, she felt the anger and tension pouring out of him. She could see it in his eyes. But the next day he left for Germany and she was left alone to dream about seeing Francheska again.

Chapter 28

In the dream there was a young blonde girl named Yanina. She was holding silks. It was Auschwitz and the silks were among the clothes taken from the thousands of prisoners who arrived by train each day. The trains never seemed to end. One after the other they came -- from Greece, from France, from Italy, from Russia. The constant knocking and banging of the trains was like a heartbeat that ever rumbled beneath the noise and silence of the camp.

Mostly it was the Jews who had silks. They had stuffed their fine clothes and few valuable belongings into little satchels, but as soon as they arrived, their belongings were taken away. The girl Yanina was in charge of going through their satchels and separating the clothes into categories.

In the dream she was holding silks. The Germans wanted the silk scarves and silk garments most of all. They wanted them for their wives and girlfriends. They were beautiful and the Germans wanted them very badly.

Yanina held up the silk scarf and admired it. It was the most beautiful scarf she had ever seen. The silk was the height of elegance. It glided gently over her fingers, between her fingers, so soft against her thin tired arm. Then the German soldier began to shout.

The shout was like a gunshot, and when Yanina looked at her hand, the silk had changed into suet. Human suet, running between her fingers, melting so slowly down her arm -- stinking, running, melted human fat! The girl Yanina screamed. She looked at her hand and screamed. Then the noises of the trains became louder, thundering out her scream, mingled with the shouts of the German soldiers, their barking dogs, their guns pointed and firing in her face.

The dream troubled Jeanette all day. Certainly the horror of it depressed her, but it was the young girl that she kept thinking about. Yanina. Jeanette knew that name from somewhere. She also knew that the dream seemed so real that it must have happened. It was more like a memory and a dream all at the same time. But Yanina -- where did that name come from? Jeanette knew that her own past had been blotted from her memory, but surely if her name had been Yanina, she would recall it now. Now that the name had appeared in her dream.

When she awoke, her heart was pounding so fast she thought she would never catch up to it. It shook the bed, it was thumping so hard. She realized her past was trying with all its might to force its way into her life again. The tought terrified her. If her dreams were so horrible, what must the realities have been?

Fortunately, both Harold and Francheska were already gone. At least Harold wouldn't stand at the end of her bed staring at her as if she were crazy. And Francheska would not be able to smirk at her in the kitchen.

Jeanette didn't know if she had screamed out loud or if it had all occured in the dream. It didn't matter anyway. No one was there to hear it.

The most important thing was to get out of bed. She knew that if she dwelled on the dream too long, she would become completely immobile. She had to move. She had to fly out of that room, that house and get to the school as soon as possible. Rehearsals didn't begin till ten o'clock and it wasn't even eight, but that didn't matter. She could spend the time loosening up. She could just dance for an hour until Kirsten arrived, then they could go over details of Giselle.

Jeanette showered quickly. She was still shaken from the dream. The image of the girl, Yanina, haunted her, thrown into the camp so young, as she herself had been. She showered with her eyes open so she wouldn't have to picture the girl's face, so she wouldn't have to think about the silks and the suet. She even let the shampoo run down her face. The soap burned her eyes, but she didn't close them.

As always, when she got to the studio, her fears subsided. Her body relaxed as she sat on the floor and began her stretches. Then she began dancing. She worked on the choreography for Giselle. There were still a few places where some of the dancers were having problems. She needed to alter a few transitional steps, perhaps drop one arabesque here or a pirouette there to get the timing right. Choreography was like that. It was organic, growing as the production developed, changing slightly to fit the abilities of the dancers. Jeanette wanted to work out all of the snags as soon as possible. There wasn't that much time until the performance.

When Kirsten arrived, the talk turned to money. Kirsten had heard from the San Francisco City College, whose facility they had rented for the ballet.

"They want their second payment," Kirsten said.

Jeanette had given the school a down payment for rental of the stage and of the stage crew that came with it. But she didn't have any more money. She figured she could stall the school for a few more weeks. That ought to give her enough time to raise the money to make the second payment. But the performance was two months away and the school had to be completely paid off before then.

Where was she going to get the money she needed? She had used up all of her own money, and Harold certainly wouldn't offer her anything. Her thoughts turned to Mr. Pearson. It was unbelievable that he had wanted her to have an affair with him in order to get his donation. Perhaps he had been kidding, she thought. Perhaps it had been a joke and she had been so caught up in her own problems that she interpreted as a proposition. But in her heart, she believed he had been serious. No, Mr. Pearson could not be counted on for a donation.

Jeanette didn't know where she was going to get the money, but she made up her mind that she would get it somewhere. She was not about to let Giselle fall through the cracks.

The dancers began to drift in for rehearsal. Jeanette was pleased with the ballet. Things were coming together. Lisa had gained confidence in her acting ability and was dancing beautifully. She was especially evocative as Giselle the Wili. For the next several hours Jeanette put the dancers through their workout. She tightened up their movements and showed them the slight alterations in the choreography she had worked out earlier. It was a good rehearsal and a good day.

The only thing that troubled her was that Francheska did not show. Jeanette tried not to worry during class. She concentrated on the dancers instead. But when class ended, she could not keep her mind off Francheska.

It was Saturday, so she could not have been tied up at school. She was gone when Jeanette awoke. Had she come home last night? She couldn't actually remember. When she left the house early Friday evening, Francheska said she was going out with Debbie, one of her school friends. Jeanette went to bed early that night. Maybe Francheska never even came home. She had been lying about so many things lately, there was no way for Jeanette to believe her.

Sickened, Jeanette decided it was time to go home. The closer she got to her home, the more her feelings of well being and satisfaction began to fade away. It was as if the world of dance she loved so much was an illusion. It was a world of beauty and order, a world in which she felt she had the power to make everything more beautiful. But it was all an illusion. It had to be. Why else would it melt and separate into tear-shaped droplets that fell from sight as soon as she came home?

By the time she walked in the door, Jeanette was so upset she did not even notice if Harold was home. He was gone more and more these days. There was even talk between them of a formal separation. She began calling Francheska's name, but there was no answer. Then the phone rang. Jeanette hurried to pick it up. "Hello?"

"Jeanette Berman?" "Yes. Who is this?"

There was a long silence. Jeanette could hear the woman on the other end of the line. She was making painful noises with her face. Then she broke into tears.

"Please make her stop! Please make your daughter stop seeing my husband. She is ruining our marriage," the woman cried.

Jeanette was speechless. She held the phone up to her mouth and breathed into it, not knowing what to believe. The woman on the other end of the line sobbed. She made sniffling noises and said one more time, "Please make her stop." Then she hung up.

Francheska came home late that afternoon. Jeanette was furious. She confronted her with the accusation. Francheska denied it at first, calling her mother a liar. But in the heat of the argument that ensued, the truth came out. Francheska had dropped out of school, she quit ballet and she said she was in love with Michael Pearson.

Jeanette could not believe her ears. The same man who had made advances at her was now dating her daughter? It was too much to take.

"Are you mad, Francheska?" she screamed. "That man is 48 years old!"

"That means nothing, Mother. I love him. He is very nice to me. He gives me a car to drive, which you never did. He takes me to nice places and wants to marry me."

"Francheska, he is married and has seven children. He will use you and leave you! He is chasing a minor and his wife is calling me about you!"

"You're lying, Mother!" Francheska shouted.

"What would I have to gain by lying to you?" Jeanette shouted back. "You are the one that has a lot to lose. He is 31 years older than you! I want you to stop seeing him!"

"I will not stop seeing him. He is a good man. You are lying to me because you're jealous, jealous because he likes me instead of you."

"You will stop seeing him! I'm calling him right now to tell him to stay away from you."

"You do that and you will regret it, Mother, for the rest of your life!"

Jeanette made the call, but it didn't settle anything. Pearson said he would not stop seeing Francheska. Jeanette threatened to call the police on him, but he said he had done nothing but take her to a few restaurants. He had not even kissed her, he said, and wouldn't until her 18th birthday.

The situation became hopeless for Jeanette. In the days that followed, she got a call from a local restaurant owner. "Your daughter is at my restaurant quite often. She is drunk and unruly. She is only a minor and her behavior is jeopardizing my license. Please keep her away from here."

Jeanette felt she could do nothing to stop her. The more she tried, the more Francheska lied about where she was. She knew Francheska was seeing Pearson on the sly, but did not know how to stop the affair. Any real communication with her daughter came to a complete halt.

Jeanette didn't think she could cope. She barely slept with all the worry. She knew Pearson was buying Francheska gifts and wooing her with false hopes, playing on her age and desire for independence. She became obsessed with her daughter and had to drag herself to the studio for rehearsals. When she was there she could not concentrate on anything. Kirsten was forced to conduct the rehearsals, while Jeanette kept herself locked in the office. She felt like a dancer who had lost her balance on stage. She tried to right herself and keep the performance moving, but with every step felt it was spinning out of control.

After a week of depression, she felt she had hit bottom. The nightmares increased. It was as if she were standing before a door, the door to her past, that bent and bowed with an enormous pressure. Her past was pushing against that door, trying desperately to free itself and force itself into Jeanette's here and now. The gyspy appeared in her dreams, over and over again, shouting, "You will lose your family! You will cross big waters!" Then her flaming red hair would fly up into the wind, red columns of hair becoming chimneys that belched out sickening sweet smoke.

The dreams consumed her. But there was something missing. Didn't the gypsy say something else. Didn't she say she would be happy after crossing the big waters? Jeanette summoned all of her strength and decided she would be happy. She would make herself happy. It is what the gypsy had promised. I am not crazy, she told herself. I am not crazy and I will not act like a crazy person.

She looked for role models. She began watching soap operas on television when she wasn't at school. She picked the strongest characters and tried to emulate their actions. She wanted to be strong and self assured. She wanted to be a calm controlled person and she copied and practiced being like her role models on television.

In a grocery store one day she bought a copy of

"Psychocybernetics". It became her bible. She read it over and over -- on her way to the studio, after rehearsals, alone in her bed. She studied how to get rid of fears, how to love, how to become emotionaly stable, how to change a habit. She carried the book with her everywhere and read and reread the chapters. They grounded her, she felt, and gave her a bit of clarity.

Jeanette knew she had a long road ahead of her, but she decided she must take it upon herself and stop waiting for someone to direct her. She had to take care of herself before she could help anyone else.

It was the same struggle all over again -- the war of being self-reliant and strong, the war of making her own decisions and making them work. She had never really known what a normal life was, so no matter how she struggled, she did not know how to create it. She only knew she had to change the tape inside her head from one that spoke of fear to one that spoke of strength. Only then could she release the struggling soul inside her and become a whole person again.

Chapter 29

When Seabolt boarded the plane for Germany, Jeanette moved to Los Angeles to look for work. She took the first job she could find -- modeling brassieres for a clothing factory. It turned out to be a fortuitous opportunity. From modeling lingerie, she moved on to hats and later junior miss clothing. Pictures of her appeared in California Girl magazine and she began getting calls from modeling agencies.

She had fully recovered the health of her leg and enrolled in ballet classes with a Russian teacher. Sympathetic with her history, and impressed by her ability, he used his connections in Hollywood to get her a part as a dance extra in a movie.

In practically no time, Jeanette Bayers made a name for herself as a hard working and talented dancer. All of the studios were still producing musicals, and she got calls for just about every one. It was a period of growth for Jeanette, a time in her life when dance again became the focus, moving her forward at a dizzying pace in and out of the circles of Hollywood. She worked for MGM, Universal Studios and others, and quickly came in contact with some of the biggest stars in the business -- Gregory Peck, Susan Hayward, Lana Turner, Mitzi Gaynor, Rex Harrison, Laurance Olivier. She was invited to glamorous parties and found herself mingling with the fine, dedicated families of the film industry, and also with the reckless crowds where honor and integrity meant nothing.

Jeanette's years with Madame Karsavina taught her to fit in easily with high society, but at least in Europe, the wealthy artists and patrons of the arts had behaved honorably. In Hollywood, she was shocked to see movie producers swimming naked with naked starlettes. She made the emotional adjustments by rejecting such behavior for herself without being judgemental of others. She pretended it was all on the screen and had nothing to do with her. As the glitz and glamour of Hollywood spun around her, she made sure she stood on the solid ground of knowing how to act like a lady. Her strength and good graces quickly gained her a reputation with important people in the movie industry, and earned her the nickname of "The Duchess."

The pace was demanding. Jeanette modeled and danced long hours, all the while hoping to hear from Seabolt about bringing Francheska to America, but she heard nothing for several months. She called Dolores Green at the Red Cross, who explained that the procedure for bringing her daughter home was very complicated, especially since her husband refused to adopt her. Jeanette was on her own.

The work continued. She was hired by the Max Factor company consulting on how to elegantly pose hands for advertising. But in spite of her successes, she felt guilty that her career was moving forward, rather than her life as a wife and mother. Once the guilt began to seep into her thoughts, it threatened to overwhelm her -- guilt from her husband's paranoia, guilt from surviving the Nazi death camps. The only way to stop it was to work even harder.

With more work came more opportunity. She was offered a screen test with one of Hollywood's powerful movie moguls -- Howard Hughes. She was petrified because she had not done any acting before. She was given a script one hour before the meeting and told to learn her lines.

When her time came, she was escorted into Mr. Hughes' office where there were four men staring at her as she walked in. Jerry Gaiser, the lawyer, spoke first and introduced Jeanette Bayers to each of the men. As she stood there trembling, Mr. Hughes spoke in a low voice, "That's what we need. She is right for the part."

"But I know nothing of acting," Jeanette said.

"That's okay," said one of the men, "Mr. Hughes here likes your looks and feels you are worth investing time and money for training. It will be hard work. You will sign a contract and work for us only."

"Thank you, Mr. Hughes," Jeanette said.

But he did not respond. He just sat and stared at her, never uttering another word.

"Let's see your legs," one of the men said, as Jerry Gaiser walked up to her and unzipped her skirt. Jeanette felt like a piece of meat. Anger grew within her as she was told to turn to the right and to the left, bend over, and shake her hips as the men snickered at her nervousness and discomfort.

The screen test was a success and Jeanette was offered a part in a movie to be directed by Cecil B. De Mille. During her interview, she and Mr. De Mille developed an instant rapport. He was charmed by Jeanette's aristocratic manners and straightforward approach, and he ended the interview by saying, "I must have you meet my wife. She'll just love you. I just wish I could talk this way with my niece, Agnes."

Jeanette's first part was to play a sexy blonde who uses men to go up in the world. It was a sizable role with a good amount of speaking lines. She was to play the dumb sister of the leading lady. But for Jeanette, it was no easy role to play. As soon as she read the script, she found herself in total conflict. The role demanded behavior that was completely against her grain. It called for her to dress in a tight skirt and a plunging blouse, and wiggle her breasts and behind. It called for her to consider all men fools and use her sex appeal to get what she wants from them. After so many years of training to be a ballerina -- an international "diplomat" -- this kind of behaviour was outrageous.

Jeanette thought of the elite, aristocratic world she had been so much a part of with Madame Karsavina, the sophistication, the elegance. She had been taught that social manners were of utmost importance and had pursued the elusive qualities of ideal beauty as a ballerina. As an actress, she was asked to be just the opposite. For the first time she realized that to succeed in this role, she would really have to act. She would really have to pretend to be someone she was not. The thought terrified her.

Adding to Jeanette's emotional pressure was the coming of Christmas. This time of year was especially painful for her. She became extremely lonely and upset as the people around her planned family gatherings and bought gifts for their sisters and brothers, their cousins, their parents and uncles. It all made her realize that she had no family, no roots. Despite her successes in Hollywood, there was no one to look over her, to dote on her and buy her gifts. Her anxieties drove her straight to the MGM cafeteria where she could tranquilize herself with food, stuff herself and lick her wounds. Food had always had this affect on her, ever since Auschwitz.

While she was eating she heard a voice next to her.

"You're going to get fat and ugly if you keep this up," a man said.

"What business is it of yours?" Jeanette responded angrily.

"I'm making it my business," he said.

Jeanette was frightened by the abrasiveness of his answer. He was a man in his 40s, with dark hair and a lean angry face. He looked like he had seen some very hard times in his life. Jeanette said nothing and continued her meal.

"Those fucking dumb waiters here. They know nothing," the man grumbled to himself. "I hate this place. I don't know what I'm doing here with these shitty people. They're all phoneys."

Jeanette was shocked at his language and wanted to move to another seat, but curiosity and need for someone to talk to made her stay. She listened to him complain and then she began to tell him a little about herself. He told her his name was John and he stood up to go.

"Be careful," he said sternly. "Don't end up wearing testicles around your neck. They love your type in this business." Then he left.

Jeanctte was completely thrown by the whole experience. She didn't know what to think of this foul mouthed person and wasn't sure what his cryptic warnings meant either. She sat and sipped her coffee and nibbled on her lemon pie. She looked up and saw a woman sitting at the next table staring at her.

"What is he talking about," Jeanette asked her.

"In this town, everyone wants to sleep with aspiring actresses. And the actresses do it because they think it's going to help their careers."

It's just like in my script, Jeanette thought. It's not a movie, it's true.

"You look like you've gone through the wringer," the woman said to her. Her soft voice was warm and lovely and her eyes were full of feeling.

"I am beat," Jeanette said, "and I'm not sure I like this business. These men treat you like they own you."

"Don't take it too seriously," the woman said. "They say that I am not a good actress, just a sex symbol. But it's not easy to be sexy all the time and make it look natural, it's hard work. I come from a small town and I know that's not really me up on the screen. It's me acting. Fortunately, it sells so I keep at it. You have to look at it as a business."

"What's your name," Jeanette asked her.

"Marilyn Monroe."

"Mine is Jeanette Bayers, but most people call me Duchess."

"That's a good name. I will call you Duchess," Marilyn said.

"Hey, why don't you come and spend the weekend at my house. I am all alone. I have no family and Christmas is here. Everyone thinks that because I am Marilyn Monroe, I am so busy. But most of the big holidays, I'm all alone."

They agreed to spend Christmas together and exchanged telephone numbers.

"And don't worry about the movie moguls," Marilyn said. "You may feel like a piece of property to them, but thank God they like you."

Jeanette and Marilyn became friends. They spent the holidays together. They walked the beach dressed in huge coats, their heads covered with scarves and wearing sun glasses so no one would recognize Marilyn. Jeanette noticed that Marilyn was very quiet by nature, a peaceful quiet.

"When you act you are always talking, always saying someone elses words. It's s nice to be quiet. I love the seclusion and quiet. I'd love to have lots of children and a fine husband. Everyone is involved in themselves here in Hollywood. They are all ego. I don't know if I will ever find a man I can love, that can put up with my stardom."

Jeanette told her about her husband and her past, about how Seabolt was always insanely angry with whatever she did. Marilyn listened and Jeanette felt close to her because she was so up front and honest.

"This is a good business, Duchess. But the hours can kill you. I never have time for dreaming. It's just work, work, work and give and give and give."

Jeanette's screen test came in and the studio was very excited about it. Marilyn, who was the only person Jeanette trusted, asked to see it and gave her full approval. Jerry Gaiser had a contract ready for her but needed both her and her husband's signature to make it legal, and had to await Seabolt's return.

Jeanette's career continued to flourish. In addition to her work with the studio, she modeled mink and linx coats at the Coconut Grove. She modeled clothes for California Girl, and gloves and hats for market week when the clothing buyers would come to town. Invitations came for more parties. She attended Eva Garner's birthday party, and met Micky Rooney, Frank Sinatra, James Mason and Deborah Kerr. Rita Hayward she already knew from her life in Europe. She had met her at the ballets with Agha Kahn and also when she danced in Maria Callas' operas.

Some nights she would see a face staring at her. It was the rude man from the cafeteria. He seemed to follow her every move and watched from cars and from across the street. One day she confronted him and told him to stop following her or she would call the police. He said he would never stop following her because he cared about her. He continued to appear out of nowhere, watching her, seeming to protect her, telling men to stay away from her.

One day Count Cedrik de Guille showed up in Hollywood. He told Jeanette he had been following her life and hoped she didn't mind.

"Of course not," she said. "Are you really here just to see how I am doing?"

"Yes, and to tell you that Madame misses you a great deal. She really needs you."

"Well, I must follow my convictions and run my life myself," Jeanette answered. It was true, she wanted to run her own life. But Jeanette also didn't know how to go back into her past. Since she was ten years old she had been trying to understand it. But it was mostly too painful to deal with. She only wanted to be happy, right now, in the present.

"So are you making your own decisions?" Cedrik asked.

"Not really" she answered. "People do it for me again and I must follow like a puppy dog. The only thing I handle is when I see that something is wrong for me. "

"I love you Duchess," Cedrik said.. "Forgive me, but my whole life is brighter because of your existence. I am fulfilled knowing you are happy."

Jeanette and Cedrik spent a day together and everywhere they went people seemed to recognize him. Jeanette felt like he was a father to her. He was gentle and kind, in contrast with most of the men she had known. But he stayed in Hollywood for only a few days and then he went back to Europe.

Jeanette missed him. She realized he made her feel safe and allowed her to contemplate her life. She thought of it like a canvas where her thoughts, emotions and acts were the paints. She wanted to paint a picture of herself that was true. In her imagination she had a dream of the person she wanted to be. She wanted to build a life. She wanted to contribute to the world around her, not destoy anything. She wanted to paint with the positive colors of her heart and spirit -- determination, patience, endurance, self-discipline, work, love and faith. She wanted to fill each moment of her life with these qualities, and instill every endeavor with them. She knew she was in love with life, with its beauty and promise, and she strove to become an ideal person so that beauty would last forever.

Chapter 30

Jeanette received a letter from her husband that he was on his way home with Francheska. She quickly called Frau Hofman in Germany to learn what had taken place there. Frau Hofman was so happy that Francheska would finally be reuinted with her mother. But she also warned Jeanette to stay away from her husband.

"Get away from him," she said. "He is a bad, sick man." Promise me you will divorce him."

"But I cannot, Frau Hofman," Jeanette said over the telephone. "I am Catholic. Marriage is forever."

"I don't want to interfere child, but you are not safe with him. He is not well."

Frau Hofman explained that during his stay in Germany he had impregnated another naive young girl and refused to take responsibility for his actions.

Jeanette knew something had to be done. But she didn't know what. There was no one to give her advice. She knew that he would have to go back to El Paso, but she did not want to go there with him. The only hope in El Paso was to talk to his doctors and to Dolores at the Red Cross.

One day the call finally came. Seabolt was in Texas with Fracheska.

"Is she safe," Jeanette asked.

"Yes, my mother is taking care of her."

Jeanette thought of that house in the middle of nowhere and Seabolt's strange family.

"Please bring her to Hollywood. I want you to bring Francheska to Hollywood," she pleaded.

It took a lot to convince him, but Seabolt finally agreed. They arrived at midnight three days later. When Francheska stepped off the train, Jeanette could not believe how wonderful it felt to see her -- her plump, cuddly little girl with huge blue eyes.

Francheska ran to her mother shouting, "Momma, Momma, I love you!"

Clinging to her, Jeanette felt that no one could ever separate them again. She would see to that.

Fortunately for the two of them, Seabolt had to stay on the base at Fort Ord. Jeanette kept Francheska at her apartment in Hollywood. In time, everyone got to know her. Clare Trevor bounced her on her knee. Clark Gable called her little Shirley Temple. Francheska was a hit everywhere. Marilyn loved her too and made Jeanette bring her along whenever they got together. Sometimes this made Jeanette quite nervous because of the crowds that Marilyn drew. Although she and Jeanette disguised themselves, somehow people would recognize her and start attacking them for autographs. Jeanette often feared that she and Francheska would be trampled to death by fans.

Jeanette appreciated so much having a friend like Marilyn, in spite of the dangers of her fame. They grew close and spent many a day at her home, hiding from the public, glad not to have to be glamorous and completely made up.

One day while Francheska was in school, the two of them decided to go to the market on Hollywood Boulevard to shop. To keep from being recognized they wore scarves, trench coats and sunglasses and no make up. With their blonde hair, similar builds and nearly identical outfits, they looked like twins. Still, Marilyn was sure no one would recognize them. But to Jeanette's chagrin, while they were loading groceries into the car, a mob of people attacked her, screaming for her autograph, calling her Marilyn and tearing at her clothes. Someone even ripped Jeanette's watch from her wrist, cutting the skin in the process.

"I'm not Marilyn!" Jeanette shouted, but no one seemed to hear, except Marilyn, herself, who was standing on the other side of the car alone, laughing hysterically. The police finally came and escorted the two of them home. Marilyn continued to laugh, but Jeanette was near tears from the ordeal.

"Are you sure you want to be part of this business?" Marilyn asked. "It's not as much fun as it seems. You will never know if people love you or if they just use you for the money and fame."

Jeanette's success continued. She attended the premieres and the academy awards events and still more Hollywood parties. One night after a party she went outside to hail a taxi, but a producer she had met there followed her outside and insisted she let him give her a ride. On the way home, he suddenly pulled to the side of the road. He unzipped his pants and tried to force Jeanette's head into his crotch. She resisted with all her might, trying to get out of the car. Then she heard a crash and the car door on her side flew open. There was Jeanette's admirer, the foul mouthed man from the cafeteria. He pulled her out of the car and then went after the producer, but the man drove off in his car.

"Okay," he said. "I know I'm a nuisance. Don't ask me why I feel the way I feel about you, but I do."

"Thanks for helping me," Jeanette said.

"I know I have no right, but Marilyn told me a lot about you and I feel you need a streetwise friend. Will you come with me to have coffee?"

Jeanette agreed and the two of them ended up at an all night diner where the waitress kept calling her "Honey." Despite the atmosphere and the evening's strange circumstances, Jeanette felt quite comfortable.

"This is a formal introduction. My name is John Fante. Remember this night."

As they sat in the diner, there was a spark, an energy that developed between the two. John ordered breakfast for them and they just stared at each other. He held both of her hands across the table and they stared into each other's eyes. They stayed in the diner for hours until the waitress finally asked them if they planned to spend the entire night there.

It was raining as they stepped into the street and John pulled Jeanette close to him to cover her with his raincoat. As they reached his car he turned and took Jeanette in his arms and kissed her passionately. She responded with equal passion and the kiss seemed to last a lifetime. Then they got into the car and he drove her home.

Jeanette's life became more complex. Seabolt was able to spend more and more time with her and she could see he greatly resented her success in the entertainment business. He knew he had to control himself but whenever he was with her, she felt his inner rage bubbling beneath the surface.

Word came from MGM that they were ready for Jeanette to sign her contract, but she still needed her husband's signature to make it official. She had arranged to have him meet her at the MGM studio and she went to work early to rehearse her scenes. Seabolt arrived in a fury.

"No wife of mine is going to be an actress! They are nothing but whores!" he shouted, waving the contract in his hand. "Nothing will make me sign this. She belongs at home, taking care of me and the child!"

Jeanette nearly died of embarrassment as he dragged her out of the studio as if she were a child.

"You will never set a foot in here again, do you hear me!" Seabolt raged.

She did return to the studio the next day, but everyone avoided her. No one wanted husband trouble, and the contract offer was permanently put on hold. Fortunately for Jeanette, Mr. De Mille still had interest in her career. He sent her an invitation to attend one of his parties. She was extremely nervous before the party, not knowing what to expect. Did he want to tell her that her career was over? Did he plan to make a pass at her like other powerful men in Hollywood often seemed to do to young actresses? She forced herself to go to the party and worked up her defenses before knocking on the door. To her surprise, a lovely woman answered the door.

"You must be Duchess," she said.

"Yes, I am," Jeanette answered hesitantly.

"Oh, I can't wait to hear your story. I understand you spent time in Auschwitz. My husband tells me you survived so much. I am Mrs. De Mille."

Jeanette was so relieved she felt the tension pour out of her like water. Inside the De Mille's home she was introduced to their niece,

Agnes, who was very a successful dancer and choreographer. She had choreographed the musical hit "Oklahoma" and spoke with Jeanette about European and American ballet.

The party was attended by actors and actresses and their families. And that skinny, silent, staring Mr. Hughes was there, too. One of the guests was a reporter from the Los Angeles times. He was extremely patronizing to her.

"So, you want to be famous?" he said to Jeanette.

"Actually, I have no particular plans for myself," she said.

"Well, you sure fell into the big time around here, and fast. Mr. Hughes and Mrs. De Mille are really taken by you. I have orders to build you up and write about your past."

"My past is ugly," Jeanette said.

"Yeah, but it makes for good reading," he said, lighting up a cigarette.

"Are you aware of your opportunities here, especially with De Mille's wife on your side?"

"I'm not sure if I really want to go on with this," Jeanette said. Marilyn, my friend, thinks I'm good, but it's a very demanding job."

"It sure is," he said. "Marilyn is so busy and so tired that she needs uppers to wake up in the morning, and downers to go to sleep."

Jeanette was shocked, but realized that what he said was true. For the first time, she thought of how many pills Marilyn always had with her, how she would take pills to relax, enjoy a few drinks and then forget she even took them. "Did I take my pills, Duchess?" she would ask. Then she would take another just to be sure.

Jeanette became a frequent visitor to the De Mille's and her friendship with them improved -- all except for Agnes. Jeanette sensed from here disdain and resentment. The more she got to know Mr. and Mrs. De Mille, the more Agnes seemed to despise her. One day Jeanette asked Mrs. De Mille about it.

"As you know, Cecil is very fond of you," she explained. "He feels you are very mature and experienced, and finds you so easy to talk to. He and Agnes have never been able to talk. I think she feels you have the relationship with her Uncle that she has never been able to have."

Hollywood continued to court Jeanette, in spite of the incident with her husband at MGM. She continued to get roles as a dance extra, including a spot in the highly successful "Seven Brides for Seven Brothers." She mingled in the right circles and was invited again to all the right social gatherings. She rarely had to buy her own clothes. Furs, dresses and hats were provided by fine shops for publicity.

Jeanette began consulting at a dance studio where many of Hollywoods dancers and actors trained. Many of the actors and actresses had no dance experience at all, but were being cast in musicals. Jeanettee showed them how to move their hands and bodies to look like they had studied dance for years. She also used the space to train her daughter. Francheska responded beautifully and was quickly becoming a skilled ballerina.

In the evenings, she would see John Fante quite often. The two of them knew something was happening between them, but neither of them was ready to bring it out into the open. Their romance was like experiencing a first love, like two people who never felt puppy love and were taking delicate, almost adolescent steps, afraid that if either of them spoke too much, it would all crumble and blow away. When Jeanette was with him life was more intense -- flowers were more fragrant, the ocean seemed louder, and if they were in a crowded restaurant, it seemed no one else was in the room.

Jeanette never made plans to meet with him. He just seemed to appear and disappear. She never asked who he really was or where he lived. He just seemed to watch over her like a guardian angel.

But her guardian angel had no one to watch over him, and his life in Hollywood began to fall apart. One day while Jeanette was having lunch at the MGM cafeteria, he appeared again. This time he was in terrible spirits. She could see on his face that he was terribly upset and felt in her heart that the two of them were reaching some kind of turning point.

John complained that as a writer, he was a failure. He wanted nothing more than to write a novel, but was forced to work for the movie studios writing scripts. He hated movies and scripts, he said. But he was just not able to complete a successful novel.

"If it wasn't for you I don't know what I'd do," he said. "You give me strength. You have such a positive attitude."

Over the next several months, Jeanette could see his anger and resentment growing because he could not sell his novel. Throughout

Hollywood, he had become quite unpopular. When Jeanette mentioned his name, people told her to stay away from him, that he was trouble. Others who knew she was seeing him acted as if they felt sorry for her.

One day, she and John went to a drive-in restaurant for lunch. It was to be their last meeting. They ate together in silence and when Jeanette looked at him she did not see why people thought he was trouble. All she saw was that he was a loving protective person. He still did not know that she was married, and she did not know if he was either.

The one person he did not protect her from was her husband. Seabolt was still on medication, but he was still boiling inside at Jeanette's Hollywood career. That night as she was entering her hotel, he pulled her into an alley and beat her till she fainted. She ended up in the hospital and Seabolt was arrested and handed over to the military.

When she was released the military told her she had to come to El Paso where he husband was to be committed. Guilt swept over Jeanette like a wave and she told her agent she had neglected her duties as a wife and mother for too long. That's why all this had happened. Her agent and Mr. De Mille told her that she should not be wasted on domestic chores, that they would write to her husband and to the military. But Jeanette took Francheska and left Hollywood.

Chapter 31

Once outside the maze of Los Angeles, the train picked up speed. Jeanette and Francheska held each other close as the cars clattered their familiar tick-tock, like the workings of a giant timepiece slowly releasing its tightly wound inner spring. Jeanette felt the train taking her again along a path set out by the hands of men she did not know, whose hammering and hard work put down tracks her life seemed destined to follow. The destination was El Paso.

For the time being, at least, she and Francheska were free of Seabolt. The Army had him in custody and its psychiatrists were determining the insane soldier's fate. His madness was hereditary, they determined. There was little hope of a cure. For Jeanette, that was no consolation. She was still married to him, still bound by laws, customs and guilt.

When she arrived in El Paso, she was met by another U.S. Army MP, one of the many employed by the army over the years to protect her from her husband. Dolores Green, the Red Cross nurse, was there too. Jeanette still wore the purple bruises her husband had left on her face, like some kind of bad make-up. She still had stitches in her lip and in her skull, hidden beneath her hat.

Dolores was livid. The anger from seeing Jeanette, beat up once again at the hands of the army's incureable madman, was more than she could take. She lashed out at Jeanette.

"You stupid girl!" she scolded, her voice trembling with anger. "You are really stupid. Don't you know that you are in a free country and you don't have to take this from anyone! You're not in Auschwitz anymore!"

Jeanette was shocked by Dolores' outrage.

"What is the matter with you?" Dolores asked, tears in her eyes and in her voice. "You have rights. You're not his prisoner, his slave to be beaten and treated like an animal."

The words were harsh, but effective. Jeanette at once knew the importance of what Dolores was saying, and for the first time, she realized that she truly did have the right to control her own life. Suddenly it dawned on her that she had been accepting the circumstances of her life as they were preordained, as if it were fate. Men are cruel brutes and women are their servents to be beaten, seduced and abused. How could she believe otherwise? From the days of her childhood this is the way it had been. In her heart she assumed that this was natural, that it was the way of life, that it was happening everywhere. Now, this nurse's words had changed everything.

It was as if a window were suddenly opened and Jeanette felt the air of freedom for the first time, a breeze that swept across her skin and filled her lungs. She breathed it in and realized that she had been imprisoned in a dungeon of fear, a dark cell filled with the stifling air of acceptance. Even with all her successes in Hollywood, it had never occurred to her that she was free to walk right out of that cell whenever she decided that she could no longer breathe. Her marriage to Seabolt had always been with her, weighing her down with fear and guilt.

It took the compasion of this nurse, crazy at the sight of Jeanette's beaten face, caring enough to tell her that she was in a different world where she had the right to choose her own life.

I have paid highly for my existence and I deserve better, Jeanette thought to herself. The realization was a gift too great to repay. Dolores also made her understand that her husband was an incurably sick man, and that an annulment could be arranged to finally free her legally from his insanity.

"I could be free of him," Jeanette whispered.

Dolores was so moved by Jeanette's plight that she offered to help her file the annulment papers with the proper authorities. She took

Jeanette under her wing completely, inviting her and Francheska to stay in her own house until she could find them an apartment.

The apartment was small and simple, but had a brand new kitchen and a furnished bedroom. Jeanette was elated. Francheska was at her side, and they could finally make a home for themselves, a place to grow together.

Dolores visited them often. "The army is discharging your husband to a private insane asylum," she told Jeanette one day. "The army will pay all of his bills; you are not to be responsible at all," she said.

"His condition is inherited. It is a good thing you and he did not have children of your own. The child most likely would have suffered the same illness."

Francheska was enrolled in a school and Dolores helped Jeanette find a job as a car hop at a drive-in restaurant. The annulment process was tedious and slow, and Jeanette didn't really understand it. She just filled out the information required of her and trusted Dolores to tell her what to do, or drive her to the annulment proceedings when her testimony was required. Jeanette decided that she should return to Paris if and when her marriage was legally undone, but Dolores tried to convince her that she deserved to stay in America, to become an American citizen, to make a life of her own.

Sending Francheska to school sent shock waves through Jeanette. It made her realize that she, herself, had not been in school since she was 10 years old. It made her question her own identity. Who am I? Who are my parents? What is my real name? As she dressed Francheska each day for school, sending her off in with her lunch in hand, she realized she knew nothing of childhood. Adult life had been forced upon her at 10 years of age, like some kind of punishment. She knew nothing really of being a mother. She could barely remember being young herself, and had her own mother taken from her so long ago that the lessons and tenderness of motherhood were a milky haze behind the memories of the terror of Auschwitz.

As Jeanette held her daughter in her arms, vowing silently to protect her from any hurt, she realized how hungry she was for a mother's love, for approval from a father, for someone that cared. She considered contacting Cedrik and accepting his offer of marriage. The annulment would be granted soon she hoped, and she would be free to do as she pleased. But she realized too that she was totally frightened of the responsibility that lay ahead of her.

The fear of not knowing gripped her heart and left her limp. She blamed it all on her lack of schooling.

"I was dragged away from my education at ten years of age, how am I to know what to do?" she cried out loud. The task of filling out applications, paying bills, getting a drivers license -- all of these frightened her terribly. She had never had to do much for herself. Even in Hollywood, her agent and the studio looked after her. She could not subtract or divide and the whole situation made her feel ashamed.

Making it worse was Francheska's questions about school and homework. Jeanette did not even understand her daughter's books. Out of ten words on a page, she knew three. She could not answer her own daughter's questions. Her lack of education wasn't limited to school, she realized; she hardly understood the normal procedures of everyday life. Simple money transactions baffled her. About the only thing she felt comfortable with was buying food. She felt more afraid, frustrated and helpless with each day that passed.

One morning after Francheska had gone off to school, Jeanette began preparing food for dinner. She turned on the gas oven to warm it for cooking, then went about washing vegetables in the sink, cleaning them and then slicing them for stew. She went back to the oven, but it was not warm yet so she took out matches to light it. At the first spark the gas ignited and blew Jeanette across the room, singing her eyebrows and hair and slamming her against the ice box. She was dazed, and lucky to be alive.

One of her neighbors, hearing the explosion, ran to her aid, helped her off the floor and made sure she was not seriously injured. After she had helped Jeanette clean herself up, she explained to her how to operate the oven properly and offered to help her out with anything she needed.

The explosion was like a personal blow, administered by some unknown authority -- even without the Nazi guards or her husband she fell victim -- who gave her what she felt she undoubtedly deserved. It sent her into a gloom. Guilt and self pity consumed her as she lamented the loss of her parents, the loneliness, the forgotten past, the shame of no education.

When Francheska returned from school that day she looked so much bigger. She told her mother of the things she had learned, of the friends she had made. Jeanette began trying to live life through her daughter; she felt as if she were going through school with her. And each day as she grew taller and prettier, Jeanette wondered more intensely about herself -- the little girl she had never been allowed to be. Who was she? What had happened to her life? The abyss in her memory into which those years had fallen seemed deeper than ever, more dangerous, and impossible to cross.

Then the dreams began:

Jeanette walked up to the great doors. They seemed taller than any doors she had ever seen, beyond the limits of her gaze, and they were adorned with white, delicately carved, enameled trim and huge brass handles. They had a familiar and welcoming quality and she took hold of the brass door knobs and gave them a firm turn. As soon as she stepped inside she felt the cold. The air was dark and chilling and at the end of the long foyer was a brown wooden box standing upright. The box was plain brown wood, but Jeanette could feel its dreadful eminations, without even touching it. Still, the compulsion to open it was overwhelming. She watched her arm reach out to open the box, unable to stop herself, and when she swung the front of the box open, a woman's head fell out and rolled to her feet.

Jeanette was horrified. She recognized the woman's face. But before she could remember who it belonged to, a flood of human limbs -- arms and feet and body parts of children, old men and women -- poured out of the box and engulfed her. For a moment Jeanette couldn't tell if it was the crushing stench or the rolling force of the limbs that was carrying her away. She was powerless to resist that flood, no matter how she struggled. The putrid smell made her gag and wretch and the limbs seemed to clutch and pull her along.

Suddenly she was in a river of human suet, caught in its current, the turbulence of bubbling fat, the sick yellow undertow pulling her down. She screamed a scream of absolute terror. She tried to swim but felt herself drowning. There was a bank to the river, she could see it, but it was so far away. She swam with all of her strength, and for a moment she thought she was getting closer. But the noxious current was hard and dragged her toward the bottom. Then she saw people on the bank.

They were watching her, pointing at her. She cried out for help, panic-stricken, her own limbs flailing in the septic liquid, but the people did not respond. She cried out louder, she knew they could hear her now, she saw it on their faces. "Help me! Help me!" But they laughed and continued pointing and laughed some more. The river of suet pulled her away from them, and down, deeper into its swirling current, deeper.

Jeanette awoke in the morning awash with tears and sweat.

"Momma, momma, why are you crying?" Francheska had crawled into her bed and was hugging her, trying to comfort her.

"Oh, Francheska. My little child," she answered, wrapping her arms around her daughter as tightly as she could. Jeanette held back her emotions, so as not to upset her sweet girl. She was terribly shaken but tried to compose herself as best she could.

"It is nothing, Francheska," she said softly. "Nothing at all. Momma just had a bad dream."

And the dreams continued. One after the next until most nights Jeanette was afraid to go to sleep. During the day she struggled to cope with the mundane duties of her new found independence. It was only the love of Francheska that made it all worthwhile. She sensed her mother's troubled nature and tried her best to comfort her. They grew closer every day, and for Jeanette, she was at least comforted by the fact that at long last her little Francheska was safe.

The annulment proceedings seemed to take forever. Months went by and no word from the authorities. Jeanette considered going back to Hollywood, but felt trapped by the uncertainty of her future. She knew she had to settle the complications of her past before she cold really attempt a life of her own. Then word came that if she had the marriage annulled, she would lose her rights as a U.S. citizen.

"What am I going to do?" she asked Dolores.

"You'll have to divorce him," she said.

Religious objections that Jeanette harbored from her Catholic upbringing faded in the face of having to spend the rest of her days with a maniac who could kill her or Francheska without provocation or warning, and had threatened to do so many times.

Jeanette took Dolores' advice and agreed that she should not give up her American rights and privileges. So a divorce it was.

In spite of Jeanette's yearning for independence, she was still easily swayed by the people around her and heavily influenced by their explanations and decisions. Jeanette relied greatly on Dolores, and during the months prior to her divorce, she met another person who became her friend and changed her life.

His name was Harold Berman. He was a handsome young officer who first noticed Jeanette during her visits with Dolores. He was greatly attracted to Jeanette, watching her from a distance at first until he worked up the courage to introduce himself. He was friendly and Jeanette took a liking to him, and as they met over coffee and movies, she learned that he was innocent and naive and had no notion of the life that she had been through.

Still, he was kind to her, and courted her. When he finally proposed marriage, Jeanette was not sure what to answer. It was Dolores who convinced her that marrying him was a good decision.

"You must marry him," she said. "You must have someone to take care of you. He is crazy about you."

To someone as afraid of being alone as Jeanette was, Berman's proposal seemed like a gift from heaven. True, she hadn't known him for very long, but the love and emotion he poured over her, combined with her anxieties about making it on her own and taking care of Francheska, outweighed any momentary doubts.

She said yes, and the two were quickly married.

Jeanette Berman left Texas for Los Angeles, a new bride, with a daughter nearly nine years of age, and her head full of promising future. She found out quickly that her new husband was at once more, and less, than he had seemed. He still had his parents and two sisters, along with a number of uncles and aunts, but he could not wait to put distance between his family and himself. His resentment toward his family was centered around his mother, and women in general. He was angry with women, and was a man who did not want to admit he was Jewish.

His emotions were stifled, held in check by some unknown inner restraints, and he spoke very little. But Jeanette convinced herself that things would be okay once they got to know each other better.

To distract herself from such concerns, she threw herself into being the perfect American housewife, the perfect mother, dedicating herself to making her new family happy.

Back in Hollywood, she was torn between the opportunities of the movie business and her desire to be a family. The whole situation put her in a constant state of discomfort. But she did take advantage of her connections in the dance community. She and Harold Christianson, from the San Francisco Ballet, had met a few times in the past and Balanchine had told Christianson about her. He encouraged Jeanette to come to San Francisco and he would help her find a position teaching ballet.

She felt it was a good decision. Perhaps if she left the conflict of Los Angeles she could put her anxieties to rest and be a good wife and a good mother to Francheska. Her husband agreed to the move, and the three of them set out to create a new life in San Francisco.

Chapter 32

Divorcing Harold Berman really wasn't any more difficult than marrying him. One day Jeanette just knew it was the thing to do. She had decided to clear her life of negative influences. For too long she had felt like a cripple. She was crippled at first by being dependent on so many people during her life, and later by being rejected by those she loved. Now she could finally be free.

The divorce went smoothly. She had the assistance of Andrew Bodisco, a San Francisco lawyer, whom she had met in Hollywood. He even claimed to know her parents before the war, but did not speak to her about it, because he also knew it was beyond her ability to comprehend the past. When he had brought up the subject of her family a few years earlier, Jeanette went blank. It was as if the information were spoken to a deaf person. Since then, Bodisco never mentioned it again, but he made a point of keeping in touch with the young ballet teacher.

Bodisco urged her to apply for alimony and child support. But she answered, "I came to my husband with nothing. I will leave with nothing." Harold offered nothing either. The only emotion she sensed from him was spite. He scoffed at the possibility of her making a living on her own. The one thing he wanted from the marriage, it seemed, was for her to fail in her bid for independence.

Jeanette continued to dream of that independence. She wanted the chance to learn and grow by struggling on her own. She wanted to change and educate her emotions so she could lead a normal life. The pieces of that life, she felt, were about to fall into place. All but one -- Francheska. Unfortunately, that missing piece nearly caused her whole life to break apart.

The rift between her and her daughter grew greater and more oppressive every day. Francheska had quit ballet completely. For several weeks at home, Jeanette and she avoid speaking to each other because it nearly always led to a fight. Jeanette had nearly given up trying to understand her, but it seemed the risk of losing Francheska completely loomed larger every day. Then one Monday, Francheska left the house and didn't come home -- not that night, not the next day, not the following night.

Jeanette was desperate. She called Francheska's high school. She called her friends, but no one had seen her. She called the police, but they said there was little they could do so soon. For three days, Jeanette called people and searched. She drove the streets of San Francisco day and night, and on Thursday, she finally recognized a car -- Pearson's. It was parked in a motel lot on Lombard street. Jeanette called the police immediately. When they came, she had them arrest Pearson and Francheska. The police urged her to have her daughter put in a juvenile hall where she could receive counseling. They told her it would be too risky for Francheska and her to go back home together. She could only be brought to her senses with outside help. Jeanette agreed.

As for Pearson, he went free. The juvenile hall determined that Francheska was still a virgin and no charges could be brought against him. Later that week he called Jeanette. She pleaded with him to leave her and her daughter alone.

"What is it you want from us? You know she is too young for you. You already have a family. Why won't you leave us alone?"

I want to talk to you in person," he said. "Let's discuss this face to face. Maybe we can work something out."

Jeanette agreed to see him that night. He picked her up at her house and insisted they talk it out over dinner. Consumed by her anxiety, Jeanette didn't even notice where he was taking her. When he stopped the car, she realized they were in the middle of nowhere.

Pearson lunged at her. "You are jealous of your own daughter," he said as he fumbled for her crotch, "because you need a man. A sexy broad like you must really need fucking."

Jeanette screamed and tried to push him away.

"No one will hear you," he shouted back. "Scream all you want. You must need a man. You're young and sexy and I see no one around you. I'm here to fix that."

Pearson forced her down on the seat and Jeanette struggled with all her might. "You will have to kill me first," she cried out. But Pearson was stronger, and as he tried to kiss her she could hear his breathing by her ear, and the sounds he made were like those of an animal. Jeanette's thoughts flashed back to her rape. As she struggled to escape his grip, she felt a metal object on the floor. At first she could not lift it, but her fear gave strength and she raised it over her head. Pearson was intent upon satisfying himself and did not see the blow coming.

Jeanette hit him across the back of the head and he became limp. His body seemed heavier and she felt like she was being crushed beneath him. When she freed herself, she hit him again, and then again. Then she realized he was not moving. There was blood on her hands and she was certain she had killed him.

She left him there and ran away from the car. It wasn't until 5 a.m. that she found her way to the dance studio. She was exhausted and terrified, wondering what was going to happen to her. She did not answer the phone when it rang. She just sat against the wall in complete shock because she was certain she had killed a man. What frightened her most was the thought of having to go to jail. She decided she would rather die than ever be imprisoned again.

A few hours later, her students showed up at the school for rehearsals, but she did not answer the door. She stayed out of sight, curled up against the wall. She spent the entire day like that, not answering the phone, not even getting up from the floor. When it became dark she returned home. She listened to the radio to learn that Pearson's body had been found. But there was nothing of it on the news. For several days she stayed inside her home, not eating a thing, not answering the telephone or even turning on the lights. Then she heard on the radio that she, herself, had been reported missing.

The report finally gave Jeanette enough courage to leave the house. She went to the police to turn herself in. When she told them of the incident with Pearson, the police said they knew nothing of a body. With her help, they went to the spot where she had been attacked, but Pearson and his car were gone.

"Apparently, you have killed no one," the policeman said.

It was too much for Jeanette to take and she collapsed on the spot from exhaustion. In the hospital she was given a complete examination. She was sent home and told to get extra rest. But the rest would not come. Francheska was released from the juvenile hall and the two of them were once again living in the same house together.

Jeanette could not hold back her anger. "Why are you doing this, Francheska? Why are you trying to destroy everything I've worked for?"

"Because I hate you!" Francheska screamed. "You think you are so pretty, you think everyone wants you, but they don't!"

Then she turned to her mother. "Besides, I am bad blood," she said. "I have the blood of the rapist inside of me and it is bad blood. They had to be bad to do what they did to you."

"But Francheska, that is all over now. There is no reason to run around with a man like Pearson."

"Mother, there is nothing you can give me. He can give me everything -- a car, fun, a good life. I don't want to be a dancer. I just want to marry him."

Jeanette could not believe it. "After all he has done!

What is it going to take to convince you he is no good?"

But Francheska would not listen. She ran out of the room and Jeanette heard the door slam behind her. She came back the next day when Jeanette was out and took all of her clothes. Then she disappeared again.

Jeanette wanted so much to put her life in control, but her obsession with finding Francheska pushed that dream further and further away. She abandoned the ballet school completely. Kirsten tried to keep things going, but without Jeanette's help, there was nothing she could do. Giselle was disappearing before their eyes. Jeanette no longer went to classes and the bills mounted up.

All she could think about was Francheska, and the pressure inside her chest. It felt as if something was trying to escape from her body, as if someone was inside her, trying to find a way out. Jeanette ignored the sensation as best she could, but it would not go away. When she drove up and down the San Francisco streets it was there. When she huddled helplessly in her bed it was there too. When she thought of Giselle the Wili, dancing about her room in her etherial gown, she felt it still, pushing against the inside of her chest and her head.

She imagined how the performance of Giselle would have gone. She saw herself directing the performance from the wings, keeping the dancers' concentration on target when it wavered, bolstering their spirits when they doubted. She imagined herself backstage like a general, moving through the halls and the dressing room, advising on make-up, helping the dancers to visualize their parts. And she imagined the performances being praised by the critics and applauded by the audience.

But that was not to be.

Jeanette knew she had to save Francheska.

Chapter 33

This time it was not a dream. The picture was too clear. It had actually happened to Yanina -- to me! Too many of the details had been real, just like her memories of the camps. Too many of the faces were faces that had become a part of her, a part of me, that had become imprinted on my psyche. Especially one face. The face was so beautiful and at the same time so odd that it had awakened me. What was wrong with it? Why had a face so beautiful disturbed me in such a way?

I, Yanina, awake for the first time in years, sat up in bed, soaked with sweat. The glimpse of memory had terrified me, but I did not know why. I leaned back against the wall and stared out across the length of my bed. I was afraid to close my eyes because the memory might return. I knew I had to see that face again, but didn't want to confront the horror it made me feel. Yet, even with my eyes open I could sense it stirring. The memory was still alive within me, and I knew that it was coming. Like a wave it was coming and there was nothing I could do to stop it. As it welled up inside me, I finally realized that it was good, it was a relief. I did not want to stop it.

Then the face of Natasha filled the room. Natasha, my friend from the camps. Natasha and Yanina. Natasha my only friend.

It was evening in Auschwitz and I stared out of the window of the lager. Outside I could see birds on the fence and the roofs and I wished I could climb on the wings of one of the birds and fly away with it.

Then the realization came that there was really no place to go. Warsaw was just as bad, full of death and suffering. I wondered if there was someplace that was safe. How about Vienna? How about Germany? Maybe this cruelty is only in Poland, I thought. There must be peace somewhere. I looked at the birds again. I wondered how far one of them could take me, how lucky they were to be able to fly.

"Take some bread," the voice behind me said. It was Natasha. "You must get strong so you can become a ballerina," she said.

Natasha was so beautiful and made me feel so safe. Fantasies had taken near total control of my life. I talked about little else besides my upcoming role as the Sugar Plum Fairy. Natasha was the only one who stood by me, who comforted me, who never called me the Sugar Plum Nut. And when Natasha was with me, I felt as if the fantasies might not be real, that they might only be dreams. Natasha was my only link to the past, to my home and my parents, to the world I had tried to put out of my mind.

"They have chosen me to go to the pleasure camps tomorrow," Natasha said suddenly.

I saw the horror on her face.

"I will not go there," she said. "I am a Catholic and I will not go there!"

"But, Natasha, you have no choice," I whispered.

"No! No! I will not go there ever. I will not let them touch my body. I want to marry a wonderful man someday. I want to be pure for him. I will never go there, you will see," she shouted.

The look on her face frightened me. I sat back against the wall, watching Natasha walk off toward her bunk. The pleasure camps almost always meant death, and I felt in my stomach that I would never see Natasha again. It was a terrifying thought. Natasha was still so beautiful and strong. She was my only friend.

In the morning after roll call, there was a little free time for the prisoners. Natasha said to me, "Walk with me." We walked out into the yard. Ahead of us was one of the Nazi guards, his boots shining, a rifle in his hands and a bayonet at his belt. As we approached, Natasha began to smile at him coyly. She pulled her striped uniform off of her shoulder and swayed her hips to get his attention. Slowly, he came near.

I was dismayed by her actions. I moved away from her and the soldier, confused.

Natasha and the Nazi exchanged words, then they moved into each other -- Natasha bringing her face close to his and gently stroking his hair. I thought that they were about to kiss. But then I saw Natasha swinging her leg back, and in an instant she had kicked the soldier with all her might, right in the crotch.

The Nazi doubled up in pain. For a moment I felt the pain too, a pain that quickly changed into mortal fear for Natasha.

She glanced back at me. The corners of her mouth were pulled back as if she were trying to smile, but I could not return the smile. The fear had turned my face to ash.

The Nazi struggled to regain his breath and right himself. Then, as quickly as the kick had come, he pulled the bayonet from his side and swung it at Natasha. The single motion happened so quickly that I thought he had slapped her, until suddenly, Natasha's head was at my feet, still wearing the awkward smile. I looked up at the soldier and could see Natasha's body fall, several feet away.

"Get rid of this body!" the soldier shouted.

I stooped down and gathered up Natasha's head. From behind I could hear trucks arriving with new prisoners and when I looked up there was a woman standing next to me.

"They have brought in new ballet students for the audition," I said to the woman. "I hope they will all make it. They have a truck full of new talent and they must be good. They had to be recommended by their teachers."

The woman was Gerda. She gently took Natasha's head from me, and wiped the blood off my hands with her shirt. "Yes, we have new talent coming in, but you are my favorite student and you will be famous someday," she said to me.

Gerda looked into my face and said gently, "Why don't you cry, child?"

"I am happy they can dance," I said.

"No, I mean cry for Natasha," Gerda said.

I looked at her blankly. "Who is Natasha?" I asked.

I held my head in my hands and wept. I wept for the face of Natasha and I wept for myself -- the young Yanina who would not let herself remember her own past. For nearly 20 years I had not allowed myself to weep for Natasha, but my friend would not let me forget. Now that we had looked into each other's eyes again, the tears came easily. The wave poured over me and washed away all of the resistance. I was Yanina once again.

Chapter 34

When I awoke in the morning, I knew my life had changed. I could not even think of myself as Jeanette anymore. I was Yanina again, suddenly transported through time, not quite certain how I came to be lying in a small bedroom in small apartment in San Francisco.

There were memories to place me, memories to take me from one event to another, but they hardly seemed real anymore. They seemed more like dreams. When I tried to retrace my steps from Auschwitz to San Francisco, I felt as though I had passed through a hundred dreams -- some, my own, and some belonging to others -- of all sorts and scope: dreams of dancing, dreams of small birds in flight, dreams of hideous violent faces, dreams of the dead and half-dead, dreams of the grand ballet, dreams of sweat on the dance floor, dreams of fingers pointing to the left and to the right, fervent dreams of a fresh young girl, bitter dreams of an angry young woman, dreams of human bodies lifting off the ground.

When the telephone rang, I wondered if I was actually hearing the bell or remembering it. I let it ring until it stopped. Then the bell began again. This time I answered the phone and heard on the other end the voice of the doctor who had examined me a few weeks ago. The tests he had taken had turned up something serious, he said. I needed to come to the hospital immediately.

The doctor looked pained when I stepped into his office, and as he closed the door gently, I could see on his face that he was struggling with his words. The he found those words and turned his face toward mine.

"You have leukemia," he said. "It is very grave. You probably have less than a year to live."

I did not know what to feel. It all seemod so odd. He was telling me that I was going to die, but how could he know? He had taken tests on Jeanette Bayers. I was Yanina Cywinska. He doesn't realize he has made a mistake.

On the way home, I hoped it was all a dream. But this thought gave me little solace, because I knew now that all the dreams were real. My life suddenly made no sense. Why had I struggled so hard for personal independence? Why had I just learned my true identity if I was going to die? There must be some mistake.

As it would turn out, I was right. There had been a mistake. It would be months before the hospital would discover its misdiagnosis and in those months, the last vestages of order in my life fell totally apart.

I was still obsessed with finding Francheska, so much so that I abandoned my school entirely. Giselle had to be cancelled and because of unpaid rent, the landlord locked me out of the building. It was a terrible feeling. I had failded my students. I had failed in my goal for independence. I had failed to bring the young Giselle to life, a girl so innocent and full of joy that she has the power to dance right through death. But all of these failures paled compared to my inability to save my own daughter and preserve my family. In the end, all I could think about was finding Francheska.

I had hired a private detective to help me, and after a few weeks of tormented sleepless nights, I got a call that he had tracked her down at the Y.M.C.A. in Oakland. My depression turned to excitement and hope that Francheska would come home and we would work out our differences. But before we got to the Y.M.C.A. she disappeared again. We met and spoke with the director who told me what he had learned about Francheska. He said that shortly after her 18th birthday and a few sexual encounters with her gentleman friend, he dumped her. She was crushed and became hysterical and violent, swearing she would follow the man wherever he went. To get rid of her, he filled her full of drugs and threw her out into the streets. She ended up in Oakland where the staff at the Y.M.C.A. helped her get back on her feet and kept her away from the temptation to take more drugs. But she refused to stay and left the facility the night before we arrived. I paid the bills she had left behind and vowed to continue my search.

It would be months before I saw her again. In that interim I joined the Leukemia Society, made my funeral arrangements, got a fine casket and resigned to do charity work for fellow victims of the disease. I was broke, but managed to make a little money doing choreography or as a guest teacher.

Then one day I stopped in Vanessi's for lunch and Mr. Vanessi told me that he saw Francheska's picture at one of the clubs on Broadway Street. She was being advertised as the latest new sexy dancer in an all naked show.

I went to the club where she was appearing and found out how I could get in touch with her. She was working for a woman named Muffin, and living with her. Muffin's address was difficult to find out, but I asked most of the club owners and businesses on Broadway and finally learned where she lived.

I arrived early in the morning at Muffin's house and Francheska was there. I didn't know whether to scream at her or try to hold her in my arms.

"If you do this nude act," I told her, "then so will I. Right after you. I have a nice body, large breasts, they will hire me on the spot. Like mother like daughter."

"Oh no you won't," Francheska responded.

"Come home with me," I said softly.

"But I like my job. Why should I come home?"

Muffin came into the room in a see-through negligee.

"Muffin, this is my mother," Francheska said.

"Oh hi, Honey," she said.

"I am not your honey," I said.

The doorbell rang and three men came in. Muffin took them all to another room. That's when it hit me -- she was running a whore house. I coudn't believe I had been so naive. The cheap furniture/ the red velvet everywhere -- how could I have not seen it the moment I walked in. I was shocked. Then Francheska stood up and told me it was time to leave because she had to go to work.

"I will walk with you," I said.

"No, I have to meet somebody in the hotel."

"Okay, well, call me," I pleaded. "Let's solve our problems and get going with your life, okay?"

"No it's not okay," Muffin said from behind me. "You just get out of here. She is of age and doesn't need you to spoil my business."

I was so stunned I nearly stumbled out of the doorway. I couldn't believe it had come to this. All my efforts to have a family to raise my daughter to feel loved -- all of it was for nothing. Everything had gone wrong. I crossed the street and found a telephone booth. I didn't even know who I was going to call. I just wanted to talk to someone. When I closed the door, I noticed the two men who had followed me from Muffin's. They came up close to the glass booth and leered at me. Then one of them took a huge knife from inside his jacket and began cleaning his fingernails with it, glancing up at me and smiling.

Fortunately, a man pulled his car up next to the phone booth and got out to wait for a chance to use the phone. Muffin's thugs walked down the block and I used the opportunity to run the other way.

When I got home the telephone was ringing.

"Hey, is this Tootsie's mother?" a man asked.

"What do you want?" I asked.

"How much a trick?"

"What?"

"How much a trick? You know, I want to screw you. How much? Fifty bucks?"

I slammed the phone down and decided to leave. The next morning I went back to Muffin's again, but she wouldn't let me in. I explained to her that I had things to work out with my daughter, but she told me to get lost.

Back at home again, the fear and depression began to overtake me. I wanted somehow to save Francheska. I wanted to tell her that I had leukemia and that I was going to die soon. And no one really cared, not even her. I felt so desperate and so trapped.

A few days later I decided to make one more attempt to see Francheska. This time Muffin let me in. Francheska was getting dressed.

She had on a tight black skirt and black boots that laced up to the knees. Her blouse was cut low so her breasts were nearly exposed. Her hair was fruzzed and bleached and ratted. She looked like a whore.

"What happened to that beautiful lady that everyone admired so?" I asked her.

"I'm still the same, Mother," she said.

"No, you're not. Look at yourself. You're not even 21 yet and you look 40."

"Mother, stay out of this," she said.

"Don't you want to come home?" I asked. But she did not answer. Muffin gave her orders and she had to leave. I left too, wandering the streets, wondering what to do. Then I heard a car screech to a halt behind me and two men grabbed me before I even turned around. They dragged me into the car and gagged me. Then one of them held my arms behind by back.

"Look, lady. Stop making trouble for Muffin. If you want to stay alive, you'll take my advice. We don't want to see you around here anymore. We don't want you calling Francheska or trying to talk to her. Get smart. Either we kill you or drug you, leave you in a motel and have you arrested for soliciting. Don't think we won't do it."

I was too terrified to even nod my head.

"This is your last warning. If you don't disappear, we will make sure that you do."

Then he kicked me in the ribs and threw me out of the car in the middle of a dark street. I lay there for awhile, too frightened to move. What was I supposed to do? How could I handle this all by myself? I was going to die anyway, so why not try to help Francheska before it's too late.

But I didn't have an idea how to save anyone. A few weeks later I was contacted by the police. They informed me Francheska had been arrested for prostitution and for stealing money and credit cards from her clients, and charging up thousands of dollars worth of merchandise for Muffin. They asked me to appear in court the following day.

When I saw Francheska in the courtroom guarded by two policemen, I was crushed. I sat there numb and helpless, feeling so alone, with no one to tell about my leukemia and my daughter's problems. People were all around me, but I was so alone. I felt I had to keep my troubles to myself and solve them myself, but I wanted someone to help me. Francheska's situation was all my fault, I believed.

In the courtroom I just stared at my daughter. Muffin came in with a lawyer and walked up to the judge. They spoke, but I was not listening. I could not take my eyes off my daughter. I blamed myself for everything and knew then I would never be able to tell her about my leukemia. She had too many problems of her own.

Looking at her, I remembered the times I held her, held that beautiful round faced little doll with her large blue eyes. I remembered the songs I sang to her, the hopes I built for her. I had lost my family and my roots, but I had always believed I could build a wonderful family with my daughter, and someday she would have little ones of her own. I sat there remembering how much I wanted her, how much I loved her, how loving and adoring she was, so sweet. She was the ideal little baby, and when she was a young girl she had adored me so. Seeing her up on the stand made me realize that little girl was gone. I was looking at a stranger.

Looking at her also made me think of myself. The little girl I had never been allowed to be was echoing within my chest. I had promised myself that I would not allow this to happen to someone else, but the actions of the Nazis still affected every aspect of my life. They had given me guilt, fear, helpless immobility. They had destroyed me and now they were destroying my daughter.

The judge called recess and I walked up to Francheska with tears in my eyes, and looked straight into hers.

"Why, my child? Why are you doing this to yourself? Please explain it to me so I can understand."

"I hate you, Mother. You're so good, so fine. Now you know I am a hooker and a thief."

"You're doing all this because you hate me and want to hurt me? What have I done to you?"

"Nothing," she said. "I just like this life."

"What are you saying, Francheska? Don't you want to get out of this?"

"Muffin will help me," she said.

"She is not helping you," one of the policemen said. "She is using you. Come to your senses. Go home with your mother. Look at her. She looks like she's ready for a nervous breakdown."

"I don't care," Francheska said. "Muffin will help me."

The judge came back into the courtroom and asked me to accompany him to his chamber. Then he asked me to sit down.

"Listen to me, Yanina. Let me give you some fatherly advice. Your daughter is in trouble, but it is her own choosing. She made her bed, now let her lie in it. She is stubborn, uncooperative, and I think she is actually enjoying all the attention. She seems especially thrilled to hurt you."

He leaned forward in his chair and continued, "We tried to reason with her. We have given her help and lots of options. She rejected them all. Now look at you. Look at how you are ruining your life with worry. I think you should put your own life back together and let Francheska be responsible for the things she has done. Get away from all this. Promise me you will do that."

I walked out of his chambers and right past my daughter, not even looking back, right past Muffin, past the court doors and outside onto the street. Then someone shouted from behind, "Yanina, could we see you at Mr. Carey's office at 10 a.m. tomorrow?"

I turned around to look and it was Muffin's lawyer. "Carey's office is representing Muffin, and we would like to talk to you."

Mr. Carey was a very powerful lawyer in San Francisco. I was at his office at 10 a.m. on the dot. I entered his office and saw him sprawled on his chair, looking so smug.

"Now we understand your daughter is a very unruly child. She has been a real trouble at home and she is a mental case," he said.

"We would like you to sign this statement to that effect so we, my client and I can have her committed."

"Sign what, Mr. Carey?" I asked.

"Sign a statement that your daughter has been a problem all your life and that she is mentally disturbed."

I was enraged. "Mr. Carey, you are the scum of the earth to ask a mother to do this to her child. You're protecting a pimp. You are the king of the tarts in this city. I didn't even think you would stoop so low."

I slammed the door and walked out. I am going to die soon, I thought, so what difference does it all make? What's the point of fighting another war?

Chapter 35

It was several days later when I received the call from the hospital. They said it was very important that I come in immediately. When I arrived, the doctor brought me into his office ahead of everyone else in the waiting room. It was not the same doctor who had examined me before.

He said that recent tests of my blood had shown that I did not have leukemia. The original diagnosis was wrong. He tried to explain to me that the mistake had been perfectly understandable. All the symptoms had pointed to leukemia. But now the hospital had improved testing methods, and had determined that my condition was not dangerous and could be cured with simple medication. I saw through his double talk. I knew they had made a big mistake and just didn't want to admit it. But I was too stunned to protest.

I walked out of the hospital and headed across town. I stopped at a butcher shop to buy some meat for myself for dinner. I put the small steak in my pocket and headed toward the Golden Gate Bridge. It was a long walk through the Presidio to get to the bridge, and by the time I stepped onto it, the sun was just getting ready to go down. The wind clawed at my skin, but I didn't turn away. I walked out onto the bridge, transfixed by the glorious sunset. Cars raced by me, some with their headlights on and some without. I knew every one of them had a destination, a place to go where there were people that loved each other. It made me realize how truly alone I was.

But when I looked at the sun, I felt released. It was so beautiful. I had already made up my mind to jump. I was tired, defeated. There was no use fighting anymore. I had accustomed myself to the fact that I was going to die soon of leukemia. Now, even though the hospital had taken that fact away, I saw no reason to feel differently. My death was inevitable, and I was going to see that it was accomplished once and for all.

The desire to fly off the bridge was overpowering, to just step into the air and soar, ever downward into the sea. I moved with grace and assurance, gently placing my leg on the railing. That's when I heard the voice. Gerda. My protector who had died in Auschwitz.

"Is this how it ends?" she asked. "The Nazis could not destroy you. They could not crush your body or your spirit, and now you are going to do it yourself?"

"Yes, Gerda," I said.

A fierce gust of wind hit me in the face. When it stopped, Gerda was still there. "I saved you from the gas chamber. I gave you breath again. I took all those chances so you could finally do the job yourself? You want to give the Nazis that satisfaction? Is that what I saved you for? For this stupid act? I am so disappointed, Yanina."

Then I remembered.

Gerda had saved me. I had finally been chosen for extermination. I was in line. The emotions were so strange.

For so long I had handed out the towels, the soap, and now I was in line to receive them. I remembered what took place inside that chamber and I knew I was finished. I was frightened. I prayed. "God please forgive me for stealing a lily. It was so beautiful, I never wanted to give it up. Please forgive me. My parents didn't. They never came to get me because they are still angry at me for stealing."

As we walked down the long hall, we were serenaded by the orchestra. The women all played violins -- the sweetest most sorrowful violins. And the music was beautiful. I wanted to scream for my life, but knew no one would ever hear me. I suppressed the urge and an old woman next to me recognized what I was going through. She took my hand and told me to cry into her body so no one would hear.

"Don't scream, my child. They will kill you on the spot. One more moment counts. In one more moment, everything can change."

The urge to scream passed. I knew in a few minutes that some fellow prisoner would be dragging my body out of the chamber, throwing it onto a truck for burning. I knew everything that was going to happen.

We were asked to strip down. The Sondercommandos ordered us to clearly mark our clothes hangers with our names if we wanted to claim them after the showers. Everyone around me felt the surge of hope and relief, but I burst out laughing. The sign over the chamber read "Disinfektionsraum", and the Sondercommandos quickly herded us into it. I stopped in my tracks, trying to find a way out, but someone pushed me into the room with a rod.

People in the chamber tried to turn on the showers, but nothing came out. Suspicion grew as the door behind us was slammed shut. The slight glimmer of hope on people's faces turned to fear and then silence. Then the lights went off and I looked up to the little window, knowing that the Nazi was up there, sprinkling his blue crystals down the shafts into the chamber.

"God, where are you?" I whispered. "I don't want do die yet. I haven't lived yet." But I knew my prayers would not be answered any more than they had been before.

As the gas poured from the holes, everyone panicked. People rushed to the door, then to each other, then to the door again. The screaming began. The stronger climbed atop the bodies in search of a precious breath of air. Someone was stepping over me. As the bodies began to fall in the corner by the door, I thought I saw my mother and father. Yes, they were there with me. It must be them. "Momma, Momma, save me!" I screamed. "Please save me, Momma!"

In a few moments, everything went blank. The coughing and the crying stopped and I saw the Sugar Plum Fairy dancing as the violins played. I continued to hear violins and voices in the distance. I could faintly hear the door opening. I thought I was dead, but I felt someone dragging me by my feet. Then I heard a woman say, "Gerda, yours is still breathing. Get the Nazi to finish her off."

"No, no!" Gerda whispered. She pressed her mouth into mine, giving me air. She breathed into me again and again.

"Gerda, they will shoot you! Take her out of here!" the other voice said.

I felt Gerda drag my body away. She stopped and then breathed into me again. I opened my eyes and she said, "Shut up. Don't move. Don't even breath. The SS men are here to finish the breathing ones."

After awhile, she dragged me a long way, and then stood me up and made me put on the clothes of one of the dead prisoners.

"Why, Yanina? Why this?" Gerda's voice brought me back from my memory, back onto the bridge.

"Because I can't do it anymore," I answered. "I have tried, but I just can't do it anymore."

"What have you tried?"

"I tried to make the world perfect," I said. "I tried to make everyone happy. I tried to be a responsible person and live a perfect life, to do my very best, to make a perfect home for my family so that terrible things would never happen again. I don't want those terrible things to ever happen again."

Gerda smiled. Then she grew taller and more transparent and I felt a hot wind blowing onto me. The warmth surrounded me as if it were a huge angel wrapping its wings around me, protecting me from the danger and the cold. And I could feel my life, the core of my life, and I was transformed. And I could see life itself, look into the heart of life and know it with all my senses.

I was alive. And that's all that mattered.

Epilogue

At long last, I have come to understand my past and am no longer bound in slavery by it. I've been able to return again to another try at life. Today, I am the maker of my character and the builder of my destiny. Every circumstance, whether pleasant or unpleasant, is grist for my personal mill. I embrace it as such, put it into my chosen pattern of living and let it serve rather than torment me through fear or worry.

I've learned to adapt to all possible circumstances and the drastic changes which my life has presented me. Yes, I have a pain that never sleeps, but the beauty of the world overpowers it.

Over the years, endless questions in my mind grew: Could I, once a destroyed human being, completely alone in the world, grasp a normal existence in my remaining years? Could I trust again? Could I love again?

The answer was yes to all these questions.

Within a short time of my liberation—perhaps too soon—I went on to build my career in ballet. Currently, I delight in my work as the Artistic Director of the Solano Civic Ballet, a non-profit organization supported by the city of Fairfield, California, and am owner of Yanina Cywinska's Ballet Academy in nearby Suisun. I teach, choreograph, and design sets. In my work, I see young people overcome personal difficulties through dance. At long last, I met my present husband,

Norman Impelman, whom I trust and am capable of receiving and returning his love. He has been my support for the last 35 years.

Letters from students in response to Yanina's speaking engagements

Andrea Mendoza

Holocaust.

When everyone first heard that you were coming to Alleman to talk to us, I think everyone was expecting the same speech that almost all speakers tell us. But you definetly proved us wrong!!!

I think I speak for everyone when I say your story was definitely touching and inspiring to all of us here. There were many parts of your story when I wanted to cry. I really got choked up & so did my friends who I was sitting with.

You are definitely with out a doubt the best speaker we have had at Alleman! I would love to have you back here again! Thank you for coming!

Israel nettles

Mrs. Cywinska

Your visit to our school changed the way a lot of us students think act and feel. Also it lets us look at life in a whole different way your story made me see that not everyone gets the great in life but doesn't mean that you have to give up. For you to come to our school and go all over telling your story and being able to stand it I feel as if people can live and do anything no matter what goes on or happens in their life. I really appreciate you coming and telling your story to our school it really touched all of us in many different ways I really respect you and everything you had to go through for you to be able to live life to your fullest after everything you went through it really inspires me to go on in anything that I desire to do and anything that I put my mind to thank you and I wish the best for you in life as you continue on living in full. Thank you so much !

Nathan Bush

Computer I-EB

Sister Ruth

13 April 2005

Holocaust Survivor

When the speaker first made an entrance onto the stage she looked light hearted and full of life which was intriguing, how someone after all she's been through can recover and love life. She was kind of short but only physical her personality and strength was amazing.

Her entire family was murdered in the first instance of death she was able to survive hungry but unscathed. It made me grateful that none of us have gone through these events, and has given me an understanding of how important the U.S. military is. I was startled by her strength as she pulled bodies from the gas chamber and didn't lose it when the baby she was holding had its head blown off (which got a reaction from every one). After serving and proving her strength she was move to the experimentation part of the camp. When there she was forced to watch a living man with his skull cap removed be tortured until his brain bubbled white from stress. Even in my imagination her experiences haunt me I have so much respect for her character. During her speech she even managed to include humor which fascinated me and may sound inappropriate but she used it tastefully and only lightened the mood of the room.

In the end I was left disturbed from her terrible life story but in awe that someone like her had the strength to pass the story on. Finally she cracked a joke at the principle when his voice squeaked. Overall she has given me a great understanding of WW II.

Lawrence

The holocaust survivor that came to talk to us about her story is in my opinion a very strong individual. She made me realize that my life is easy. I know now when I go to church I should feel lucky I'm not putting my life in danger because of my faith. All she did was fight for those who could not fight for themselves. I personally think there is a reason for her living still today; that is to tell her story and touch peoples lives. She showed me how ruthless humans can be to one another. Hearing her talk has changed my way of thinking and going about things; I don't take anything as a free lunch ticket any more; I work harder and cherish what I have and before I did not. I've heard many holocaust stories but none this tragic and touching. Ever since I heard her story and how bad they treated her, I have decided to turn my act around and be nice to people because I don't want to hurt people. Overall I am glad that she came to speak to us and I believe I am better off for having heard her story.

CPSIA information can be obtained at www.ICGtesting.com
Printed in the USA
BVOW071724220812

298480BV00001B/5/A

9 781434 342423